Arthur Herbert Dyke Acland

A Guide to the Choice of Books for Students and General Readers

Arthur Herbert Dyke Acland

A Guide to the Choice of Books for Students and General Readers

ISBN/EAN: 9783337424251

Printed in Europe, USA, Canada, Australia, Japan

Cover: Foto ©Lupo / pixelio.de

More available books at **www.hansebooks.com**

A GUIDE

TO THE

CHOICE OF BOOKS

O for a Booke and a shadie nooke
  eyther in-a-doore or out ;
With the grene leaves whisp'ring overhede,
  or the Streete cryes all about.
Where I maie Reade all at my ease,
  both of the Newe and Olde ;
For a jollie goode Booke wherein to looke
  is better to me than Golde.

A GUIDE

TO THE

CHOICE OF BOOKS

FOR

STUDENTS & GENERAL READERS

EDITED BY

ARTHUR H. D. ACLAND, M.P.

HONORARY FELLOW OF BALLIOL COLLEGE, OXFORD

Books are not absolutely dead things, but doe contain a potencie of life in them to be as active as that soule was whose progeny they are: . . . I know they are as lively, and as vigorously productive, as those fabulous Dragons' teeth; and being sown up and down may chance to spring up armed men.—MILTON.

The point is not that men should have a great many books, but that they should have the right ones, and that they should use those that they have.—JOHN MORLEY.

LONDON: EDWARD STANFORD
26 & 27 COCKSPUR STREET, CHARING CROSS, S.W.
1891

Read not to contradict and confute; nor to believe and take for granted; nor to find talk and discourse; but to weigh and consider.
BACON.

Books are no more education than laws are virtue; and, just as profligacy is easy within the strict limits of law, a boundless knowledge of books may be found with a narrow education. A man may be, as the poet saith, "deep vers'd in books and shallow in himself."
F. HARRISON.

There are three classes of readers; some enjoy without judgment, others judge without enjoyment, and some there are who judge while they enjoy and enjoy while they judge.   GOETHE.

PREFACE

FOR those who have competent advisers at hand who can tell them "What to read" this little book is not intended. They are fortunate persons in an enviable position, more fortunate and more envied than they often know. The making of these lists arose from the frequent demands made upon myself and some of my friends by two different classes of persons. There were those with no advisers, who asked for the names of some of the best books on the subjects in which they were interested; and there were those who were responsible for providing libraries of books for popular or general use. It has been impossible to discharge the task satisfactorily, and I am not sure whether the result in any way justifies the great amount of labour that has been given to the work, or whether those whose needs we have tried to meet will not be disappointed. Possibly only those who make the attempt know what the difficulties of the task really are. But whether the result is bad or good, I owe the best parts of the book to my Oxford and Cambridge friends and others who have so kindly helped me, and they are not to blame if its general arrangement is unsatisfactory, or if there are bad omissions and mistakes.

I hope that the book will be useful to the Committees of the smaller Free Libraries, to the Educational Departments of Working Men's Co-operative and other Societies, to some of those who are attending University Extension Lectures, to Home Reading Circles and Mutual Improvement Societies, and also to a good many isolated students engaged in efforts to educate themselves. Few people who have had a good education realise how great are the difficulties of many whose opportunities have been narrowly limited, who desire guidance, but who are unable, in an age when books pour forth from the printing presses in an unceasing torrent, to discriminate between the good, the bad, and the indifferent. There are still in many provincial towns and many out of the way homes those who cannot get at any good advisers, who want to use libraries or buy books intelligently, but know not how. Except in London and a very few large towns, readers cannot get sufficient help from booksellers, and too many circulating or public libraries are inadequately furnished with the books which are best adapted to the needs of students who desire to inform themselves upon literary, scientific, historical, and economical subjects. The experience of University Extension Lecturers and others has shown again and again that time is disastrously wasted by those who read antiquated and second-rate books because they know no better. Some read antiquated books on scientific and similar subjects, when the newer books would be far more useful. Others who read general literature jump at "the latest book out," and know little of the stores of interest and wisdom to be found in the masterpieces of older writers.

I have some hope too that the book will be of special service in Public Libraries to those many librarians who so industriously try to lift by degrees the taste of their readers from the indifferent and second-rate books to the good. The grants for Free Library salaries given by many of the municipal bodies are often so small, and the amount of mechanical duty therefore so great, that there is little opportunity for librarians to help their readers in the choice of books as much as they would wish to do. But as a truer conception of municipal life and duty grows among us, the better recognition of such work may be confidently expected.

The number of subjects on which lists have been given is, when compared with the ordinary library catalogue, very limited, and the principle on which the selection has been made is arbitrary. This was inevitable if the book was to be moderate in size and cheap. The case of the ordinary reader or student of certain subjects of literature, history, art, science, economics, philosophy, has been kept in view, with some consideration for children and "the home." Large classes of books have inevitably been ruled out altogether. There are practically no technical books on trades, professions, amusements, sport. There are no theological books. The list of works of fiction is limited, and a great deal of what is called light literature of all sorts is omitted, because it is just on this point that information is very easy to obtain. There are no foreign books unless translated (except in the books for beginners in languages), and hardly any books which are out of print, this last being a rule which keeps out a grievously large number of important works.

The question of advice as to the merit of different books is a difficult matter, and it may be said that there is very little guidance in a book of this sort after all. I can only say that I have studied many lists which profess to describe books or to classify them according to their merits, which exhaust and repeat all the epithets of praise, faint or unmeasured, and those which mark with asterisks certain selected books. I believe little that is of practical value can be gained by such means, unless comments are given at far greater length than would be possible here. A few words of suggestion or advice have been given here and there where it seemed advisable at the beginning of the lists. In certain cases the books are classified into Elementary, Advanced, and Reference books. The price of a book frequently gives some guidance as to its character. Beyond this it is difficult to go with any satisfactory results.

It is no doubt the case that, notwithstanding all efforts to keep out bad or indifferent books, in some of the lists—such, for instance, as Biography—it is not easy to exclude books of very moderate value. But, on the whole, a biography of even moderate merit is better than none. Ladders must be built for miscellaneous readers to lead them on to the higher and better books. Mr. Frederic Harrison, in his wise essay on the Choice of Books, has uttered many wholesome warnings against the "cataract of printed stuff which honest compositors set up." But he could not withstand the temptation in his younger days, as he tells us himself. And however true and sane his advice may be, the lesser books must continue for many to be the starting-points from which a desire for the greater books will arise. Thus children's books, domestic economy books, popular biography and history, elementary science books, popular or indifferent books on social economy, even blue books, may become stepping-stones to something better.

I fear that it is a very humble measure of assistance which this book will give to those who need advice and guidance. But I hope that those who may use it will remember that whatever devotion they may give to science, political economy, philosophy, or history, they will always need the help which comes from a study of the great books which will be found mainly under the head of Literature, with a few additions from the other lists. Unless they would be one-sided men and women, let them not fail to turn again and again to the great masterpieces of all time, to the books which are strong, dignified, inspiring, in which the wisdom and experience of many generations is enshrined.

It should be added that none of those who have kindly given their advice in the selection of books are to be regarded as solely responsible for the lists as finally printed. Several friends of acknowledged authority have helped me, whose names I do not feel at liberty to give, as for want of space and other reasons the lists have had to be modified since passing out of their hands. I have to thank various friends at Oxford and Cambridge, and at the University College, Bangor, and the Yorkshire College, Leeds, for invaluable help. To the following, among others, I desire to make special acknowledgments:— Mr. G. N. Richardson, Mr. Charles W. Sutton, Mr. D. S. Maccoll, Mr. H. J. Mackinder, Mr. S. Alexander, Mr. D. G. Ritchie, Mr. F. York Powell, Mr. O. Elton, Mr. M. E. Sadler, Mr. G. R. Benson, Mr. H. Llewellyn Smith, Miss Sharp. To my wife and Miss M. Roberts I owe a great deal of assistance, without which the book would never have been brought to completion.

The grouping of the books under large headings, which is a more educational method than a mere alphabetical list of each minor subject apart from its proper surroundings, may lead to a little difficulty in finding a subject or a book. This can only be remedied by a constant use of the Index (which is, I hope, pretty complete) or the Table of Contents, till those who use the book are familiar with its arrangement.

There is room for criticism in every page of the book by those who miss in each of the lists some of the books which they know and which they like. But, in a small and handy work of this sort, if only the books that are in the lists are in the main fairly good, this is the best that can be hoped for. For after all, to read all the books even in two or three only of the larger subjects would be quite out of the reach of those for whom these lists are intended. To be on friendly terms with one-tenth part of them would be an achievement difficult enough. I shall be much indebted to those who will suggest improvements or correct mistakes in case a new edition of the book should be required.

    CLYNNOG, CARNARVON,
      January 1891.

> Mark there. We get no good
> By being ungenerous, even to a book,
> And calculating profits,—so much help
> By so much reading. It is rather when
> We gloriously forget ourselves and plunge
> Soul-forward, headlong, into a book's profound,
> Impassioned for its beauty and salt of truth—
> 'Tis then we get the right good from a book.
>
>   MRS. BROWNING.

NOTES AND EXPLANATIONS

The Index must be habitually used by those who have any difficulty in finding a book or a subject. The Index contains the names of all the subjects dealt with in the book, and of all the authors (with a few exceptions in the case of Biography) whose books are in the lists.

The Table of Contents gives an outline (with sub-headings) of the main subjects on which lists are given. These are arranged in alphabetical order in the body of the book, and the name of the subject is given on the top of each page. Those who are familiar with the Table of Contents will find little necessity for using the Index as far as subjects are concerned.

In the choice of Editions of the cheaper books, especially under the heading Literature, the object has been to choose those which were both cheap and fairly good, not necessarily the cheapest in every case. Some excellent cheap series of books which contain short single works or small selections have been hardly noticed in these lists for want of space, as, for instance, *Cassell's National Library* (each volume 3d. in paper, 6d. in cloth), which, in a form really available for the pocket, contains much excellent matter from great authors, both English and foreign.

The Standard Library Editions of the works of the great authors are not always mentioned in these lists, as the object of the book is to draw the reader to study the masterpieces in the handiest available form. Many of the standard editions of collected works are out of print. But in a large number of cases they can be obtained second-hand at very moderate prices. It is outside the scope of this book to give the prices of second-hand books, but the information can easily be obtained from any of the larger booksellers.

In the choice of Manuals on various subjects it should be clearly understood that the best, on the whole, within the knowledge of the person making the selection has been chosen, and that sometimes the advantage in favour of one manual which is chosen over one which is left out may be but slight.

ABBREVIATIONS.

ed. = edited by.
O. P. = out of print, but probably to be procured second-hand.

sep. = separately.
trans. = translation, or translated by.

NOTICE

ALL the books in this list remaining in print and published in Great Britain (with a few exceptions in the case of those not published on the usual terms) can be supplied at a discount of 25 per cent for cash by Edward Stanford, 26 and 27 Cockspur Street, London, S.W.

Adjust your proposed amount of reading to your time and inclination—this is perfectly true to every man; but whether that amount be large or small, let it be varied in its kind, and widely varied. If I have a confident opinion on any one point connected with the improvement of the human mind, it is on this.

Dr. Arnold.

TABLE OF CONTENTS

	PAGE
BOOKS OF REFERENCE, DICTIONARIES, ETC. .	xvii, xviii
ANTIQUITIES AND ARCHÆOLOGY	1-3
I. Egyptian and Oriental	1
II. Greek . . .	2
III. Roman . . .	2
IV. General and British .	3
ART . .	4-8
I. Painting	4
II. Sculpture .	6
III. Architecture . . .	6
IV. Decorative Art . . .	7
V. Practice of Drawing and Painting	7
BIOGRAPHY (INCLUDING LETTERS, SPEECHES, AND AUTOBIOGRAPHIES) . .	9-23
I. Artists	9
II. Economists	10
III. Leaders of Industry and Inventors .	11
IV. Men and Women of Letters . . .	11
V. Men and Women of Science . . .	15
VI. Musicians	15
VII. Religious Leaders and Writers .	16
VIII. Soldiers and Sailors .	18

BIOGRAPHY—*Continued.*

	PAGE
IX. STATESMEN AND SOVEREIGNS	19
X. TRAVELLERS AND DISCOVERERS	21
XI. GENERAL	22

CHILDREN'S BOOKS — 24-26

I. STORIES AND TALES	24
II. POETRY	25
III. PICTURE BOOKS	26
IV. SCIENCE BOOKS	26

DOMESTIC ECONOMY — 27, 28

I. CARE OF CHILDREN	27
II. COOKERY	27
III. GARDENING	28
IV. HEALTH AND THE HOUSE	28

EDUCATION — 29, 30

I. ELEMENTARY	29
II. TECHNICAL	29
III. SECONDARY	30
IV. UNIVERSITIES	30
V. EDUCATIONAL METHODS	30
VI. HISTORY OF EDUCATION	30

GEOGRAPHY AND TRAVEL — 31-36

I. GENERAL	31
II. PHYSICAL	32
III. HISTORICAL	32
IV. COMMERCIAL	33
V. TRAVELS	33
1. General	33
2. Europe	34
3. Asia	34
4. Africa	34
5. America	35
6. Arctic and Antarctic	35
VI. GUIDE BOOKS	35
VII. MAPS	36
1. English Atlases	36
2. German Atlases	36
3. Wall Maps	36
4. Government Maps	36

	PAGE
GOVERNMENT PUBLICATIONS	37, 38

[REPORTS OF COMMISSIONS, STATISTICAL ABSTRACTS, ETC.]

HISTORY	39-54
I. ANCIENT HISTORY	39
1. General and Oriental . . .	39
2. Egyptian	40
3. Jewish	40
4. Greek	41
5. Roman	41
II. MEDIÆVAL AND MODERN HISTORY .	42
1. Europe	42
a. Great Britain and Ireland . . .	43
i. England	43
(A) Political . . .	43
(B) Constitutional . . .	46
ii. Scotland . . .	47
iii. Ireland . . .	48
b. Austria and Hungary . . .	49
c. France	49
d. Germany	49
e. Italy	50
f. Netherlands . . .	50
g. Russia	51
h. Scandinavia . . .	51
i. Spain and Portugal . . .	51
k. Switzerland . . .	51
l. Turkey and Greece . . .	52
2. British Colonies and India . . .	52
3. America	54
LANGUAGES (BOOKS FOR BEGINNERS)	55-57
I. GREEK . .	55
II. LATIN . .	55
III. FRENCH . .	56
IV. GERMAN . .	56
LITERATURE . . .	58-73
I. INTRODUCTORY (HISTORICAL AND CRITICAL) .	58
II. POETRY	60
1. Collections of Poems . . .	60
2. Best Cheap Editions of English Poets . .	60
3. Foreign Poets, Ancient and Modern (translations) .	63

LITERATURE—*Continued.*

		PAGE
III. FICTION .		64
1. Novels		64
a. English		64
b. American		67
c. Foreign (translations)		67
2. Historical Novels and Tales		68
IV. ESSAYS, LECTURES, AND STUDIES		70
1. English		70
2. American		72
V. SOME FAMOUS BOOKS		72

PHILOSOPHY   74-77

I. METAPHYSICS	74
II. ETHICS	75
III. LOGIC	76
IV. PSYCHOLOGY	76
V. MISCELLANEOUS BOOKS	76
VI. HISTORY OF PHILOSOPHY	77

POLITICAL AND SOCIAL ECONOMY   78-89

I. GENERAL	78
1. Economic Theory	78
2. Standard Works	79
3. Economic and Commercial History	79
4. Method and History of Economic Science	79
II. ORGANISATION OF INDUSTRY	79
1. Division of Labour and Modern Production	79
2. Factory System	80
3. Guilds	80
4. Trades Unions and Strikes	80
5. The Wages Question	80
6. Conciliation and Adjustment of Wages	81
7. Profit-Sharing	81
8. Co-operation	81
III. LAND, AGRICULTURE, AND MINING	81
1. Land Tenure	81
2. Land Transfer	81
3. Rent and Tenancy	82
4. Commons and Enclosures	82
5. Allotments and Cottage Farming	82
6. Mining and Royalties	82
7. Village Communities	82

POLITICAL AND SOCIAL ECONOMY—*Continued.*

PAGE

- IV. CONDITION OF THE PEOPLE . . . 82
    1. General 82
    2. Population and Vital Statistics . . 83
    3. Thrift and Temperance . . . 83
    4. Poor Law and Pauperism . . . 83
    5. Charities and Charity Organisation . . 84
- V. CURRENCY, BANKING, AND TRADE . . 84
    1. Money, Credit, and Banking . . . 84
    2. Speculation, Markets, and Exchanges . 85
    3. Prices 85
    4. Foreign Trade and Foreign Exchanges . 85
- VI. FINANCIAL POLICY 85
    1. Taxation 85
    2. National Finance 86
    3. National Debts 86
- VII. FREE TRADE AND PROTECTION . . 86
    1. Protection to Trade . . . 86
    2. Protection to Labour . . . 86
- VIII. PRIVATE ENTERPRISE AND PUBLIC CONTROL . 87
    1. Individualism 87
    2. Socialism 87
    3. The Province and Policy of State Intervention . 88
- IX. LITERARY WORKS DEALING WITH ECONOMIC PROBLEMS 88
- X. WORKS OF REFERENCE AND PERIODICAL LITERATURE 89

POLITICAL SCIENCE 90-93

- I. SOCIOLOGY 90
- II. POLITICS 91
    1. General Political Science . . 91
    2. Special Political Questions . . 91
    3. Famous Older Books of Political Theory . 91
    4. English Constitution and Practical Works . 92
    5. British Colonies 93
    6. American Constitution . . . 93
    7. Various Constitutions of the World . 93

SCIENCE 94-112

- I. MATHEMATICS 94
    1. Pure Mathematics . . . 95
    2. Mixed Mathematics . . . 96
    3. Histories and Miscellaneous . . 98

SCIENCE—*Continued.*

                                                  PAGE

- II. PHYSICS 98
    1. General Physics 98
    2. Mechanics (including Dynamics and Hydrostatics) . . 99
    3. Sound 99
    4. Heat 100
    5. Light 100
    6. Electricity and Magnetism 101
    7. The Theory of Energy 101
    8. Miscellaneous 102
    9. Method 102
- III. CHEMISTRY 102
    1. General 102
    2. Applied 103
- IV. BIOLOGY 104
    1. Zoology 104
        - a. Zoology (general) 104
        - b. Evolution 104
        - c. Anatomy and Physiology . . . 105
        - d. Natural History 105
    2. Botany 108
    3. Anthropology 109
- V. GEOLOGY 110
    1. General 110
    2. Palæontology 111
    3. Mineralogy 111
- VI. ASTRONOMY 112
    1. Popular and Descriptive 112
    2. Mathematical 112
    3. Historical 112

> If time is precious no book that will not improve by repeated readings deserves to be read at all.—CARLYLE.

BOOKS OF REFERENCE, DICTIONARIES, ETC.

[*This list includes a few of the more essential books for a small Public Library.*]

I. GENERAL

		£	s.	d.
Encyclopædia Britannica. 24 vols. and Index.	*Black*	37	0	0
Chambers's Encyclopædia. 10 vols. (New edition in course of publication.)	*Chambers*	5	0	0
The Encyclopædic Dictionary. 7 vols.	*Cassell*	7	7	0

II. DICTIONARIES, ETC.

		£	s.	d.
Skeat, Etymological Dictionary of the English Language.	*Clarendon Press*	2	4	0
,, Concise Edition.		0	5	6
Ogilvie's Imperial Dictionary. 4 vols.	*Blackie*	5	0	0
Webster's International Dictionary.	*Bell*	1	11	6
Murray, New English Dictionary (in course of publication). Vol. I.	*Clarendon Press*	2	12	6
Brachet, Etymological Dictionary of French.	*Clarendon Press*	0	7	6
Whitney, Compendious German Dictionary.	*Macmillan*	0	7	6
Baretti, Italian Dictionary.	*Houlston*	1	1	0
Neuman and Baretti, Spanish Dictionary.	*Houlston*	1	8	0
,, Abridged Edition.	*Houlston*	0	6	0
Liddell and Scott, Greek-English Lexicon.	*Clarendon Press*	1	16	0
,, Abridged Edition.	*Clarendon Press*	0	12	6
Lewis and Short, Latin Dictionary.	*Clarendon Press*	1	5	0
Roget's Thesaurus of English Words and Phrases.	*Longmans*	0	10	6

III. CHRONOLOGY, GEOGRAPHY, AND BIOGRAPHY

		£	s.	d.
Haydn, Dictionary of Dates.	*Ward, Lock*	0	18	0
Lippincott, Gazetteer of the World.	*Lippincott*	3	3	0
Bartholomew, Gazetteer of the British Isles.	*Black*	1	16	0
Stephen, L., Dictionary of National Biography. 25 vols. published.	*Smith, Elder.* Each	0	15	0
Haydn, Universal Index of Biography (in course of publication).				
Hole, Brief Biographical Dictionary.	*Macmillan*	0	4	6

IV. CONTEMPORARY EVENTS, STATISTICS, ETC.

		£	s.	d.
Irving, Annals of Our Time. 2 vols.	*Macmillan*	1	16	0
Annual Register. Yearly.	*Longmans*	0	18	0
Hazell's Annual.	*Hazell*	0	3	6
Whitaker's Almanack.	*Whitaker*	0	2	6
The Statistical Abstract (United Kingdom).	*Eyre, Spottiswoode*	0	1	0
The Statesman's Year-book.	*Macmillan*	0	10	6
Sergeant, The Government Handbook.	*Unwin*	0	10	6
The Royal Kalendar.	*Allen*	0	7	0
The County Councils and Municipal Corporations Companion.	*Waterlow*	0	10	0
The Metropolitan Year-book.	*Cassell*	0	1	0
Kelly's Handbook to the Titled, Landed, and Official Classes.	*Kelly*	0	16	0
Men and Women of the Time.	*Routledge*	0	15	0

[*For various Colonial and Foreign Year-books see the Lists of Books of Reference in the Statesman's Year-book under the different Countries.*]

V. BOOKS OF REFERENCE FOR LIBRARIANS

		£	s.	d.
Allibone, Dictionary of Authors. 3 vols.	*Lippincott*	5	8	0
Poole, Index to Periodical Literature.	*Trübner*	3	13	6
,, First Supplement, 1882-87.	*Trübner*	1	16	0
English Catalogue of Books, 1835-80, 3 vols. (Vols. I. and II. O.P., Vol. III. 42s.) Index, 1837-80, 3 vols. (Vol. I. O.P., Vol. II. 42s., Vol. III. 18s.) 1881 and after annually.	*Low.* Each	0	5	0
Reference Catalogue of Current Literature (published every four or five years, latest vol. 1889).	*Whitaker*	O. P.		
Lowndes, Bibliographer's Manual. 4 vols.	*Bell*	2	2	0
Sonnenschein, The Best Books.	*Swan Sonnenschein*	1	11	6
Greenwood, Public Libraries.	*Simpkin, Marshall*	0	2	6

[*For Classical, Historical, and other Dictionaries see the various lists. For Trade, Commercial and Technical Dictionaries reference must be made to other catalogues.*]

> We talk of food for the mind, as of food for the body: now a good book contains such food inexhaustibly; it is a provision for life, and for the best part of us; yet how long most people would look at the best book before they would give the price of a large turbot for it!—RUSKIN.

ANTIQUITIES AND ARCHÆOLOGY

[NOTES AND SUGGESTIONS.—*A few leading books only have been mentioned under this heading. For further books larger catalogues must be consulted. Much of the best information is to be found scattered in periodicals.*]

> Antiquity! thou wondrous charm, what art thou? that being nothing, art everything! When thou *wert*, thou wert not antiquity—then thou wert nothing, but hadst a remoter *antiquity*, as thou calledst it, to look back to with blind veneration; thou thyself being to thyself flat, jejune, *modern!* What mystery lurks in this retroversion? or what half Januses are we, that cannot look forward with the same idolatry with which we for ever revert!—CHARLES LAMB.

I. EGYPTIAN AND ORIENTAL

1. EGYPTIAN

		£	s.	d.
Maspero, Egyptian Archæology (*trans.*)	Grevel	0	10	6
Mariette, Monuments of Upper Egypt (*trans.*)	Trübner	0	7	6
Perrot and Chipiez, History of Art in Ancient Egypt (*trans.*) 2 vols.	Chapman, Hall	2	2	0

2. ASSYRIAN, &c.

		£	s.	d.
Perrot and Chipiez, History of Art in Chaldæa and Assyria (*trans.*) 2 vols.	Chapman, Hall	2	2	0

3. PHŒNICIAN

		£	s.	d.
Perrot and Chipiez, History of Art in Phœnicia and its Dependencies (*trans.*) 2 vols.	Chapman, Hall	2	2	0

4. COPTIC

		£	s.	d.
Butler, A. J., The Coptic Churches of Egypt. 2 vols.	Chapman, Hall	1	4	0

Antiquities and Archæology—Egyptian and Oriental, continued

5. SARACENIC

	£	s.	d.
Lane-Poole, S., The Art of the Saracens in Egypt. *Chapman, Hall*	0	4	0
Smith, R. Murdoch, Persian Art. *Chapman, Hall*	0	2	0

6. INDIAN

Prinsep, Indian Antiquities. 2 vols. *Murray*		O.	P.	
Fergusson, History of Architecture. Vol. III. *Murray*	2	2	0	
Thomas, Pathan Kings of Delhi. *Trübner*	1	8	0	
Birdwood, Industrial Arts of India. *Chapman, Hall*	0	14	0	
Cunningham, Reports of the Archæological Survey of India. Vols. I. to XXIII. *Trübner.* Each 10s. and 12s.				

7. NUMISMATICS

	£	s.	d.
Lane-Poole and Others, Coins and Medals. 3 vols. *Stock*	1	16	0
British Museum Catalogue of Oriental, Persian, and Indian Coins. 13 vols. 7 vols. (Oriental) out of print, 6 vols. *British Museum*	6	7	0

II. GREEK

1. ELEMENTARY.

	£	s.	d.
Mahaffy, Greek Antiquities. *Macmillan*	0	1	0
Harrison, J. E., Introductory Studies in Greek Art. *Unwin*	0	7	6
Collignon, Manual of Greek Archæology (*trans.*) *Cassell*	0	5	0
Upcott, An Introduction to Greek Sculpture. *Clarendon Press*	0	4	6

2. ADVANCED.

	£	s.	d.
Newton, Sir C. T., Essays on Art and Archæology. *Macmillan*	0	12	6
Mitchell, History of Ancient Sculpture. *Kegan Paul*	2	2	0
Gardner, Types of Greek Coins. *Cambridge Press*	1	11	6
Hicks, Manual of Greek Historical Inscriptions. *Clarendon Press*	0	10	6
Pausanias, Description of Greece (*trans.*) 2 vols. *Bell*	0	10	0
Becker, Charicles (*trans.*) *Longmans*	0	7	6
Mahaffy, Social Life in Greece from Homer to Menander. *Macmillan*	0	9	0
Schömann, Antiquities of Greece: the State. *Rivington*	O.	P.	

III. ROMAN

1. ELEMENTARY.

	£	s.	d.
Wilkins, Roman Antiquities. *Macmillan*	0	1	0

Antiquities and Archæology—Roman, continued

2. ADVANCED.

		£	s.	d.
Becker, Gallus.	*Longmans*	0	7	6
Ramsay, Roman Antiquities.	*Griffin*	0	8	6
Middleton, Ancient Rome in 1888.	*Black*	1	1	0
Burn, Old Rome.	*Bell*	0	10	6
Dyer, Pompeii.	*Bell*	0	7	6

IV. GENERAL AND BRITISH

		£	s.	d.
Jewitt, Ll., Half hours among English Antiquities.	*Allen*	0	5	0
Lubbock, Prehistoric Times.	*Norgate*	0	18	0
Hildebrand, The Industrial Arts of Scandinavia in Pagan Times.	*Chapman, Hall*	0	2	6
Worsaae, Industrial Arts of Denmark from the Earliest Times to the Danish Conquest of England.	*Chapman, Hall*	0	3	6
Montelius, Civilisation of Sweden in Heathen Times (*trans.*)	*Macmillan*	0	14	0
Greenwell, British Barrows, Excavations, etc. A Record of the Examination of Sepulchral Mounds in various parts of England.	*Clarendon Press*	1	5	0
Evans, The Ancient Stone Implements, Weapons, and Ornaments of Great Britain and Ireland.	*Longmans*	1	8	0
„ The Ancient Bronze Implements, Weapons, and Ornaments of Great Britain and Ireland.	*Longmans*	1	5	0
Rhys, Celtic Britain.	*S.P.C.K.*	0	3	0
Scarth, Roman Britain.	*S.P.C.K.*	0	2	6
Allen, Grant, Anglo-Saxon Britain.	*S.P.C.K.*	0	2	6
Evans, The Coins of the Ancient Britons. (Engraved by F. W. Fairholt.)	*J. R. Smith*	1	1	0
Akerman, Coins of the Romans.	*J. R. Smith*	0	10	6
Henfrey, A Guide to the Study and Arrangement of English Coins (edited by C. F. Keary).	*Bell*	0	6	0
Allen, Romilly, Early Christian Symbolism.	*Whiting*	0	15	0
„ „ Monumental History of the British Church.	*S.P.C.K.*	0	3	0

SCOTCH.

		£	s.	d.
Anderson, Scotland in Pagan Times. 2 vols. (*illus.*)	*Douglas.* Each	0	12	0
„ Scotland in Early Christian Times. 2 vols. (*illus.*)	*Douglas.* Each	0	12	0

IRISH.

		£	s.	d.
Wilde, Descriptive Catalogues in the Museum of Royal Irish Academy. 2 vols.	*Williams, Norgate*	0	13	6
Stokes, M., Early Christian Architecture in Ireland.	*Bell*	1	1	0
„ „ Early Christian Art in Ireland.	*Chapman, Hall*	0	7	6

ART

> For don't you mark? we're made so that we love
> First, when we see them painted, things we have passed
> Perhaps a hundred times, nor cared to see.
> And so they are better painted—better to us,
> Which is the same thing: Art was given for that.
>
> R. BROWNING: *Fra Lippo Lippi.*

Let our artists be those who are gifted to discern the true nature of beauty and grace; then will our youth dwell in the land of health, amid fair sights and sounds; and beauty, the effluence of fair works, will visit the eye and ear, like a healthful breeze from a purer region, and insensibly draw the soul even in childhood into harmony with the beauty of reason.   PLATO'S *Republic.*

I. PAINTING

[NOTES AND SUGGESTIONS.—*The reading about Pictures is useless without the study of paintings also. For this purpose a particular master should be fixed upon in any accessible gallery, and his works compared with those in other galleries by means of prints and photographs. The most recent historical catalogues of foreign galleries should be made use of in visiting them to correct older information given in text-books; other books will give information about the life, training, and subjects of the Painters, and the derivation of their style.*]

1. HANDBOOKS TO GALLERIES

	£	s.	d.
Thompson, Kate, Handbook to the Galleries of Europe. *Macmillan*	O.	P.	
Cook, E. T., A Popular Handbook to the National Gallery. *Macmillan*	0	14	0

2. WORKS OF REFERENCE AND GENERAL HISTORY

Middleton, Article "Painting" in Encyclopædia Britannica.
Woltmann, and Woermann, K., History of Painting (to the Renaissance). 2 vols.   *Kegan Paul*   3 10 0

Art—Painting, continued

	£	s.	d.
Bryan, Dictionary of Painters and Engravers. (ed. Graves and Armstrong). 2 vols. *Bell*	3	3	0
Eastlake, Materials for a History of Oil Painting (technical). 2 vols. *Longmans*	1	6	0
Jameson, Mrs., Sacred and Legendary Art (on Christian Paintings).			
Legends of the Saints and Martyrs. 2 vols. *Longmans*	1	0	0
Legends of the Monastic Orders. *Longmans*	0	10	0
Legends of the Madonna. *Longmans*	0	10	0
History of our Lord. 2 vols. *Longmans*	1	0	0
Husenbeth, Emblems of Saints, in works of Art. *Longmans*		O. P.	
Ruskin, Modern Painters. 5 vols. *G. Allen*	6	6	0
,, Studies of Mountain Form. In Montibus Sanctis. Parts I. and II. *G. Allen.* Each	0	1	6
,, Studies of Cloud Form. Cœli Enarrant. Part I. *G. Allen*	0	1	6
Gilbert, Landscape in Art, to the time of Claude and Salvator. *Murray*	1	10	0

3. HANDBOOKS TO SEPARATE SCHOOLS

	£	s.	d.
Kugler (ed. Layard), Handbook to Italian Schools. 2 vols. *Murray*	1	10	0
Vasari, Lives of Painters. (Italian). 6 vols. *Bell.* Each	0	3	6
Wauters, Flemish School of Painting (*trans.*) *Cassell*	0	5	0
Conway, Early Flemish Painters. *Seeley*	0	7	6
Buxton, Wilmot, and Poynter, German, Flemish, and Dutch Painting. *Low*	0	5	0
Havard, Dutch School of Painting (*trans.*) *Cassell*	0	5	0
Smith, G., Spanish and French Artists. *Low*	0	5	0
Redgrave, R. and S., A Century of English Painters. *Low*	0	10	6
Chesneau, English School of Painting (*trans.*) *Cassell*	0	5	0

4 INDIVIDUAL PAINTERS

See Biography (Artists)

[*For fuller lists of books on the whole subject see Catalogue of Library, South Kensington Museum, viz. List of Works on Painting* (1s.) *and List of Biographies of Artists* (1s. 4d.), *to be bought at the Museum.*]

Art, continued

II. SCULPTURE

[NOTES AND SUGGESTIONS.—*It is quite necessary in studying this subject to have photographs. A good library should contain a portfolio of mounted photographs, if possible platinotypes, at least of the groups from the pediments, metopes, and frieze of the Parthenon in the British Museum. These can be got from the British Museum, or, with other good Greek examples, from Mansell's in Oxford Street. Photographs of Italian Sculpture should be obtained from Alinari, Via Tornabuoni, Florence. A selection from the following works is suggested: Niccolo Pisano, Pulpit in the Baptistery at Pisa; Giacomo della Quercia, sculpture Doorway at S. Petronio, Bologna, and Boys with Garlands, Bargello, Florence; Ghiberti, Gates of Baptistery, Florence; Donatello, Bronze David, St. George, and one of his groups of Madonna and Child; the Della Robbias, some of the glazed terra cotta groups in the Bargello; Luca della Robbia, Dancing Boys and Girls (Bargello); Mino da Fiesole, Madonna (Bargello); a Monument of Bishop Salutati, Cathedral, Fiesole; Verrocchio, David (Bargello); Sansovino, Baptism of Christ, Baptistery, Florence; Michael Angelo, sculptures on Medici Tomb, Florence.*]

		£	s.	d.
Redford, Sculpture.	*Low*	0	5	0
Mullins, Roscoe, Primer of Sculpture.	*Cassell*	0	2	6
Murray, History of Greek Sculpture. 2 vols.	*Murray*	1	16	0
Newton, Essays on Art and Archæology. 2 vols.	*Macmillan*	0	12	6
Parry, Gambier, The Ministry of the Fine Arts.	*Murray*	0	14	0
Waldstein, Catalogue of Casts in Fitzwilliam Museum, Cambridge.	*Macmillan*	0	1	6
Parry, Catalogue of Casts in South Kensington Museum. Department of Science and Art.		0	0	6
Guides to the Department of Greek and Roman Antiquities, the Vase Rooms, and the Department of Coins and Medals in the British Museum.	Various prices			
Perkins, Historical Handbook of Italian Sculpture.	*Remington*	0	15	0

[*For Mediæval Sculpture the best authority is the article (in French) on Sculpture in the Dictionnaire Raisonnée de l'Architecture, Viollet le Duc.*]

III. ARCHITECTURE

[NOTES AND SUGGESTIONS.—*In Architecture, as in other Arts, books alone will carry the student only a very little way. Only by a careful study of good examples, of which fortunately there are many in this country, can progress be made and real knowledge secured.*]

ELEMENTARY.

		£	s.	d.
Parker, Concise Glossary.	*Parker*	0	7	6
" A B C of Gothic Architecture (*illus.*)	*Parker*	0	3	0
" Introduction to Study of Gothic Architecture (*illus.*)	*Parker*	0	5	0
Rosengarten, Handbook of Styles (*illus.*)	*Chatto*	0	7	6

Art—Architecture, continued

ADVANCED.

		£	s.	d.
Fergusson, History of Architecture of all Countries (*illus.*) 4 vols. *Murray*		6	16	6
Or separately—I and II, Ancient and Mediæval.		3	3	0
III, Indian and Eastern.		2	2	0
IV, Modern.		1	11	6
Freeman, Historical and Architectural Sketches, chiefly Italian (*illus.*) *Macmillan*		0	10	6
Ruskin, Seven Lamps of Architecture (*illus.*) *G. Allen*		0	7	6
,, Stones of Venice. 3 vols. (*illus.*) *G. Allen*		4	9	0
,, ,, Selections. 2 vols. *G. Allen*. Each		0	5	0
,, Examples of the Architecture of Venice (15 plates). *G. Allen*		3	3	0
,, The Bible of Amiens. *G. Allen*		0	6	0

SPECIAL.

	£	s.	d.
Viollet le Duc, Lectures on Architecture (*trans.*) (*illus.*) 2 vols. *Low*	3	3	0
,, Habitations of Man in all Ages (*trans.*) *Low*	0	16	0
Pugin, A. W. Principles of Pointed or Christian Architecture. *Weale*	0	15	0
Stanley, Dean, Historical Memorials of Westminster Abbey (*illus.*) *Murray*	0	15	0
Mackmurdo, Wren's City Churches. *G. Allen*	0	5	0

IV. DECORATIVE ART

	£	s.	d.
Jones, Owen, Grammar of Ornament. *Quaritch*	5	5	0
Redgrave, R., A Manual of Design. *Chapman, Hall*	0	2	6
Day, Lewis, Everyday Art. *Batsford*	0	7	6
,, Anatomy of Pattern. *Batsford*	0	3	6
Collingwood, Philosophy of Decoration. *G. Allen*	0	5	0
Poynter, E. J., Ancient Decorative Art, in "Lectures on Art." *Chapman, Hall*	0	9	0
Wornum, Analysis of Ornament. *Chapman, Hall*	0	8	0
Moody, Lectures on Art. *Bell*	0	4	6
Mahew, Decorative Composition. *Virtue*	0	6	0

V. PRACTICE OF DRAWING AND PAINTING

1. GENERAL.

	£	s.	d.
Ruskin, Laws of Fésole. *G. Allen*	0	10	0
Gullick and Timbs, Painting popularly explained. *Crosby Lockwood*	0	5	0

Art—Practice of Drawing and Painting, continued

	£	s.	d.
Taylor, E. R., Elementary Art Teaching. *Chapman, Hall*	0	10	6
Hamerton, Landscape in Nature, Literature, and Painting. *Seeley*	5	5	0
„ Imagination in Landscape Painting. *Seeley*	1	1	0
Da Vinci, Leonardo, Treatise on Painting (*trans.* Rigaud). *Bell*	0	5	0

2. PERSPECTIVE

	£	s.	d.
Dennis, H. J. Second Grade Perspective. *Bailliere*	0	2	6
„ Third Grade Perspective. *Bailliere*	0	15	0
James, H. A., Handbook to Perspective. *Chapman, Hall*	0	2	6
Puckett, R. C., Sciography or Radial Projection of Shadows. *Chapman, Hall*	0	6	0

3. GEOMETRICAL, ARCHITECTURAL, AND MECHANICAL DRAWING

	£	s.	d.
Burchett, Practical Plane Geometry. *Chapman, Hall*	0	5	0
Bradley, T., Elements of Geometrical Drawing. 2 vols. *Chapman, Hall*	1	12	0
Binns, Elementary Orthographic Projection. *Spon*	0	9	0
„ Second Course of „ „ *Spon*	0	10	6
Heather, Descriptive Geometry. *Lockwood*	0	2	0
„ A Treatise on Mathematical Instruments. *Lockwood*	0	1	6

4. ETCHING AND ENGRAVING

	£	s.	d.
Ruskin, Ariadne Florentina (Wood and Metal Engraving). *G. Allen*	0	7	6
„ Lecture on Leech and Tenniel, "The Art of England." *G. Allen*	0	1	0
Short, Treatise on Etching. *Dunthorne*	0	5	0
Conway, The Woodcutters of the Netherlands in the Fifteenth Century. *Cambridge Press*	0	10	6
Wedmore, Four Masters of Etching. *Fine Art Society*	1	1	0
Hamerton, Etching and Etchers. *Macmillan*	7	7	0

5. COLOUR

	£	s.	d.
Church, A. H., Colour. *Cassell*	0	3	6
Chevreul, The Principles of Harmony and Contrast of Colours. *Bell*	0	5	0
Field, Chromatography. Modernised by Taylor. *Winsor, Newton*	0	5	0

6. ANATOMY

	£	s.	d.
Marshall, John, Anatomy for Artists. *Smith, Elder*	1	11	6
Sparkes, Artistic Anatomy. *Bailliere*	0	7	6

BIOGRAPHY

INCLUDING LETTERS, SPEECHES, AND AUTOBIOGRAPHIES

[NOTES AND SUGGESTIONS.—*The number of first-rate biographies in the English language could probably be counted on the fingers of one hand. But after all an indifferent biography is, on the whole, better than none. Some good biographies are unfortunately out of print.*]

"Let us now praise famous men."—ECCLESIASTICUS.

I. ARTISTS

> It's not your chance to have a bit of chalk,
> A wood-coal or the like? or you should see!
> Yes, I'm the painter since you style me so.
> R. BROWNING : *Fra Lippo Lippi.*

	£	s.	d.
Cellini, Benvenuto, Autobiography (trans. by J. A. Symonds) *Nimmo*	0	9	0
Correggio, Heaton. *Low*	0	2	6
Della Robbia and Cellini, Scott. *Low*	0	2	6
Durer, Albrecht, Heath. *Low*	0	3	6
" Scott. *Longmans*	0	16	0
Fra Angelico, Masaccio, and Botticelli, Scott. *Low*	0	3	6
Fra Bartolommeo, Albertinelli, and Andrea del Sarto, Scott. *Low*	0	3	6
Gainsborough and Constable, Arnold. *Low*	0	3	6
Ghiberti and Donatello, Scott. *Low*	0	2	6
Giotto, Quilter. *Low*	0	3	6
" " *Low*	0	15	0
Hogarth, Dobson. *Low*	0	3	6
Holbein, Cundall. *Low*	0	3	6
" Woltman (*trans.*) *Bentley*	1	11	6
Landseer, Stevens. *Low*	0	3	6
Lawrence and Romney, Gower. *Low*	0	2	6
Leonardo da Vinci, Richter. *Low*	0	3	6
Lorrain, Claude le, Dullea. *Low*	0	3	6
Mantegna and Francia, Dullea. *Low*	0	3	6

Biography—Artists, continued

		£	s.	d.
Meissonier, Mollett.	Low	0	2	6
Michelangelo, Clément.	Low	0	3	6
,, Grimm. 2 vols.	Smith, Elder	1	4	0
Millet, Sensier.	Macmillan	0	16	0
Murillo, Minor.	Low	0	2	6
Overbeck, Atkinson.	Low	0	3	6
Raphael, d'Anvers.	Low	0	3	6
,, Crowe and Cavalcaselle. 2 vols.	Murray	1	13	0
Rembrandt, Mollett.	Low	0	3	6
Reynolds, Pulling.	Low	0	3	6
Rossetti, D. G., Sharp.	Macmillan	0	10	6
Rubens, Kett.	Low	0	3	6
Thorvaldsen, Thiele (*trans.*)	Chapman, Hall	0	9	0
Tintoretto, Osler.	Low	0	3	6
Titian, Heath.	Low	0	3	6
,, Crowe and Cavalcaselle. 2 vols.	Murray	1	1	0
Turner, Monkhouse.	Low	0	3	6
,, Hamerton.	Seeley	0	7	6
Vandyck and Hals, Head.	Low	0	3	6
Velasquez, Stowe.	Low	0	3	6
Vernet and Delaroche, Rees.	Low	0	3	6
Watteau, Mollett.	Low	0	2	6
Wilkie, Mollett.	Low	0	3	6

		£	s.	d.
Crowe and Cavalcaselle, Lives of the Early Flemish Painters.	Murray	0	7	6
Jameson, Mrs., Memoirs of the Early Italian Painters (Cimabue to Bassano).	Murray	0	12	0
Vasari, Lives of Painters, Sculptors, and Architects. 6 vols.	Bell. Each	0	3	6

II. ECONOMISTS

A person is not likely to be a good economist who is nothing else.
A. & M. P. MARSHALL.

		£	s.	d.
Fawcett, Leslie Stephen.	Smith, Elder	0	12	6
,, Speeches.	Macmillan	0	10	6
Jevons (Letters and Journal), Mrs. Jevons.	Macmillan	0	14	0
Malthus, Bonar.	Macmillan	0	12	6
Mill, James, Bower.	Low	0	3	6
Mill, John Stuart, Courtney.	Walter Scott	0	1	0
,, ,, Autobiography.	Longmans	0	7	6
Ricardo (Letters to Malthus), Bonar.	Clarendon Press	0	10	6
,, M'Culloch.	Murray	0	16	0
Smith, Adam, Haldane.	Walter Scott	0	1	0
,, ,, Farrer.	Low	0	3	6

Biography, continued

III. LEADERS OF INDUSTRY AND INVENTORS

To be a noble Master, among noble workers, will again be the first ambition with some few: to be a rich Master only the second. —CARLYLE.

		£	s.	d.
Brassey, Helps.	*Bell* {	0	1	6
		0	6	0
Caxton, Blades.	*Trübner*	0	5	0
Denny, Bruce.	*Hodder, Stoughton*	0	12	0
Hill, Sir Rowland, Birkbeck Hill.	*De La Rue*	0	16	0
Moore, George, Smiles.	*Routledge*	0	6	0
Nasmyth, Smiles.	*Murray*	0	6	0
Stephenson, Smiles.	*Murray*	0	2	6
Men of Invention and Industry, Smiles.	*Murray*	0	6	0
Industrial Biography, or Iron-workers and Tool-makers, Smiles.	*Murray*	0	6	0
Heroes of Industry, Major Jones.	*Low*	0	7	6
Lives of the Engineers, Smiles. 5 vols.	*Murray.* Each	0	7	6

IV. MEN AND WOMEN OF LETTERS

O thou who art able to write a book, which once in the two centuries or oftener there is a man gifted to do, envy not him whom they name city-builder, and inexpressibly pity him whom they name conqueror or city-burner! Thou too art a conqueror and victor, but of the true sort—namely, over the Devil.—CARLYLE.

		£	s.	d.
Addison, Courthope.	*Macmillan*	0	1	6
Austen, Jane, Mrs. Madden.	*Allen*	0	3	6
,, ,, Tytler.	*Cassell*	0	3	6
,, ,, Goldwin Smith.	*Walter Scott*	0	1	0
Bacon, Abbott.	*Macmillan*	0	14	0
,, Church.	*Macmillan*	0	1	6
,, **Letters and Life,** Spedding. 7 vols.	*Longmans*	4	4	0
Bentley, Jebb.	*Macmillan*	0	1	6
Blake, Gilchrist. 2 vols.	*Macmillan*	2	2	0
Brontë, Charlotte, Mrs. Gaskell.	*Smith, Elder*	0	2	6
,, ,, Reid.	*Macmillan*	0	6	0
,, ,, Birrell.	*Walter Scott*	0	1	0
,, **Emily,** Robinson.	*Allen*	0	3	6
Browning, Elizabeth Barrett, Ingram.	*Allen*	0	3	6
Browning, Robert, Sharp.	*Walter Scott*	0	1	0
Buckle, Huth. 2 vols.	*Low*	1	12	0
Bunyan, Froude.	*Macmillan*	0	1	6
,, Venables.	*Walter Scott*	0	1	0

Biography—Men and Women of Letters, continued

		£	s.	d.
Burke, J. Morley.	*Macmillan*	0	1	6
„ A Historical Study, J. Morley.	*Macmillan*	0	5	0
Burns, Carlyle. Essays. Vol. II.	*Chapman, Hall*	0	1	0
„ Blackie.	*Walter Scott*	0	1	0
„ Shairp.	*Macmillan*	0	1	6
Byron, Nichol.	*Macmillan*	0	1	6
„ Noel.	*Walter Scott*	0	1	0
„ **Letters and Journals,** Moore.	*Chatto*	0	7	6
Carlyle, R. Garnett.	*Walter Scott*	0	1	0
„ Froude. History of First Forty Years of Carlyle's Life (1795–1835). 2 vols.	*Longmans*	1	12	0
„ Froude. History of Carlyle's Life in London (1834–1881). 2 vols.	*Longmans*	1	12	0
„ Froude. Cheap edition of above. 4 vols.	*Longmans*	0	14	0
Casaubon, Pattison.	*Longmans*	0	18	0
Chaucer, A. W. Ward.	*Macmillan*	0	1	6
Clarendon, Life by himself. 2 vols.	*Clarendon Press*	1	2	0
Coleridge, Traill.	*Macmillan*	0	1	6
„ Caine.	*Walter Scott*	0	1	0
Congreve, Gosse.	*Walter Scott*	0	1	0
Corneille, Trollope.	*Blackwood*	0	2	6
Cowper, Goldwin Smith.	*Macmillan*	0	1	6
Crabbe, Kebbel.	*Walter Scott*	0	1	0
Dante, Mrs. Oliphant.	*Blackwood*	0	2	6
„ Symonds. Introduction to the Study of.	*Smith, Elder*	0	7	6
Defoe, Minto.	*Macmillan*	0	1	6
De Quincey, Masson.	*Macmillan*	0	1	6
„ Page. 2 vols.	*Hogg*	0	12	0
Dickens, A. W. Ward.	*Macmillan*	0	1	6
„ Marzials.	*Walter Scott*	0	1	0
„ Forster.	*Chapman, Hall*	0	7	0
Diderot and the Encyclopædists, J. Morley. 2 vols. *Macmillan.* Each		0	5	0
Dryden, Saintsbury.	*Macmillan*	0	1	6
Edgeworth, Maria, Zimmern.	*Allen*	0	3	6
Eliot, George, Blind.	*Allen*	0	3	6
„ Cross.	*Blackwood*	0	7	6
„ Oscar Browning.	*Walter Scott*	0	1	0
Emerson, Conway.	*Trübner*	0	10	6
„ Garnett.	*Walter Scott*	0	1	0
Ewing, Mrs., and her books, Gatty.	*S.P.C.K.*	0	1	0
Fielding, Dobson.	*Macmillan*	0	1	6
Gibbon, Autobiography and Correspondence.	*Ward, Lock*	0	3	6
„ Morison.	*Macmillan*	0	1	6
Godwin, Kegan Paul. 2 vols.	*Kegan Paul*	1	8	0
Goethe, Autobiography. 2 vols.	*Bell* Each	0	3	6

Biography—Men and Women of Letters, continued

		£	s.	d.
Goethe, Hayward.	*Blackwood*	0	2	6
„ Sime.	*Walter Scott*	0	1	0
„ Lewes (abridged).	*Smith, Elder*	0	7	6
Goldsmith, Black.	*Macmillan*	0	1	6
„ Dobson.	*Walter Scott*	0	1	0
„ J. Forster. Life and Times of.	*Ward, Lock*	0	2	0
Gray, Gosse.	*Macmillan*	0	1	6
Grote, Mrs. Grote.	*Murray*	0	12	0
Hawthorne, Henry James.	*Macmillan*	0	1	6
„ Conway.	*Walter Scott*	0	1	0
Heine, Stigand. 2 vols.	*Longmans*	1	8	0
„ Sharp.	*Walter Scott*	0	1	0
Hugo, Victor, Barnett Smith.	*Ward, Downey*	0	6	0
„ „ Marzials.	*Walter Scott*	0	1	0
Hume, Huxley.	*Macmillan*	0	1	6
Johnson, Dr., Boswell, ed. Napier. 6 vols.	*Bell*	1	1	0
„ „	*Nimmo*	0	5	0
„ „ ed. by Birkbeck Hill. 6 vols.	*Clarendon Press*	3	3	0
„ Symonds.	*Longmans*	0	1	6
„ Leslie Stephen.	*Macmillan*	0	1	6
„ Grant.	*Walter Scott*	0	1	0
Keats, Colvin.	*Macmillan*	0	1	6
„ Rossetti.	*Walter Scott*	0	1	0
Kingsley, Edited by his Wife.	*Kegan Paul*	0	6	0
Lamb, Ainger.	*Macmillan*	0	1	6
Landor, Colvin.	*Macmillan*	0	1	6
„ Forster.	*Chapman, Hall*	0	12	0
Lessing, Rolleston.	*Walter Scott*	0	1	0
„ Sime. 2 vols.	*Trübner*	1	1	0
Locke, Fowler.	*Macmillan*	0	1	6
Longfellow, Robertson.	*Walter Scott*	0	1	0
Macaulay, Morison.	*Macmillan*	0	1	6
„ Miscellaneous Writings and Speeches.	*Longmans*	0	2	6
„ Life and Letters. Trevelyan.	*Longmans*	0	2	6
Marryat, Hannay.	*Walter Scott*	0	1	0
Martineau, Harriet, Mrs. Miller.	*Allen*	0	3	6
„ „ Autobiography. 3 vols.	*Smith, Elder*	1	12	0
Milton, Pattison.	*Macmillan*	0	1	6
„ Stopford Brooke.	*Macmillan*	0	1	6
„ Garnett.	*Walter Scott*	0	1	0
„ Masson. 6 vols.	*Macmillan*	5	8	0
Molière, Mrs. Oliphant and Tarver.	*Blackwood*	0	2	6
More, Sir Thomas, Roper.	*Cambridge Press*	0	3	6
Motley, O. W. Holmes.	*Trübner*	0	6	0
Motley, Letters of. 2 vols.	*Murray*	1	10	0
Pascal, Tulloch.	*Blackwood*	0	2	6

Biography—Men and Women of Letters, *continued*

		£	s.	d.
Petrarch, Reeve.	*Blackwood*	0	2	6
Poe, Woodberry.	*Low*	0	2	6
Pope, Leslie Stephen.	*Macmillan*	0	1	6
„ Elwin and Courthope, Vol. V. of Works.	*Murray*	0	10	6
Rabelais, Walter Besant.	*Blackwood*	0	2	6
Rossetti, D. G. (see Artists)				
Rousseau, J. Morley. 2 vols.	*Macmillan*	0	10	0
Ruskin, Praeterita: Scenes of my Past Life. 2 vols. *George Allen.* Each		0	13	0
Sand, George, Thomas.	*Allen*	0	3	6
Schiller, Carlyle.	*Chapman, Hall*	0	1	0
„ Nevinson.	*Walter Scott*	0	1	0
„ Sime.	*Blackwood*	0	2	6
Scott, Sir W., Hutton.	*Macmillan*	0	1	6
„ Yonge.	*Walter Scott*	0	1	0
„ Lockhart. *Black.* 10 vols., £1 : 10s., and abridged		0	6	0
„ Journal. 2 vols.	*Douglas*	1	12	0
Sévigné, Miss, Thackeray.	*Blackwood*	0	2	6
Sidney, Sir Philip, Symonds.	*Macmillan*	0	1	6
Shakespere, Hudson. 2 vols.	*Boston.* Each	0	12	0
„ Halliwell-Phillipps. 2 vols.	*Longmans*	1	1	0
Shelley, Dowden. 2 vols.	*Kegan Paul*	1	16	0
„ Sharp.	*Walter Scott*	0	1	0
„ Symonds.	*Macmillan*	0	1	6
Sheridan, Mrs. Oliphant.	*Macmillan*	0	1	6
Smith, Sydney, Lady Holland.	*Longmans*	0	3	6
Smollett, Hannay.	*Walter Scott*	0	1	0
Southey, Dowden.	*Macmillan*	0	1	6
Spenser, Church.	*Macmillan*	0	1	6
Steele, Dobson.	*Longmans*	0	1	6
Sterling, Carlyle.	*Chapman, Hall*	0	1	0
Sterne, Traill.	*Macmillan*	0	1	6
Swift, Leslie Stephen.	*Macmillan*	0	1	6
„ Craik.	*Murray*	0	18	0
Thackeray, Trollope.	*Macmillan*	0	1	6
„ Letters.	*Smith, Elder*	0	12	6
Thoreau, H. A. Page.	*Chatto*	0	2	6
Voltaire, J. Morley.	*Macmillan*	0	5	0
Walpole, Horace, Letters. 9 vols.	*Bentley*	4	14	6
Wordsworth, Myers.	*Macmillan*	0	1	6
Johnson, Lives of the Poets, Selected (M. Arnold)	*Macmillan*	0	4	6

(*For Ancient Writers reference should be made to Ancient Classics for English Readers, Blackwood, each 2s. 6d., which contain some biographical matter. For some of the Philosophers see Philosophy. The English Men of Letters Series published by Macmillan, quoted above at 1s. 6d., can also be had at 1s. in paper covers.*)

Biography, continued

V. MEN AND WOMEN OF SCIENCE

Who ever knew Truth put to the worse in a free and open encounter.
MILTON: *Areopagitica.*

		£	s.	d.
Agassiz, Louis, Agassiz. 2 vols.	*Macmillan*	0	18	0
Brewster, By his daughter.	*Douglas*	0	2	6
Buckland, Bompas.	*Smith, Elder*	0	5	0
Darwin, Charles, Grant Allen.	*Longmans*	0	1	6
„ „ Bettany.	*Walter Scott*	0	1	0
„ „ F. Darwin. 3 vols.	*Murray*	1	16	0
„ **Erasmus**, Charles Darwin.	*Murray*	0	7	6
Davy, Mayhew.	*Routledge*	0	3	6
Faraday, Life and Letters. Bence Jones. 2 vols.	*Longmans*	1	8	0
„ As a Discoverer. Tyndall.	*Longmans*	0	3	6
Galileo, Private Life of.	*Macmillan*	0	7	6
Herschel, Mrs. Herschel.	*Murray*	0	7	6
Humboldt, A., Bruhns. 2 vols.	*Longmans*	1	16	0
Linnæus, Miss Brightwell.	*Van Voorst*	0	3	6
Lyell, Mrs. Lyell. 2 vols.	*Murray*	1	10	0
Maxwell, Clerk, Campbell and W. Garnett.	*Macmillan*	0	7	6
Murchison and his Contemporaries, Geikie. 2 vols.	*Murray*	1	10	0
Newton, I., Brewster.	*Tegg*	0	6	0
Somerville, Mary, Personal Recollections.	*Murray*	0	12	0
Astronomers, Morton.	*S.P.C.K.*	0	4	0
Botanists, Zoologists, and Geologists, Duncan.	*S.P.C.K.*	0	4	0
Chemists, Muir.	*S.P.C.K.*	0	4	0
Mechanicians, Lewis.	*S.P.C.K.*	0	4	0
Physicists, W. Garnett.	*S.P.C.K.*	0	4	0

VI. MUSICIANS

I can always leave off talking when I hear a Master play.
R. BROWNING: *A Toccata of Galuppi's.*

		£	s.	d.
Bach, R. Lane Poole.	*Low*	0	3	0
Beethoven, Nohl.	*W. Reeves*	0	3	6
Chopin, Liszt.	*W. Reeves*	0	6	0
Handel, Marshall.	*Low*	0	3	0
„ Hadden.	*Allen*	0	1	6
„ Rockstro.	*Macmillan*	0	10	6
Liszt, De Beaufort.	*Ward, Downey*	0	6	0
„ Ramann (*trans.*) 2 vols.	*Allen*	1	1	0
Mendelssohn, Rockstro.	*Low*	0	3	0
„ Hadden.	*Allen*	0	1	6

Biography—Musicians, continued

		£	s.	d.
Mendelssohn, Letters. 2 vols.	*Macmillan*	0	10	0
Mozart, Gehring.	*Allen*	0	1	6
„ Otto.	*Novello*	1	11	6
Purcell, Cummings.	*Low*	0	3	0
Schubert, Kreisle.	*Allen*	0	6	0
Schumann, Balfe.	*Low*	0	3	0
Wagner, Hueffer.	*Low*	0	3	0
Hueffer, Musical Studies.	*Black*	0	6	0

VII. RELIGIOUS LEADERS AND WRITERS

> Just are the ways of God,
> And justifiable to men.
> MILTON : *Samson Agonistes.*

		£	s.	d.
Athanasius, Reynolds.	*Religious Tract Society*	0	2	6
„ Bush.	*S.P.C.K.*	0	2	6
Anselm, R. W. Church.	*Macmillan*	0	6	0
Augustine, Cutts.	*S.P.C.K.*	0	2	0
Baxter, Boyle.	*Hodder, Stoughton*	0	2	6
Bede (The Venerable), Browne.	*S.P.C.K.*	0	2	0
Bernard, Morison.	*Macmillan*	0	6	0
Buddha, Rhys Davids.	*S.P.C.K.*	0	2	6
Bunyan. See "Men of Letters."				
Calvin, Guizot. In "Great Christians of France" (St. Louis and Calvin).	*Macmillan*	0	6	0
„ **Early Years of**, McCrie and Ferguson.	*Douglas*	0	6	0
Chalmers, Hanna. 2 vols.	*Douglas*	0	12	0
Channing, Memoirs and Correspondence. 2 vols.	*Routledge*	0	7	0
Chrysostom, Stephens.	*Murray*	0	7	6
„ Bush.	*Religious Tract Society*	0	5	0
Erasmus, Seebohm in "Oxford Reformers of 1498."	*Longmans*	0	14	0
„ Drummond. 2 vols.	*Smith, Elder*	1	1	0
Francis of Assisi, Mrs. Oliphant.	*Macmillan*	0	6	0
Francis de Sales, Mrs. Lear.	*Longmans*	0	3	6
Francis Xavier, H. J. Coleridge. 2 vols.	*Burns, Oates*	0	18	0
Hook, Dean, Stephens.	*Bentley*	0	6	0
Hutten, Ulrich von, Strauss.	*Daldy*	0	10	6
Irving, Edward, Mrs. Oliphant.	*Hurst, Blackett*	0	5	0
Jerome, Cutts.	*S.P.C.K.*	0	2	0
Keble, J. T. Coleridge.	*Parker*	0	6	0
Ken, Plumptre. 2 vols.	*Isbister*	1	12	0
Kingsley. See "Men of Letters."				
Knox, McCrie.	*Blackwood*	0	3	6
„ **Portraits of**, Carlyle.	*Chapman, Hall*	0	1	0
Latimer, Demaus.	*Religious Tract Society*	0	5	0

Biography—Religious Leaders and Writers, continued

		£	s.	d.
Luther, Froude.	*Longmans*	0	1	0
„ Koestlin (*trans.*)	*Longmans*	0	16	0
„ Tulloch in "Leaders of the Reformation."	*Blackwood*	0	7	6
„ Rae.	*Hodder, Stoughton*	0	7	6
Maurice, F. D. 2 vols.	*Macmillan*	0	16	0
Memoirs of the Oxford Methodists, L. Tyerman.	*Hodder, Stoughton*	0	10	6
Mohammed, Wollaston.	*Allen*	0	6	0
„ Muir.	*Smith, Elder*	0	14	0
„ „	*Religious Tract Society*	0	5	0
Mohammed and Mohammedanism, Bosworth Smith.	*Smith, Elder*	0	8	6
Newman, J. H., Apologia Pro Vita Sua.	*Longmans*	0	3	6
„ „ Hutton.	*Methuen*	0	2	6
Parker, Theodore, Frothingham.	*Boston*	0	15	0
Patteson, Yonge.	*Macmillan*	0	12	0
Penn, Stoughton.	*Hodder, Stoughton*	0	7	6
Robertson, F. W., Stopford Brooke.	*Kegan Paul*	0	6	0
Savonarola, Villari. 2 vols. (*trans.*)	*Unwin*	1	1	0
Selwyn, Tucker. 2 vols.	*Wells Gardner*	1	4	0
Simeon, Charles, Seeley.	*Seeley*	0	5	0
Stanley, Dean, Recollections of, Bradley.	*Murray*	0	3	6
Wesley, John, Tyerman. 3 vols.	*Hodder, Stoughton*	0	18	0
„ „ Southey. Life of Wesley, and Rise and Progress of Methodism.	*Bell*	0	5	0
„ Samuel, Tyerman.	*Hodder, Stoughton*	0	7	6
„ „ Stevenson. Memorials of the Wesley Family.	*Partridge*	0	7	6
„ Susanna, Eliza Clarke.	*Allen*	0	3	6
Whitfield, Gledstone.	*Longmans*	0	14	0
Wiclif, J. E. T. Rogers. In "Historical Gleanings." Vol. II.	*Macmillan*	0	6	0
„ Lechler (*trans.*)	*Religious Tract Society*	0	8	0
„ Pennington.	*S.P.C.K.*	0	3	0
„ Matthew.	*S.P.C.K.*	0	0	6
Wilberforce, Bishop, Ashwell and R. Wilberforce. 3 vols.	*Murray*	2	5	0
Walton, Izaac, Lives (Herbert, etc.)	*S.P.C.K.*	0	2	6
Christian Leaders of Last Century, Ryle.	*Nelson*	0	7	6
Chief Actors in Puritan Revolution, Bayne.	*Clarke*	0	12	0
Oxford Reformers of 1498 (Colet, Erasmus, More), Seebohm.	*Longmans*	0	14	0
Essays in Ecclesiastical Biography, Sir J. Stephen.	*Longmans*	0	7	6
English Puritanism and its Leaders, Tulloch.	*Blackwood*		O. P.	

(*See also under Men and Women of Letters.*)

Biography, continued

VIII. SOLDIERS AND SAILORS

> And is not War a youthful king,
> A stately hero clad in mail?
> Beneath his footsteps laurels spring;
> Him earth's majestic monarchs hail,
> Their friend, their playmate; and his cold bright eye
> Compels the maiden's love-confessing sigh.—COLERIDGE.

		£	s.	d.
Blake, Admiral, Hannay.	*Longmans*	0	1	6
Cæsar, Froude.	*Longmans*	0	3	6
Charles XII., Voltaire.	*Bell*	0	1	6
„ By the King of Sweden (*trans.*)	*Bentley*	0	12	0
Clive, Wilson.	*Macmillan*	0	2	6
Columbus. See "Travellers and Discoverers."				
Cook. „ „				
Cromwell. See "Statesmen."				
Clyde, Phillips.	*Cassell*	0	1	0
Dampier, Clark Russell.	*Macmillan*	0	2	6
Drake, Corbett.	*Macmillan*	0	2	6
Frederick the Great. See "Statesmen."				
Garibaldi, Autobiography. 3 vols.	*Smith, Innes*	1	11	6
„ Blackett.	*Walter Scott*	0	2	6
Gordon, General, Butler.	*Macmillan*	0	2	6
„ „ Barnes.	*Macmillan*	0	1	0
Gustavus Adolphus, Stephens.	*Bentley*	0	15	0
„ „ Trench.	*Kegan Paul*	0	4	0
Havelock, Forbes.	*Macmillan*	0	2	6
„ Marshman.	*Longmans*	0	3	6
Hawke, Burrows.	*Allen*	1	1	0
Henry V, Church.	*Macmillan*	0	2	6
Howe, Barrow.	*Murray*	0	12	0
Marlborough, Saintsbury.	*Longmans*	0	1	6
„ Coxe. 3 vols.	*Bell.* Each	0	3	6
„ Butler.	*Macmillan*	0	2	6
Monk, Corbett.	*Macmillan*	0	2	6
Montcalm and Wolfe, Parkman. 2 vols.	*Macmillan.* Each	0	12	6
Moore, Sir John, Maurice.	*Macmillan*	0	2	6
Montrose, Morris.	*Macmillan*	0	2	6
Napier, Sir Charles, Bruce.	*Murray*	0	12	0
„ Butler.	*Macmillan*	0	2	6
Napoleon, Bingham. Selections from Letters and Despatches. 3 vols.	*Chapman, Hall*	2	2	0
„ Lanfrey. 4 vols. (*trans.*)	*Macmillan*	O. P.		

A GUIDE TO THE CHOICE OF BOOKS

Biography—Soldiers and Sailors, continued

		£	s.	d.
Napoleon, Seeley.	*Seeley*	0	5	0
Nelson, Southey.	*Bell*	0	5	0
,, Clarke and MacArthur. 3 vols.	*Jackson*	O. P.		
,, Despatches and Letters (selected), Laughton.	*Longmans*	0	16	0
Outram, Goldsmid. 2 vols.	*Smith, Elder*	1	12	0
Peterborough, Stebbing.	*Macmillan*	0	2	6
Raleigh, Gosse.	*Longmans*	0	1	6
Roberts, Sir Frederick, Low.	*Allen*	0	7	6
Rodney, Hannay.	*Macmillan*	0	2	6
Suvoroff, Spalding.	*Chapman, Hall*	0	6	0
Washington. See "Statesmen."				
Wellington, Hooper.	*Macmillan*	0	2	6
,, Gleig.	*Longmans*	0	3	6
,, Yonge. 2 vols.	*Chapman, Hall*	2	2	0
,, Despatches, etc. 23 vols.	*Murray.* Each	1	0	0
William III. See "Statesmen."				

Lives of Indian Officers, Kaye. 2 vols.	*Allen.* Each	0	6	0
Four Famous Soldiers (Sir H. Edwardes, Hodson of Hodson's Horse, Sir C. Napier, and Sir W. Napier) Holmes.	*Allen*	0	6	0

IX. STATESMEN AND SOVEREIGNS

When you separate the common sort of men from their chieftains, so as to form them into an adverse army, I no longer know that venerable object called the People. —BURKE.

		£	s.	d.
Althorp, Myers.	*Bentley*	0	3	6
Bacon. See "Men and Women of Letters."				
Beaconsfield, Kebbel.	*Allen*	0	2	6
,, Froude.	*Low*	0	3	6
Bismarck, Lowe. 2 vols.	*Cassell*	0	10	6
Bolingbroke, Hassall.	*Allen*	0	2	6
,, Collins.	*Murray*	0	7	6
,, Macknight.	*Chapman, Hall*	0	18	0
Bright, John, Barnett Smith.	*Hodder, Stoughton*	0	7	6
,, Speeches.	*Macmillan*	0	3	6
Brougham, Life of, written by himself. 3 vols.	*Blackwood.* Each	0	16	0
Burke. See "Men and Women of Letters."				
Canning, Hill.	*Longmans*	0	1	6
Clarendon. See "Men of Letters."				
Cobden, J. Morley.	*Chapman, Hall*	0	2	0
		0	7	6

Biography—Statesmen and Sovereigns, continued

		£	s.	d.
Cobden, Speeches, etc., edited by J. Bright.	Macmillan	0	3	6
Coligny, Besant.	M. Ward	0	2	6
Cromwell, F. Harrison.	Macmillan	0	2	6
,, Goldwin Smith in "Three English Statesmen."	Macmillan	0	5	0
,, Carlyle. (Letters and Speeches.) 5 vols. Chapman, Hall. Each		0	1	0
Dalhousie, Trotter.	Allen	0	2	6
,, Hunter.	Clarendon Press	0	2	6
Derby, Kebbel.	Allen	0	2	6
Elizabeth, Beesley.	Macmillan	0	2	6
Edward I., York Powell. (forthcoming)	Macmillan	0	2	6
Fawcett. See *Economists*.				
Forster, Reid.	Chapman, Hall	0	10	6
Fox, Wakeman.	Allen	0	2	6
,, Life and Times of, Lord John Russell.	Bentley	0	12	0
,, Early History of (1749-74), Trevelyan.	Longmans	0	6	0
Frederick the Great, Brackenbury.	Chapman, Hall	0	4	0
,, ,, Carlyle. 10 vols.	Chapman, Hall	0	10	0
Gambetta, Marzials.	Allen	0	2	6
Gladstone, Barnett Smith.	Cassell	0	3	6
		0	1	0
Grattan, Dunlop.	Allen	0	2	6
,, Speeches, edited by Madden.	Duffy	0	2	6
Hampden, Lord Nugent.	Bell	0	3	6
,, Goldwin Smith in "Three English Statesmen."	Macmillan	0	5	0
Hastings, Warren, Trotter.	Clarendon Press	0	2	6
,, ,, Lyall.	Macmillan	0	2	6
Henry II., Mrs. Green.	Macmillan	0	2	6
Henry V. See "Soldiers."				
Henry VII., Gairdner.	Macmillan	0	2	6
Lincoln, Abraham, Stoddard.	Sonnenschein	0	15	0
Mary Queen of Scots, Mignet.	Bentley	0	6	0
,, ,, Leland.	M. Ward	0	2	6
Mazarin, Gustave Masson.	S.P.C.K.	0	3	6
Melbourne, Torrens.	Ward, Lock	0	2	0
,, Dunckley.	Low	0	3	6
Metternich, Prince, Malleson.	Allen	0	2	6
Mirabeau, Carlyle in "Essays." Vol. V.	Chapman, Hall	0	1	0
,, Macaulay. ,,	Longmans	0	2	6
Northcote, S. (Lord Iddesleigh), Lang.	Blackwood	0	7	6
O'Connell, Hamilton.	Allen	0	2	6
,, Speeches.	Duffy	0	2	0
Palmerston, Sanders.	Allen	0	2	6
,, Dalling and Bulwer, and Ashley. 2 vols.	Bentley	0	12	0

Biography—Statesmen and Sovereigns, continued

		£	s.	d.
Peel, Thursfield.	*Macmillan*	0	2	6
,, Dalling and Bulwer.	*Bentley*	0	7	6
,, Montague.	*Allen*	0	2	6
Peter the Great, Schuyler. 2 vols.	*Low*	1	12	0
Pitt, Stanhope. 3 vols.	*Murray*	1	16	0
,, Macaulay in "Essays."	*Longmans*	0	2	6
,, Goldwin Smith in "Three English Statesmen."	*Macmillan*	0	2	6
Pym, ,, ,,	*Macmillan*	0	2	6
Richelieu, Gustave Masson.	*S.P.C.K.*	0	3	6
Russell, Lord John (Earl), Walpole. 2 vols.	*Longmans*	1	16	0
Shaftesbury (First Earl), Traill.	*Longmans*	0	1	6
,, ,, Christie. 2 vols.	*Macmillan*	1	4	0
Shelburne, Fitzmaurice. 3 vols. *Macmillan.* Each		0	12	0
Stein, Seeley. 3 vols.	*Cambridge Press*	1	10	0
Strafford, Traill.	*Macmillan*	0	2	6
Walpole, Sir R., J. Morley.	*Macmillan*	0	2	6
,, Coxe. 4 vols.	*Longmans*	O. P.		
Washington, Washington Irving. 4 vols.	*Bell*	0	14	0
,, Marshall. 2 vols.	*Philadelphia*	1	5	0
Wellesley, Malleson.	*Allen*	0	2	6
William the Conqueror, Freeman.	*Macmillan*	0	2	6
William III., Traill.	*Macmillan*	0	2	6
,, Torriano.	*Allen*	0	2	6
Wolsey, Cardinal, Creighton.	*Macmillan*	0	2	6

(*See also under History, De Montfort, Machiavelli, Cavour, and others.*)

X. TRAVELLERS AND DISCOVERERS

Go from the east to the west, as the sun and the stars direct thee,
Go with the girdle of man, go and encompass the earth.
Not for the gain of the gold; for the getting, the hoarding, the having,
But for the joy of the deed; but for the Duty to do.—A. H. CLOUGH.

		£	s.	d.
Barents.	(forthcoming) *Philip*	0	4	6
Batuta, Ibn.	,, *Philip*	0	4	6
Bruce, Scott Keltie.	*Philip*	0	4	6
Cartier, Jacques.	(forthcoming) *Philip*	0	4	6
Columbus, Washington Irving. 2 vols.	*Bell*	0	7	0
,, Helps.	*Bell*	0	6	0
Cook, Walter Besant.	*Macmillan*	0	2	6
Dampier.	(forthcoming) *Philip*	0	4	6
Davis, John, Markham.	*Philip*	0	4	6
Erikson, Leif.	(forthcoming) *Philip*	0	4	6

Biography—Travellers and Discoverers, continued

		£	s.	d.
Franklin, Markham.	*Philip*	0	4	6
Gama, Vasco de, Ravenstein.	*Philip*	0	4	6
Humboldt.	(forthcoming) *Philip*	0	4	6
Livingstone, Thomas Hughes.	*Macmillan*	0	2	6
„ Johnston.	*Philip*	0	4	6
„ Blaikie.	*Murray*	0	6	0
Magellan, Guillemard.	*Philip*	0	4	6
Park, Mungo, Thomson.	*Philip*	0	4	6
Polo, Marco.	(forthcoming) *Philip*	0	4	6
Ross, Mackinder.	*Philip*	0	4	6
Saussure, Freshfield.	*Philip*	0	4	6

XI. GENERAL

		£	s.	d.
Albert, Prince, Martin.	*Smith, Elder*	0	5	0
„ „ 5 vols.	*Smith, Elder.* Each	0	18	0
Arnold, Dr., Stanley. 2 vols.	*Murray*	0	12	0
„ „	*Ward, Lock*	0	2	0
Buxton, Sir T. F., C. Buxton.	*Murray*	0	5	0
Carlyle, Jane Welsh, Letters of, Froude. 3 vols.	*Longmans*	1	16	0
Chambers, Robert, W. Chambers.	*Chambers*	0	3	6
Cooper, Thomas, Life, by himself.	*Hodder, Stoughton*	0	3	6
Davis, Thomas (Ireland), G. Duffy.	*Kegan Paul*	0	12	0
Dick, Robert (geologist), Smiles.	*Murray*	0	12	0
Dora, Sister, Margaret Lonsdale.	*Kegan Paul*	0	2	6
Edward, Thomas (naturalist), Smiles.	*Murray*	0	6	0
Fox, Caroline, Extracts from Journals.	*Smith, Elder*	0	7	6
Fry, Elizabeth, Mrs. Pitman.	*Allen*	0	3	6
Houghton, Lord, Reid. 2 vols.	*Cassell*	1	12	0
Howard (Prison Reformer), Stoughton.	*Hodder, Stoughton*	0	7	6
Kemble, Frances ("Fanny"), Records of my Girlhood.	*Bentley*	0	6	0
„ „ Records of Later Life.	*Bentley*	0	6	0
Lawrence, Henry, Edwards and Merivale.	*Smith, Elder*	0	12	0
„ Temple.	*Macmillan*	0	2	6
Lawrence, Lord, Bosworth Smith. 2 vols.	*Smith, Elder*	1	1	0
Mazzini, Joseph, Life and Writings. 6 vols.	*Smith, Elder.* Each	0	4	6
More, Hannah, Charlotte Yonge.	*Allen*	0	3	6
Osborne, Dorothy, Letters.	*Griffith, Farran*	0	6	0
Roland, Mme., Mathilde Blind.	*Allen*	0	3	6
Shaftesbury, 7th Earl, Hodder.	*Cassell*	0	7	6
Siddons, Mrs., Mrs. Kennard.	*Allen*	0	3	6
Stael, Madame de, Miss Duffy.	*Allen*	0	3	6
Tyndale, Demaus.	*Religious Tract Society*	0	5	0
Wilberforce, William, Bishop Wilberforce.	*Murray*	0	6	0

Biography—General, continued

	£	s.	d.
Lives of Archbishops of Canterbury, Hook. 12 vols. *Bentley*	9	0	0
Lives of the Lord Chancellors, Campbell. 10 vols. *Murray.* Each	0	6	0
Lives of the Judges of England, Foss. 9 vols. *Murray*		O. P.	
Lives of the Chief Justices, Campbell. 4 vols. *Murray.* Each	0	6	0
Plutarch's Lives, Stewart and Long. 4 vols. (*Bohn's Library*) *Bell.* Each	0	3	6

[*For Dictionaries of Biography see Books of Reference.*]

CHILDREN'S BOOKS

[NOTES AND SUGGESTIONS.—*It has been possible to make only a small selection from the multitude of children's books in existence. The books named have been carefully chosen as being either old-established favourites or new books which bid fair to become so; and all have passed the test of having been actually enjoyed by intelligent children.*]

I. STORIES AND TALES

		£	s.	d.
Alcott, Little Women (and others).	*Routledge*	0	1	0
Andersen, Hans, Fairy Tales.	*Bell*	0	3	0
Arabian Nights.	*Paterson*	0	5	0
Austin, Stella, Stumps.	*Masters*	0	2	6
„ Rags and Tatters.	*Masters*	0	3	0
Ballantyne, The Coral Island.	*Nelson*	0	3	6
„ The Dog Crusoe and his Master (and others).	*Nelson*	0	3	6
Blue Fairy Book, A. Lang.	*Longmans*	0	6	0
Burnett, Mrs. F. H., Little Lord Fauntleroy.	*Warne*	0	6	0
Brock, Mrs. Carey, Children at Home.	*Seeley*	0	5	0
Carroll, Alice's Adventures in Wonderland.	*Macmillan*	0	2	6
„ Through the Looking Glass.	*Macmillan*	0	2	6
Cedar Creek.	*Religious Tract Society*	0	2	0
Charlesworth, Miss, Ministering Children.	*Seeley*.	0	2	6
Church, A. J., Stories from Homer.	*Seeley*	0	5	0
„ Stories from Virgil.	*Seeley*	0	5	0
„ Stories from Herodotus.	*Seeley*	0	5	0
„ Stories from the Greek Tragedians.	*Seeley*	0	5	0
„ Three Greek Children.	*Seeley*	0	3	6
„ Heroes and Kings.	*Seeley*	0	1	6
Cooper, The Last of the Mohicans (and others).	*Routledge*	0	1	0
Defoe, Robinson Crusoe.	*Macmillan*	0	4	6
Elliott, Miss, Copsley Annals, preserved in Proverbs.	*Seeley*	0	5	0
Ewing, Mrs., Jan of the Windmill (and others). *Bell.* Each		0	3	0
Gatty, Mrs., Aunt Judy's Tales.	*Bell*	0	3	6
Grimm, Fairy Tales.	*Warne*	0	2	6
Hans Brinker, or The Silver Skates.	*Low*	0	1	0
Hawthorne, N., Tanglewood Tales.	*Routledge*	0	2	0
„ The Wonder Book.	*Routledge*	0	2	0
Henty, Facing Death (and others).	*Blackie*	0	5	0

Children's Books—Stories and Tales, continued

		£	s.	d.
Hughes, Tom Brown's School Days.	Macmillan	0	2	0
Keary, Miss, The Heroes of Asgard.	Macmillan	0	2	6
Kingsley, C., The Water Babies.	Macmillan	0	3	6
" Madam How and Lady Why.	Macmillan	0	3	6
" The Heroes.	Macmillan	0	3	6
Kingston, Three Midshipmen (and others).	Griffith, Farran	0	3	6
Lamb, Tales from Shakespeare.	Macmillan	0	4	6
Marryat, Children of the New Forest.	Routledge	0	2	0
" Masterman Ready.	Routledge	0	2	0
" Settlers in Canada.	Routledge	0	2	0
Martineau, Miss, Feats on the Fiord.	Routledge	0	1	0
" Peasant and Prince.	Routledge	0	1	0
" Settlers at Home.	Routledge	0	1	0
Mayne Reid, Boy Hunters (and others).	Routledge	0	2	6
Molesworth, Mrs.,	Macmillan. Each	0	2	6
Carrots. A Christmas Child.				
Us. The Cuckoo Clock.				
Rosy. Grandmother Dear.				
" Four Winds Farm.	Macmillan	0	4	6
Ouida, Bimbi.	Chatto	0	3	0
" Dog of Flanders.	Chatto	0	2	0
Paget, The Charcoal Burners.	Masters	0	1	0
" The Hope of the Katzekopfs.	Masters	0	2	0
Stevenson, Treasure Island.	Cassell	0	5	0
" Kidnapped.	Cassell	0	5	0
Thackeray, The Rose and the Ring.	Smith, Elder	0	1	6
The Bishop's Little Daughter.	Masters	0	2	0
The Children of Blackberry Hollow.	Nisbet	0	1	6
The Cherry Stones.	Routledge	0	2	0
The Swiss Family Robinson.	Routledge	0	2	6
Tip Cat.	Smith, Innes	0	3	6
Verne, Tigers and Traitors (and others).	Low	0	2	0
Warner, Miss, The Christmas Stocking.	Nisbet	0	1	6
" Mr. Rutherford's Children.	Nisbet	0	1	6
Wilberforce, Bishop, Agathos (and other Sunday Stories)	Seeley	0	1	0
Witt, Myths of Hellas (trans. Younghusband).	Longmans	0	3	6
Yonge, Miss, A Book of Golden Deeds.	Macmillan	0	4	6
" The Little Duke (and others).	Macmillan	0	2	6

(See also *Historical Novels and Tales*.)

II. POETRY

		£	s.	d.
Patmore, The Children's Garland from the Best Poets.	Macmillan	0	4	6
Stevenson, A Child's Garden of Verses.	Longmans	0	5	0
Woods, Miss, Three School Poetry Books. (1)	Macmillan	0	2	6
" " " (2) and (3)	Macmillan. Each	0	4	6

Children's Books, continued

III. PICTURE BOOKS

			£	s.	d.
Caldecott, 16 Picture Books.	*Routledge.* Each	0	1	0
,, ,, in 2 vols.	*Routledge.* Each	0	10	6
,, ,, in 4 vols.	*Routledge.* Each	0	5	0
Crane, The Baby's Opera.	*Routledge*	0	5	0
,, The Baby's Bouquet.	*Routledge*	0	5	0
,, The Baby's Own Æsop.	*Routledge*	0	5	0
,, Aladdin's Picture Book.	*Routledge*	0	5	0
,, 5 Picture Books.	*Routledge.* Each	0	1	0
,, 21 ,, on linen.	*Routledge.* Each	0	1	0
Greenaway, Kate, Marigold Garden.	*Routledge*	0	6	0
,, The Pied Piper of Hamelin.	*Routledge*	0	6	0
,, The Language of Flowers.	*Routledge*	0	3	6
,, Under the Window (Rhymes).	*Routledge*	0	6	0
,, A Day in a Child's Life.	*Routledge*	0	5	0
,, Little Ann and other Poems.	*Routledge*	0	5	0
,, Mother Goose. *Routledge* 1s., 1s. 6d., and		0	2	0
Lear, Nonsense Drolleries.	*Warne*	0	1	6
,, Book of Nonsense.	*Warne*	0	6	0

IV. SCIENCE BOOKS

Common objects of the Country.	*Routledge*	0	1	0
Buckland, F. T., Curiosities of Natural History, 4 series.	*Bentley.* Each	0	3	6
Buckley, Arabella, Life and Her Children.	*Stanford*	0	6	0
,, Winners in Life's Race. 2 vols.	*Stanford.* Each	0	4	6
,, Fairy Land of Science.	*Stanford*	0	6	0
,, Through Magic Glasses.	*Stanford*	0	6	0
Giberne, Agnes, The World's Foundations.	*Seeley*	0	5	0
,, Sun, Moon, and Stars.	*Seeley*	0	5	0
,, Among the Stars.	*Seeley*	0	5	0
Henslow, Botany for Beginners.	*Stanford*	0	2	6
Kingsley, C., Madam How and Lady Why.	*Macmillan*	0	3	6
,, Glaucus, or Wonders of the Sea Shore.	*Macmillan*	0	3	6
Kitchener, A Year's Botany.	*Longmans*	0	5	0
Wood, J. G., Homes without Hands.	*Longmans*	0	10	6
,, Romance of Animal Life.	*Isbister*	0	3	6
,, Insects at Home.	*Longmans*	0	10	6

(*For other books see Natural History and Botany.*)

DOMESTIC ECONOMY

To be happy at home is the ultimate result of all ambition, the end to which every enterprise and labour tends, and of which every desire prompts the prosecution.
— Dr. Johnson.

I. CARE OF CHILDREN

A mother is only a woman; but she needs the love of Jacob, the patience of Job, the wisdom of Moses, the foresight of Joseph, and the firmness of Daniel.—Anon.

		£	s.	d
Babies and how to Rear them.	*Sonnenschein*	0	0	6
Barrett, Howard, Management of Infancy.	*Routledge*	0	2	6
West, Dr. Charles, Mother's Manual of Children's Diseases.	*Longmans*	0	2	6
Suggestions to Mothers on the Management of their Children, by a Mother. Revised by a Physician.	*Churchill*	0	10	6
Mason, Home Education.	*Kegan Paul*	0	3	6

II. COOKERY

"Mind me and mark me; don't neglect your cookery. Kissing don't last, cookery do."—Mrs. Berry in *The Ordeal of Richard Feverel*.

		£	s.	d
Buckton, Mrs., Health in the House.	*Longmans*	0	2	0
,, Food and Home Cookery.	*Longmans*	0	2	6
Tegetmeier, Household Management and Cookery.	*Macmillan*	0	1	0
Church, A. H., Food.	*Chapman, Hall*	0	3	0
Buck, Mrs., The Little Housewife.	*Simpkin*	0	1	0
Williams, Mattieu, The Chemistry of Cookery.	*Chatto*	0	6	0
Lincoln, Boston School Kitchen Text Book.	*Roberts Brothers*	0	2	6
Thompson, Sir H., Food and Feeding.	*Warne*	0	3	6
Wright, Miss Guthrie, The School Cookery Book.	*Macmillan*	0	1	0

Domestic Economy, continued

III. GARDENING

To have a garden well ordered needs memory, decision, and forethought.—ANON.

		£	s.	d.
Watts, Flowers and the Flower Garden.	*Warne*	0	1	0
Jerrold, Our Kitchen Garden.	*Chatto*	0	1	6
Wood, Hardy Perennials and Old-Fashioned Garden Flowers.	*Upcott Gill*	0	5	0
Buckton, Mrs., Window Gardening.	*Longmans*	0	3	6
,, My Lady's Garden.	*M. Ward*	0	1	0
Robinson, The English Flower Garden.	*Murray*	0	15	0

IV. HEALTH AND THE HOME

The House is a fine house when good folks are within.—GEORGE HERBERT.

		£	s.	d.
Barnett, Mrs., The Making of the Home.	*Cassell*	0	1	6
Buckton, Mrs., Health in the House.	*Longmans*	0	2	0
Chambers, Manual of Diet in Health and Disease.	*Smith, Elder*	0	10	6
Combe, Physiology applied to Health and Education.	*Simpkin*	0	4	6
Corfield, Health.	*Kegan Paul*	0	6	0
,, The Laws of Health.	*Longmans*	0	1	6
Health Lectures for the People, Birmingham, Edinburgh, and Manchester Series.	*Heywood.* Each	0	1	0
Kingsley, C., Sanitary and Social Essays.	*Macmillan*	0	3	6
Miller, Mrs., The House of Life.	*Chatto*	0	2	6
Newsholme, A Manual of Personal Hygiene and Public Health.	*Sonnenschein*	0	2	6
Parkes, Personal Care of Health.	*S.P.C.K.*	0	1	0
Richardson, Dr., Health and Life.	*Daldy*	0	7	6
,, Health and Occupation.	*S.P.C.K.*	0	1	0
Wilson, Healthy Life and Healthy Dwellings.	*Churchill*	0	5	0
,, Handbook of Hygiene and Sanitary Science.	*Churchill*	0	10	6
Handicrafts for Handy People.	*Simpkin, Marshall*	0	2	0

EDUCATION

[NOTES AND SUGGESTIONS.—*There are a large number of books about Education, of which the following are among the best. A very complete list of books on the subject will be found at the end of the Cyclopædia of Education (Sonnenschein, 12 parts, 7d. each, or complete, 7s. 6d.) The Blue-books and Reports quoted here refer mainly to England and Wales.*]

Be sure everybody suffers when education goes wrong. The failures are the lives of men. The teacher's workshop floor is strewed, not with shavings and wasted wood, but with wasted years and broken lives.—THRING.

I. ELEMENTARY

		£	s.	d.
Craik, The State and Education. *Macmillan*		0	3	6
Arnold, Matthew, Reports on Elementary Schools. *Macmillan*		0	3	6
" Essay on "Schools" in vol. ii. "Reign of Queen Victoria." 2 vols. *Smith, Elder*		1	12	0
Owen, Elementary Education Acts (England and Wales). *Knight*		0	15	0
Royal Commission on Elementary Education, 1886, Final Report. *Eyre, Spottiswoode*		0	1	0
(*Nine other volumes contain evidence, returns, etc.*)				
Annual Report of Committee of Council on Education. *Eyre, Spottiswoode.* About		0	3	0
The Education Code, published annually. *Eyre, Spottiswoode.* About		0	0	6
Instructions to Inspectors, published annually. *Eyre, Spottiswoode.* About		0	0	6

II. TECHNICAL

	£	s.	d.
Magnus, Industrial Education. *Kegan Paul*	0	6	0
Playfair, Subjects of Social Welfare. *Cassell*	0	7	6
Technical Education in England and Wales,	0	1	0

[*For the above and other pamphlets and leaflets apply to the National Association for the Promotion of Technical and Secondary Education, 14 Dean's Yard, Westminster.*]

	£	s.	d.
Royal Commission on Technical Instruction, 1881, General Report. *Eyre, Spottiswoode*	0	3	2
Science and Art Department Directory, *Eyre, Spottiswoode.* About	0	0	6
" " " Annual Report. *Eyre, Spottiswoode*	0	1	6
" " " Calendar and General Directory. *Eyre, Spottiswoode*	0	1	4

Education, continued

III. SECONDARY

	£	s.	d.
Arnold, M., "Porro Unum" in "Mixed Essays." *Smith, Elder*	0	9	0
" Higher Schools and Universities in France. *Macmillan*	0	6	0
Royal Commission on Public Schools, 1864, Report. *Eyre, Spottiswoode*	0	3	6
(*Three other volumes of evidence, etc.*)			
Schools Enquiry Commission (Endowed and Middle Class Schools), Report. *Eyre, Spottiswoode*	0	4	6
(*Twenty other volumes, containing Reports on England and Foreign Countries, Evidence, etc.*)			
Annual Report of Charity Commission. *Eyre, Spottiswoode* About	0	1	0

IV. UNIVERSITIES

Laurie, Lectures on the Rise of Universities. *Kegan Paul*	0	6	0
Mullinger, History of the University of Cambridge. *Longmans*	0	2	6
Brodrick, " " Oxford. *Longmans*	0	2	6
Boase, Oxford (Historic Towns). *Longmans*	0	3	6

[For Reports of Examinations of Schools by Oxford, Cambridge, London University, and the College of Preceptors; Reports of Local Examinations of Oxford and Cambridge; Reports of Extension Work of Oxford, Cambridge, and London (address Charterhouse), apply to the various Secretaries. For general information about Universities and University Colleges, see the various Calendars published locally.]

V. EDUCATIONAL METHODS

Abbott, E. A., Hints on Home Teaching. *Seeley*	0	3	0
Ascham, Scholemaster. *Bell*	0	1	0
Bain, Education as a Science. *Kegan Paul*	0	5	0
Colbeck, Teaching of Modern Languages. *Cambridge Press*	0	2	0
Fearon, School Inspection. *Macmillan*	0	2	6
Fitch, Lectures on Teaching. *Cambridge Press*	0	5	0
Geikie, A., The Teaching of Geography. *Macmillan*	0	2	0
Landon, School Management (Elementary). *Kegan Paul*	0	6	0
Locke, Thoughts on Education (Ed. Quick). *Cambridge Press*	0	3	6
Shirreff, Miss, The Kindergarten. *Sonnenschein*	0	1	4
Spencer, Herbert, Education. *Williams, Norgate*	0	2	6
Sully, Teacher's Handbook of Psychology. *Longmans*	0	6	6
Thring, Theory and Practice of Education. *Cambridge Press*	0	4	6
" Addresses. *Unwin*	0	5	0

VI. HISTORY

Compayré, History of Pedagogy. *Sonnenschein*	0	6	0
Quick, Essays on Educational Reformers. *Longmans*	0	5	0

GEOGRAPHY AND TRAVELS

[NOTES AND SUGGESTIONS.—*In Section 5, "Travels," some books out of print are set down. Very few of the best books of Travel are now to be had new. They must be read at a Library, or bought second hand.*

In the same section, the sub-section "Europe" appears very incomplete. The ordinary Guide Books (section 6) to a large extent take the place of Narratives.

In section 7, "Atlases," some German works are put down. German maps are the finest, and the German names will present few difficulties to any one with the very slightest knowledge of a few German words.]

Many shall run to and fro, and knowledge shall be increased.
DANIEL xii. 4.

I. GENERAL

1. TEXT-BOOKS

	£	s.	d.
Grove, Sir George, Primer of Geography. *Macmillan*	0	1	0
Geikie, Elementary Geography of the British Isles. *Macmillan*	0	1	0
Green, J. R. & A. S., Short Geography of the British Isles. *Macmillan*	0	3	6
Chisholm, Longman's School Geography. *Longmans*	0	3	6
Mill, H. R., Elementary General Geography. *Macmillan*	0	3	6
Johnston, Keith, Physical, Historical, Political, and Descriptive Geography. *Stanford*	0	12	0

2. REFERENCE

	£	s.	d.
Reclus, Universal Geography, translated. Europe, 5 vols.; Asia, 4 vols.; Africa, 3 vols.; more to follow. *Virtue* Each	1	1	0
Stanford's Compendium of Geography and Travel. 6 vols. 1. "Europe," by Rudler and Chisholm; 2. "Asia," by Keane; 3. "Africa," by Keith Johnston and Ravenstein; 4. "N. America," by Hayden and Selwyn; 5. "S. America," by Bates; 6. "Australasia," by Wallace. *Stanford* Each	1	1	0
Hunter, Imperial Gazetteer of India. 2d edition. 14 vols. *Trübner*	3	3	0
Bartholomew, Gazetteer of the British Isles. *Black*	1	16	0

Geography and Travels, continued

II. PHYSICAL

1. GENERAL TEXT-BOOKS

		£	s.	d.
Geikie, A., Primer of Physical Geography. *Macmillan*		0	1	0
„ Elementary Lessons in Physical Geography. *Macmillan*		0	4	6
Hinman, Eclectic Physical Geography. *Van Antwerp* N. York		0	6	0
Reclus, The Earth, translated by Keane. *Virtue*		1	1	0
„ The Ocean, translated by Keane. *Virtue*		1	1	0

2. SPECIAL SUBJECTS

		£	s.	d.
Findlay, Text-book of Ocean Meteorology, edited by Martin. *Laurie*		0	12	0
Wallace, A. R., Tropical Nature. *Macmillan*		0	12	0
„ Island Life. *Macmillan*		0	18	0
„ The Geographical Distribution of Animals. 2 vols. *Macmillan*		2	2	0

3. SPECIAL REGIONS

		£	s.	d.
Ramsay, Sir A., The Physical Geology and Geography of Great Britain. 5th edition. *Stanford*		0	15	0
Geikie, A., The Scenery of Scotland. *Macmillan*		0	12	6
Hull, The Physical Geology and Geography of Ireland. *Stanford*		0	7	0
Blanford, Climates and Weather of India. *Macmillan*		0	12	6

III. HISTORICAL

1. GEOGRAPHY APPLIED TO HISTORY

		£	s.	d.
Taylor, I., Words and Places. *Macmillan*		0	6	0
Freeman, The Historical Geography of Europe. 2 vols. *Longmans*		1	11	6
„ English Towns and Districts. *Macmillan*		0	14	0
Lucas, Introduction to a Historical Geography of the British Colonies. *Clarendon Press*		0	4	6
„ Historical Geography of the British Colonies. Vol. I. 5s.; vol. II. 7s. 6d. *Clarendon Press*		0	12	6

2. HISTORY OF GEOGRAPHY

a. ANCIENT.

		£	s.	d.
Tozer, Primer of Classical Geography. *Macmillan*		0	1	0
Kiepert, Manual of Ancient Geography. *Macmillan*		0	5	0
Bunbury, A History of Ancient Geography. 2 vols. *Murray*		1	1	0

Geography and Travels—History, continued

b. MEDIÆVAL.

		£	s.	d.
Yule, Book of Sir Marco Polo. 2 vols.	*Murray*	3	3	0
Marco Polo, Wright	*Bell*	0	5	0

c. MODERN.

		£	s.	d.
Major, Prince Henry the Navigator.	*Asher*	1	5	0
Markham, Threshold of the Unknown Region.	*Low*	0	7	6
The World's Great Explorers and Explorations. *Philip*				
1. John Davis, by C. Markham.				
2. Palestine, by Major Conder.				
3. Magellan, and the Pacific, by Dr. Guillemard.				
4. Mungo Park and the Niger, by J. Thomson (and others).				
	Each	0	4	6
Markham, Fifty Years' Work of the Royal Geographical Society.	*Murray*		O. P.	
Palestine Exploration Fund. Twenty-one Years' Work in the Holy Land.	*Bentley*	0	3	6

IV. COMMERCIAL

1. TEXT-BOOKS

		£	s.	d.
Mill, Elementary Commercial Geography.	*Cambridge Press*	0	1	0
Chisholm, Handbook of Commercial Geography.	*Longmans*	0	16	0

2. REFERENCE

		£	s.	d.
Yeats, Manuals of Commerce. *Philip.*	Each	0	6	0
1. Natural History of the Raw Materials of Commerce.				
2. Technical History of Commerce.				
3. Growth and Vicissitudes of Commerce.				
4. Recent and Existing Commerce.				
Yeats, The Golden Gates of Trade.	*Philip*	0	4	6
,, Map Studies of the Mercantile World.	*Philip*	0	4	6

V. TRAVELS

(See also Travellers and Discoverers under Biography.)

1. GENERAL

		£	s.	d.
Cook, Captain, First Voyage by Hawksworth, Second and Third by Himself.	*Black*	0	3	6
Darwin, C., Naturalist's Voyage round the World.	*Murray*	0	3	6
also	*Ward, Lock*	0	2	0

Geography and Travels—Travels, continued

		£	s.	d.
Moseley, Notes of a Naturalist on the *Challenger*.	*Macmillan*	1	1	0
Dilke, Greater Britain.	*Macmillan*	0	6	0
„ Problems of Greater Britain.	*Macmillan*	0	12	6
Galton, Vacation-Tourists. 3 vols.	*Macmillan*		O. P.	

2. EUROPE

		£	s.	d.
Peaks, Passes, and Glaciers. 3 vols.	*Longmans*		O. P.	
Gilbert and Church, The Dolomite Mountains.	*Longmans*		O. P.	
King, Italian Valleys of the Alps.	*Longmans*		O. P.	
Freshfield, The Italian Alps.	*Longmans*		O. P.	
Whymper, Scrambles amongst the Alps.	*Murray*		O. P.	
Tyndall, Hours of Exercise in the Alps.	*Longmans*		O. P.	
Borrow, The Bible in Spain.	*Murray*	0	2	6
Wallace, D. Mackenzie, Russia.	*Cassell*	0	5	0
Forbes, Norway and its Glaciers.	*Black*		O. P.	
Seebohm, H., Siberia in Europe.	*Murray*		O. P.	

3. ASIA

		£	s.	d.
Freshfield, The Central Caucasus and Bashan.	*Longmans*		O. P.	
Grove, The Frosty Caucasus.	*Longmans*		O. P.	
Bryce, Transcaucasia and Ararat.	*Macmillan*	0	9	0
Stanley, Dean, Sinai and Palestine.	*Murray*	0	12	0
Kinglake, Eothen.	*Blackwood*	0	6	0
Tristram, Land of Israel.	S. P. C. K.	0	10	6
Palmer, Desert of the Exodus. 2 vols.	*Deighton, Bell*		O. P.	
Palgrave, W. G., Central and Eastern Arabia.	*Macmillan*	0	6	0
Burnaby, A Ride to Khiva.	*Cassell*	0	1	6
Curzon, Russia in Central Asia.	*Longmans*	1	1	0
Vambéry, Travels in Central Asia.	*Murray*	1	1	0
Seebohm, H., Siberia in Asia.	*Murray*	0	14	0
Tennent, Ceylon. 2 vols.	*Longmans*		O. P.	
Hooker, Himalayan Journals. 2 vols.	*Murray*		O. P.	
Williams, The Middle Kingdom. 2 vols.	*Allen*	2	2	0
Gill, The River of Golden Sand.	*Murray*	0	7	6
Guillemard, Voyage of the *Marchesa*.	*Murray*	1	1	0
Wallace, A. R., The Malay Archipelago.	*Macmillan*	0	6	0

4. AFRICA

		£	s.	d.
Hooker and J. Ball, Morocco and the Great Atlas.	*Macmillan*	1	1	0
Thomson, Joseph, Travels in the Atlas.	*Philip*	0	9	0
Livingstone, Missionary Travels in South Africa.	*Murray*	0	7	6
„ Expedition to the Zambesi.	*Murray*	0	7	6
„ Last Journals. 2 vols.	*Murray*	0	15	0

Geography and Travels—Travels—Africa, continued

		£	s.	d.
Thomson, Through Masai Land. *Low*		0	7	6
Burton, Sir R., Zanzibar. 2 vols. *Tinsley*		O. P.		
Speke, Source of the Nile. *W. Blackwood*		O. P.		
Baker, Sir S., Great Basin of the Nile. 2 vols. *Macmillan*		O. P.		
Stanley, H. M., Through the Dark Continent. *Low*		0	3	6
„ In Darkest Africa. 2 vols. *Low*		2	2	0
Schweinfurth, The Heart of Africa. 2 vols. *Low*		0	15	0
Drummond, Tropical Africa. *Hodder, Stoughton*		0	3	6
Galton, Travels in South Africa. *Ward, Lock*		0	2	0

5. AMERICA

	£	s.	d.
Butler, W. F., The Great Lone Land. *Low*	0	7	6
Marshall, W. G., Through America. *Low*	0	7	6
Belt, Naturalist in Nicaragua. *Murray*	0	12	0
Bates, Naturalist on the Amazons. 2 vols. *Murray*	1	8	0
„ Cheaper Edition, but not complete.	0	7	6
Wallace, A. R., Travels on the Amazon and Rio Negro. *Ward, Lock*	0	2	0
Wells, Three thousand miles through Brazil. 2 vols. *Low*	1	12	0
Ball, Notes of a Naturalist in South America. *Kegan Paul*	0	8	6
Humboldt, Personal Narrative of Travels in America. 3 vols. (*Bohn's Library*.) *Bell*	0	15	0

6. ARCTIC AND ANTARCTIC

	£	s.	d.
Ross, Sir James, Voyage in the Southern and Antarctic Regions. 2 vols. *Murray*	O. P.		
Dufferin, Lord, Letters from High Latitudes. *Murray*	0	7	6
Osborn, Discovery of a N. W. passage by Captain M'Clure. *Blackwood*	O. P.		
M'Clintock, Fate of Sir John Franklin. *Murray*	0	7	6
Nordenskiöld, The Voyage of the *Vega*. 2 vols. (Popular Edition, 6s.) *Macmillan*	2	5	0
Payer, New Lands within the Arctic Circle. 2 vols. *Macmillan*	1	12	0

VI. GUIDE BOOKS

	£	s.	d.
Ball, J., The Alpine Guide. 3 vols. (Separately—East, 10s. 6d.; West, 6s. 6d.; Central, 7s. 6d.) *Longmans*	1	4	6
Baedeker's Guides are perhaps best for the beaten tracks, and contain the best maps. *Dulau*	Various		
Murray's Guides are perhaps best for the towns and out-of-the-way places. *Murray*	Various		
Hare's Volumes on Italy, France, Spain, etc., are also useful. *G. Allen*	Various		

Geography and Travels - Guide Books, continued

		£	s.	d.
Baddeley and Ward's Thorough Guides are the best for the Tourist districts of the British Isles. *Dulau*			Various	
Galton, The Art of Travel. *Murray*		0	7	6
Freshfield and Wharton, Hints to Travellers. *Royal Geographical Society*		0	6	0

VII. MAPS

1. ENGLISH ATLASES

		£	s.	d.
"Multum in Parvo" of the World.	*W. and A. K. Johnston*	0	2	6
Pocket Atlases, England, Scotland, Ireland.	*J. Walker and Co.* Each	0	1	0
„ World, British Colonies.	*J. Walker and Co.* Each	0	2	6
"Handy Reference" of World.	*J. Walker and Co.*	0	7	6
Longman's "New." Edit. Chisholm.	*Longmans*	0	12	6
"Cosmographic."	*W. and A. K. Johnston*	1	1	0
"London."	*Stanford*	1	10	0
"Handy Royal."	*W. and A. K. Johnston*	2	12	6
"Royal."	*W. and A. K. Johnston*	6	6	0
"Imperial."	*Philip*	8	0	0
"Historical."	*W. and A. K. Johnston*	0	2	6

2. GERMAN ATLASES

		£	s.	d.
Andrée's Atlas.	*Velhagen and Klasing, Leipzig*	2	0	0
Droysen's Historischer Hand Atlas.	*Velhagen and Klasing, Leipzig*	2	5	0
Stieler's Hand Atlas.	*Perthes, Gotha*	3	15	0
„ New Edition coming out in 32 parts. Each		0	2	0
Berghaus Physikalischer Atlas.	*Perthes, Gotha*	6	6	0
„ „ New Edition coming out in 25 parts. Each		0	3	6
Spruner-Menke Historischer Atlas. 3 vols.	*Perthes, Gotha*	9	0	0

3. WALL MAPS

Either Stanford's or Philip's or W. and A. K. Johnston's Library Maps,—a Map of the World, a Continent, or one of the three Kingdoms, mounted on rollers, costs from one to two guineas.

4. GOVERNMENT MAPS

The Agents for the Ordnance and Geological Maps are—In England and Wales, EDWARD STANFORD; in Scotland, J. MENZIES & CO.; in Ireland, HODGES, FIGGIS, & CO. The Agent for the Admiralty Charts is S. C. POTTER. Official Catalogues are published both of the Maps and the Charts, also Index-Maps.

GOVERNMENT PUBLICATIONS

In proportion as the structure of a Government gives force to public opinion, it is essential that public opinion should be enlightened.   WASHINGTON.

A convenient list of some of the more important Parliamentary papers, Reports of Commissions and Committees, Acts of Parliament, and the like, can be obtained for 6d. from Messrs. Eyre and Spottiswoode, East Harding Street, London, E.C., to whom all correspondence about Government Publications should be addressed, if local booksellers are not willing or able to procure what is required; and from whom all the publications mentioned below can be obtained by post.

The annual amount of matter published is enormous. Thus for the year 1888 *the papers printed for the House of Commons alone are spread over* 111 *large volumes, divided as follows:—*

Volumes 1-7.—**Public Bills** introduced by the Government or by private Members, most of which do not become law.

Volumes 8-23.—**Reports from Select Committees**, specially appointed by Parliament on subjects such as Army and Navy Estimates, Poor Law Relief, Sea Fisheries, Sunday Closing Acts, Sweating System, Town Holidays, and the like. These include as a rule a great deal of evidence from witnesses.

Volumes 24-65.—**Reports from Royal Commissions and Departments.** These include Reports from Royal Commissions on *e.g.* Elementary Education Acts, Market Rights and Tolls; reports from Permanent Government Departments, such as the Education Department or the Local Government Board; and Reports as to Births, Deaths, and Marriages, Factories, Prisons, Police, and the like.

Volumes 66-111.—**Accounts, Returns, and Miscellaneous Reports and Statistics.** These include the Army and Navy and Civil Service Estimates for the Year; Commercial Reports from our Consuls and others; Railway, Trade, Friendly Society, etc. Returns; and some valuable volumes of general statistics.

A full list of all the above will be found in an annual volume called *Numerical List of Sessional Papers*, price about 2s. 3d.

A few words only as to the above mass of printed material and other blue-books can be given here.

Government Publications, continued

1. Copies of **Bills** which are before Parliament in either House can be obtained during the Session from Eyre and Spottiswoode, by post, at prices from 1d. upwards.

2. **Acts of Parliament** are bound up after the Session in volumes, price about 3s.; but all modern Acts of Parliament can be bought singly at prices from 1d. upwards, seldom exceeding 1s. A cheap edition of all the Statutes from the beginning is being published at 7s. 6d. a volume; the whole, down to the present time, to cost about 8 guineas.

3. **Reports of Select Committees and Royal Commissions.**—The actual Reports are published separately as a rule, and do not cost much, say from 3d. to 4s. But the volumes of evidence, which are often more valuable than the Reports themselves, may rise to 8s. or more, the price depending on the size and number of maps or tables. Any one ordering these should insist on having the **Index to the Evidence**, (sometimes published separately) which is a most valuable help.

Many valuable Reports of past Commissions and Committees may still be had, *e.g.* Technical Instruction, Friendly Societies, Ordnance, Forestry, Housing of the Working Classes, Irish Industries, National Insurance, Depression of Trade, Intemperance, and the like.

4. **Reports of Departments published annually.**—The Report of the Local Government Board costs about 3s. 6d.; that of the Education Department about 4s. 6d. There are many others.

5. **Miscellaneous Papers.**—There are many papers, such as Consular Reports from abroad, Reports on Agriculture, Mining, Merchant Shipping, Poor Rates, Building and Friendly Societies, particulars of which can be had from Eyre and Spottiswoode on inquiry.

6. **Statistics.**—There are some very useful volumes published annually on many subjects. The Labour Statistics (Trade Unions, etc.) should be specially noted. The following cheap collections of statistics, taken from the larger volumes and published annually, should be in every public library; and the first, commonly called *the* Statistical Abstract, should be more widely known, as it gives many interesting and valuable tables about the United Kingdom.

				£	s.	d.
Statistical Abstract,	United Kingdom.	*Eyre, Spottiswoode*		0	1	0
,,	,,	British India.	*Eyre, Spottiswoode*	0	1	0
,,	,,	Colonies.	*Eyre, Spottiswoode*	0	1	0
,,	,,	Foreign Countries.	*Eyre, Spottiswoode*	0	1	0

HISTORY

[NOTES AND SUGGESTIONS. —"*No one can really study any particular period of history unless he knows a great deal about what preceded and what came after it. He cannot seriously study a generation of men as if it could be isolated and examined like a piece of inorganic matter. He has to bear in mind that it is a portion of a living whole which is under his observation. The work of the constructive imagination comes in where the work of investigation ends. In the end this is a work which every man must do for himself. He will have to pick out from the manifold facts of history those which seem to him to be more important than the others, and it will never happen that any two men will be precisely agreed as to the relative importance of any set of facts.*"
— S. R. GARDINER.

Some books on the History of Civilisation will be found under II. 1. Europe. Neither the History of Religion nor Military and Naval History are dealt with in detail here, but a few of the best books will be found in the following list. See also Biography, Religious Leaders and Soldiers and Sailors.]

The years teach much which the days never know.—EMERSON.

> Before man parted for this earthly strand,
> While yet upon the verge of heaven he stood,
> God put a heap of letters in his hand,
> And bade him make with them what word he could.
>
> And man has turned them many times; made Greece,
> Rome, England, France;—yes, nor in vain essay'd
> Way after way, changes that never cease!
> The letters have combined, something was made.
> MATTHEW ARNOLD.

I. ANCIENT HISTORY

1. GENERAL AND ORIENTAL

1. **ELEMENTARY BOOKS.**

	£	s.	d.
Smith, Philip, Student's Ancient History of the East. *Murray*	0	7	6
Bosworth Smith, Carthage and the Carthaginians. *Smith, Elder*	0	5	0
Sayce, Light from Ancient Monuments. *Religious Tract Society*	0	2	6

History—Ancient, continued

	£	s.	d.
Sayce, Assyria, her Princes and People. *Religious Tract Society*	0	2	6
„ Ancient Empires of the East. *Macmillan*	0	6	0
See also **Non-Christian Systems, Buddhism,** and others. *S.P.C.K.* Each	0	2	6

2. MORE ADVANCED BOOKS.

	£	s.	d.
Duncker, History of Antiquity (*trans.* Abbott). 6 vols. *Bentley.* Each	1	1	0
Layard, Nineveh and its Remains. *Murray*	0	7	6
Ranke, Von, Universal History (*trans.*) Vol. I. *Kegan Paul*	0	16	0
Rawlinson, Five Great Monarchies. 3 vols. *Murray*	2	2	0
Records of the Past. 12 vols. *Bagster.* Each	0	3	6
„ New series. *Bagster.* Each	0	4	6

2. EGYPTIAN

	£	s.	d.
Birch, Egypt from the Earliest Times to B.C. 300. *S.P.C.K.*	0	2	0
Rawlinson, Ancient Egypt. *Unwin*	0	5	0
Encyclopædia Britannica, Article "Egypt." *Black*			
Brugsch-Bey, Egypt under the Pharaohs. 2 vols. *Murray*	1	12	0

3. JEWISH

(*The Revised Versions of the Old and New Testaments can be purchased separately at various prices. The Oxford Bible for Teachers (Clarendon Press), the notes to which can be had separately, will be found very useful*).

	£	s.	d.
Maclear, A Class Book of Old Testament History. *Macmillan*	0	4	6
Student's Old Testament History. *Murray*	0	7	6
Edersheim, The Bible History. 7 vols. *Religious Tract Society.* Each	0	2	6
Geikie, C., Hours with the Bible. 6 vols. *Cassell.* Each	0	6	0
Stanley, Dean, Lectures on the Jewish Church. 3 vols. *Murray*	0	18	0
„ Sinai and Palestine. *Murray*	0	12	0
Men of the Bible Series. *Nisbet.* Each	0	2	6
Ewald, History of Israel (*trans.*) 8 vols. *Longmans*	5	18	0
Wellhausen, Prolegomena to the History of Israel (with a reprint of the Article "Israel" from the Encyclopædia Britannica). *Black*	0	15	0
Schürer, The Jewish People in the Time of Jesus Christ. 3 vols. *T. & T. Clark*	1	11	6
Milman, History of the Jews. 3 vols. (Vol. III. includes the Period from the Christian era.) *Murray*	0	12	0

History—Jewish, continued

	£	s.	d.
Outlines of Jewish History from B.C. 586 to Christian era 1885. *Longmans*	0	3	6
Smith, Dr. W., Dictionary of the Bible. 3 vols. *Murray*	5	5	0
,, ,, ,, abridged	1	1	0
	0	7	6
Josephus, Whiston's Translation. 2 vols. *Bell*	0	7	0

4. GREEK

1. ELEMENTARY.

	£	s.	d.
Fyffe, Greek History. *Macmillan*	0	1	0
Cox, Athenian Empire. *Longmans*	0	2	6
Sankey, Spartan and Theban Supremacies. *Longmans*	0	2	6
Plutarch, Lives (*trans.* Langhorne). 4 vols. *Warne*	0	8	0
Smith, Dr. W., Student's History of Greece. *Murray*	0	7	6
Mahaffy, Social Life in Greece. *Macmillan*	0	7	6
,, Alexander's Empire. *Unwin*	0	5	0

2. ADVANCED.

	£	s.	d.
Abbott, E., History of Greece. *Longmans*	0	10	6
Grote, History of Greece. 10 vols. *Murray.* Each	0	5	0
Curtius, History of Greece (*trans.* Ward). 5 vols. *Bentley.* Each	0	18	0
Wordsworth, Greece, edited by Tozer (Geography). *Murray*	1	11	6
Herodotus, Translated by G. C. Macaulay. 2 vols. *Macmillan*	0	18	0
Thucydides, Translated by Jowett. 2 vols. (2d vol. being notes on Greek). *Clarendon Press*	1	12	0
Xenophon, Translated by Dakyns. Vol. I. *Macmillan*	0	10	6

3. REFERENCE.

	£	s.	d.
Schömann, Antiquities of Greece. *Rivington*		O. P.	
Harrison, J. E., Monuments and Mythology of Athens. *Macmillan*	0	10	0
Abbot, E., Skeleton Outline of Greek History. *Longmans*	0	2	6
Tozer, Lectures on Greek Geography. *Murray*	0	9	0

5. ROMAN

1. ELEMENTARY.

	£	s.	d.
Creighton, Roman History. *Macmillan*	0	1	0
Merivale, A general History of Rome. *Longmans*	0	7	6
Ihne, Rome to its Capture by the Gauls. *Longmans*	0	2	6
Arnold, Dr., The Second Punic War, ed. W. T. Arnold. *Macmillan*	0	8	6

History—Roman, continued

		£	s.	d.
Merivale, The Roman Triumvirates.	*Longmans*	0	2	6
Capes, Early Roman Empire.	*Longmans*	0	2	6
,, Age of the Antonines.	*Longmans*	0	2	6
The Student's Gibbon.	*Murray*	0	7	6

2. ADVANCED.

Mommsen, History of Rome (*trans.* Dickson). 4 vols.
Vols. I. and II. 21s. ; Vol. III. 10s. 6d. ;
Vol. IV. 15s. *Bentley* 2 6 6
  ,, History of the Roman Provinces. 2 vols. *Bentley* 1 16 0
Merivale, The Romans under the Empire. 8 vols.
Longmans. Each 0 6 0
Gibbon, Decline and Fall of the Roman Empire. 8 vols.
(Also *Warne.* 4 vols. Each 2s.) *Murray* 3 0 0

3. REFERENCE, CHRONOLOGY, ETC.

Ramsay, Manual of Roman Antiquities.	*Griffin*	0	8	6
Matheson, Skeleton outline of Roman History.	*Longmans*	0	2	0
Dyer, History of the City of Rome.	*Bell*	0	5	0
Burn, Old Rome.	*Bell*	0	10	6

(*See for both Greek and Roman History—Smith's Classical Dictionary, Murray, 18s., and Dictionary of Greek and Roman Antiquities, 2 Vols., Murray, 31s. 6d. each (cheaper editions of both 7s. 6d.); also the Public School Atlas of Ancient Geography, Longmans, 7s. 6d.*)

II. MEDIÆVAL AND MODERN HISTORY

1. EUROPE

1. ELEMENTARY.

Freeman, General Sketch of European History.	*Macmillan*	0	3	6
Church, R. W., The Beginning of the Middle Ages.				
	Longmans	0	2	6
Gibbon, The Student's Gibbon.	*Murray*	0	7	6
Seebohm, The Era of the Protestant Revolution.	*Longmans*	0	2	6
Lodge, R., Modern Europe.	*Murray*	0	7	6
Nichol, Tables of European Literature, History, and Art, 200-1882.	*Maclehose*	0	7	6

2. ADVANCED.

Gibbon, Complete Edition. 8 vols.	*Murray*	3	0	0
Hallam, Middle Ages. 3 vols.	*Murray*	0	12	0
Bryce, Holy Roman Empire.	*Macmillan*	0	7	6
Freeman, Historical Essays. Series I.	*Macmillan*	0	10	6

History—Europe, continued

	£	s.	d.
Creighton, Papacy during the Reformation. 4 vols. *Longmans*	2	14	0
Ranke, Latin and Teutonic Nations. *Bell*	0	3	6
Häusser, Period of the Reformation. 2 vols. *Strahan*	0	18	0
Gardiner, Thirty Years' War. *Longmans*	0	2	6
Dyer, Modern Europe. 6 vols. *Bell*	2	12	6
Fyffe, Modern Europe, 1792-1848. 3 vols. *Cassell.* Each	0	12	0
Rose, A Century of Continental History, 1780-1880. *Stanford*	0	6	0

(For the relation of Europe to the Saracens see Freeman, The Saracens, Macmillan, 3s. ; and Bosworth Smith, Mohammed and Mohammedanism, Smith, Elder, 8s. 6d.)

3. HISTORY OF CIVILISATION.

	£	s.	d.
Guizot, History of Civilisation from the fall of the Roman Empire to the French Revolution. 3 vols. *Bell* Each	0	3	6
Lecky, History of European Morals from Augustus to Charlemagne. 2 vols. *Longmans*	0	16	0
Lecky, History of Rationalism in Europe. 2 vols. *Longmans*	0	16	0
Burckhardt, Civilisation of the Renaissance in Italy. *Sonnenschein*	0	15	0
Symonds, The Renaissance in Italy. 7 vols. *Smith, Elder*	5	12	0

a. GREAT BRITAIN AND IRELAND
i. ENGLAND (A) POLITICAL

1. ELEMENTARY.

a. GENERAL

	£	s.	d.
Gardiner, Outline of English History. *Longmans*	0	2	6
Ransome, A Short History of England. *Longmans*	0	3	6
Gardiner, A Student's History of England. 3 vols. Vol. I. (55-1509), Vol. II. (1509-1689), Vol. III. (forthcoming). *Longmans.* Each	0	4	0
Green, J. R., Short History of the English People. *Macmillan*	0	8	6
Powell, Mackay, and Tout, History of England to 1887. 3 parts. *Longmans.* Each	0	2	6
Bright, J. F., History of England. 4 vols. Separately, Vol. I. 4s. 6d.; II. 5s.; III. 7s. 6d.; IV. 6s. *Longmans*	1	3	0

b. SPECIAL.

	£	s.	d.
Freeman, Old English History. *Macmillan*	0	6	0
English History from Contemporary Writers, edited by F. York Powell. *Nutt.* Each	0	1	0

[Already published, Edward III. and his Wars, 1327-1360; Misrule of Henry III. 1236-1251; Simon of Montfort, 1251-1265; Crusade of Richard I. (2s.); Strongbow's Conquest of Ireland; Church and State under Henry II.; England under Charles II.]

History—England, continued

	£	s.	d.
Epochs of Modern History. *Longmans.* Each	0	2	6

(*Note especially Stubbs, The Early Plantagenets; Seebohm, The Era of the Protestant Revolution; Creighton, The Age of Elizabeth; Gardiner, The First Two Stuarts and the Puritan Revolution.*)

	£	s.	d.
Twelve English Statesmen, edited by Professor M. Creighton. *Macmillan.* Each	0	2	6

[Already published, William the Conqueror, Henry II. Henry VII. Wolsey, Oliver Cromwell, William III. Walpole.]

	£	s.	d.
Historic Towns, edited by Professor Freeman and W. Hunt. *Longmans.* Each	0	3	6

[Already published, London, Exeter, Bristol, Oxford, Cinque Ports, Colchester, Carlisle, Winchester.]

	£	s.	d.
Cordery and Phillpotts, King and Commonwealth. *Seeley*	0	5	0
Molesworth, History of England, 1832-1874, abridged. *Chapman, Hall*	0	7	6

For Chronology—

	£	s.	d.
Acland and Ransome, Handbook of English Political History, from B.C. 55 to A.D. 1890. *Longmans*	0	6	0

(Abridged editions 1s. 6d. and 9d.)

2. ADVANCED BOOKS (arranged in chronological order).

	£	s.	d.
Gardiner and Mullinger, Introduction to the Study of English History. *Kegan Paul*	0	9	0
Early Britain, A series of books dealing with English History before 1100. *S.P.C.K.* Each	0	2	6
Anglo-Saxon Chronicle, with Bede's Ecclesiastical History of England (*trans.*) *Bell*	0	5	0
Green, J. R., Making of England. *Macmillan*	0	16	0
„ Conquest of England. *Macmillan*	0	18	0
Bright, W., Early English Church History. *Clarendon Press*	0	12	0
Freeman, History of the Norman Conquest. 6 vols. *Clarendon Press*	5	9	6
„ Reign of William Rufus. 2 vols. *Clarendon Press*	1	16	0
Church, R. W., Life of S. Anselm. *Macmillan*	0	5	0
Norgate, The Angevin Kings. 2 vols. *Macmillan*	1	12	0
Prothero, Simon de Montfort. *Longmans*	0	9	0
Longman, History of Edward III. 2 vols. *Longmans*	1	8	0
Wylie, History of England under Henry IV. 1st vol. published. *Longmans*	0	10	6
Gairdner, The Paston Letters. 3 vols. *Arber*	1	1	0
„ History of Richard III. *Longmans*	0	10	6

History—England, continued

	£	s.	d.
More, Sir Thos., History of Richard III. (ed. Lumby). *Cambridge Press*	0	3	6
Jusserand, English Wayfaring Life in the Middle Ages. *Unwin*	0	12	0
Oman, The Art of War in the Middle Ages. *Unwin*	0	3	6
Bacon, Lord, History of the Reign of Henry VII. (ed. Lumby). *Cambridge Press*	0	3	0
Brewer, Reign of Henry VIII. 2 vols. *Murray*	1	10	0
Cavendish, Life of Wolsey. *Routledge*	0	1	0
Seebohm, The Oxford Reformers. *Longmans*	0	14	0
Froude, History of England (1529 to 1588). 12 vols. *Longmans*	2	2	0
Dixon, History of the Church of England during the Reformation. 3 vols. *Routledge.* Each	0	16	0
Gardiner, History of England, 1603-1642. 10 vols. Each 6s. *Longmans*	3	0	0
„ History of the Great Civil War, 1642-1647. 2 vols. Vol. I. 21s.; II. 24s. *Longmans*	2	5	0
Ranke, History of England in the 17th Century (*trans.*) 6 vols. *Clarendon Press*	3	3	0
Clarendon, History of the Great Rebellion, edited Macray. 6 vols. *Clarendon Press*	2	5	0
Masson, Life and Times of Milton. 6 vols. *Macmillan*	5	8	0
Carlyle, Letters and Speeches of Oliver Cromwell. 5 vols. *Chapman, Hall*	0	5	0
Hutchinson, Mrs., Memoirs of the Life of Colonel Hutchinson, edited Firth. 2 vols. *Nimmo*	2	2	0
Pepys, Diary. 4 vols. *Bell.* Each	0	5	0
Evelyn, Diary. 4 vols. *Bell.* Each	0	5	0
Burnet, Bishop, History of his own Times (1669-1713). *Reeves*	0	18	0
Macaulay, History of England (latter part 17th Century). 2 vols. *Longmans*	0	5	0
„ „ „ 8 vols. *Longmans*	2	8	0
„ Essays. *Longmans*	0	2	6
Stanhope, Earl, History of the Reign of Queen Anne. 2 vols. *Murray*	0	10	0
„ „ History of England, 1713-1783. 7 vols. *Murray*	1	15	0
„ „ Life of Pitt. 3 vols. *Murray*	1	16	0
Lecky, History of England in the 18th Century. 8 vols. *Longmans*	7	4	0
Seeley, Expansion of England. *Macmillan*	0	4	6
Massey, History of England during the reign of George III. 4 vols. *Longmans*	1	4	0
Abbey and Overton, The English Church in the 18th Century. *Longmans*	0	7	6

History—England, continued

		£	s.	d.
Thackeray, The Four Georges. *Smith, Elder*		0	1	6
Napier, History of the Peninsular War. 6 vols. *Warne*		1	1	0
Martineau, Miss, History of England, 1800-1815. *Bell*		0	3	6
Walpole, Spencer, History of England, from 1815. 6 vols. *Longmans.* Each		0	6	0
Cory, Guide to Modern English History (1815-1835). 2 vols. *Kegan Paul*		1	4	0
M'Carthy, J., History of our own Times (1837-1880). 2 vols. *Chatto*		0	15	0
Molesworth, History of England, 1832-1874. 3 vols. *Chapman, Hall*		0	18	0
Kinglake, History of the Invasion of the Crimea. 9 vols. *Blackwood.* Each		0	6	0
Greville's Journals. 8 vols. *Longmans*		2	8	0
The Annual Register. *Longmans.* Yearly		0	18	0

(*See also under Biography, especially Statesmen, and for Social History, etc., see Political and Social Economy, Political Science, and Government Publications.*)

3. REFERENCE.

	£	s.	d.
Pulling and Low, Dictionary of English History. *Cassell*	1	1	0
Stephen, L., Dictionary of National Biography. 25 vols. Published. *Smith, Elder.* Each	0	15	0
Doyle, Official Baronage of England. 3 vols. *Longmans*	5	5	0
Haydn, Book of Dignities. *Allen*	1	10	0
„ Dictionary of Dates. *Ward, Lock*	0	18	0
Colbeck, Historical Atlas. *Longmans*	0	5	0

(B) CONSTITUTIONAL

1. ELEMENTARY.

	£	s.	d.
Freeman, Growth of the English Constitution. *Macmillan*	0	5	0
Hassall and Wakeman, Constitutional Essays. *Longmans*	0	5	0
Smith, P. V., English Institutions. *Longmans*	0	3	6
Langmead, Taswell, Constitutional History. *Stevens, Haynes*	1	1	0

2. ADVANCED.

	£	s.	d.
Stubbs, Constitutional History of England (to 1485). 3 vols. *Clarendon Press*	1	16	0
Hallam, Constitutional History of England (1485-1760). 3 vols. *Murray*	0	12	0
May, Constitutional History of England (1760-1870). 3 vols. *Longmans*	0	18	0
Gneist, History of the English Constitution (*trans.*) 2 vols. *Clowes*	1	12	0
Bagehot, The English Constitution. *Kegan Paul*	0	7	6
Hearn, The Government of England. *Longmans*	0	16	0

(*See also Political Science.*)

History, continued

ii. SCOTLAND

[NOTES AND SUGGESTIONS.—*A picturesque and vivid, if not always trustworthy, elementary view of Scottish History can be got from Scott's delightful Tales of a Grandfather, which should be supplemented by a more recent and less imaginative summary, such as MacArthur's. Burton's History is the best general authority after the thirteenth century; for the earlier period, however, Skene and Robertson should be substituted for it. Many periods of Scottish History are fully treated of in books on English History, such as Froude, Macaulay, and Lecky. By far the best account of the seventeenth century is in S. R. Gardiner's History of England, 1603-1642, and History of the Great Civil War.*]

1. ELEMENTARY.

		£	s.	d.
Rhys, Celtic Britain.	*S.P.C.K.*	0	3	0
MacArthur, Scotland.	*Macmillan*	0	2	0
Armitage, The Connection between England and Scotland. *Longmans*		0	1	6
Scott, Sir Walter, Tales of a Grandfather. 2 vols. *Black*		0	7	0
Mackenzie, History of Scotland.	*Nelson*	0	5	0
The Scottish Church from the Earliest Times to 1881. (St. Giles's Lectures. First Series.) *Chambers*		0	5	0

2. ADVANCED.

		£	s.	d.
Skene, Celtic Scotland: a History of Ancient Albion. 3 vols. *Douglas.* Each		0	15	0
Robertson, Scotland under her Early Kings. 2 vols. *Douglas*		1	16	0
Burton, J. H., History of Scotland (up to 1748). 9 vols. *Blackwood*		3	3	0
Innes, Sketches of Early Scottish History. *Edmonston, Douglas*			O. P.	
„ Lectures on Scottish Legal Antiquities. *Edmonston, Douglas*			O. P.	
M'Crie, Life of John Knox.	*Blackwood*	0	3	6
„ Life of Andrew Melville.	*Blackwood*	0	6	0
Mignet, Mary Stuart (*trans.* by Scoble).	*Bentley*	0	6	0
Hosack, Mary Queen of Scots and her Accusers. 2 vols. *Blackwood*		1	1	0
Skelton, Maitland of Lethington.	*Blackwood*	0	12	6
Chambers, Domestic Annals of Scotland. 3 vols. *Chambers*		2	0	0
Napier, Mark, Life and Times of Montrose. 2 vols. *Blackwood*			O. P.	
„ „ Memorials of Dundee. 3 vols. *Blackwood*			O. P.	

History—Scotland, continued

		£	s.	d.
Stewart, Sketches of the Characters of the Highlanders of Scotland and of the Highland Regiments. 2 vols. *Longmans*			O.	P.
Story, William Carstares (1649-1715). *Macmillan*		0	12	0
Grub, Ecclesiastical History of Scotland. 4 vols. *Hamilton*		2	2	0
Annals of the Disruption. *Simpkin*		0	5	0

iii. IRELAND

[NOTES AND SUGGESTIONS.—*Hallam, Froude, Gardiner, Macaulay, and Lecky have each devoted special attention to the History of Ireland, so far as it synchronises with the periods of English History of which they treat, and the student will do well to consult their works as part of his advanced reading.*]

1. ELEMENTARY.

		£	s.	d.
Lawless, Miss, Ireland. *Unwin*		0	5	0
Walpole, C. G., Short History of Ireland. *Kegan Paul*		0	6	0
Thursfield, England and Ireland. *Longmans*		0	1	6
Sullivan, New Ireland. *Cameron*		0	1	0

2. ADVANCED.

		£	s.	d.
Stokes, G. T., Ireland and the Celtic Church. *Hodder, Stoughton*		0	9	0
" Ireland and the Anglo-Norman Church. *Hodder, Stoughton*		0	9	0
O'Curry, Manners and Customs of the Ancient Irish. (Edited Dr. Sullivan.) 3 vols. *Williams*		2	2	0
Richey, Short History of the Irish People. *Hodges, Figgis*		0	14	0
Bagwell, Ireland under the Tudors. 2 vols. *Longmans*		1	12	0
Hassencamp, Dr., History of Ireland (*trans.*) *Sonnenschein*		0	9	0
Reid, History of the Presbyterian Church. 3 vols. *Griffin*		0	12	6
Carte, Life of the Duke of Ormond. 6 vols. *Clarendon Press*		1	5	0
Hickson, Ireland in the 17th Century. 2 vols. *Longmans*		1	8	0
Prendergast, Cromwellian Settlement of Ireland. *Longmans*		O.	P.	
" Ireland 1660-1690. *Longmans*		O.	P.	
Froude, English in Ireland. 3 vols. *Longmans*		0	18	0
Lecky, Leaders of Public Opinion in Ireland. *Longmans*		O.	P.	
Two Centuries of Irish History. Ed. Bryce. *Kegan Paul*		0	16	0
O'Brien, Barry, Fifty Years of Concessions to Ireland. 2 vols. *Low.* Each		0	16	0
Duffy, Young Ireland. *Simpkin, Marshall*		0	5	0

History—Ireland, continued

		£	s.	d.
De Beaumont, Ireland, Social, Political, Religious (*trans.*) 2 vols.	*Bentley*		O. P.	
Kane, Industrial Ireland.	*Murray*	0	6	0
Gilbert, J. T., Viceroys of Ireland.	*Duffy*	0	16	0

(*See especially Lecky's History of England in the 18th Century.*)

b. AUSTRIA AND HUNGARY

		£	s.	d.
Coxe, House of Austria. 4 vols.	*Bell*	0	14	0
Vambéry, Hungary.	*Unwin*	0	5	0
Ward, House of Austria during the Thirty Years' War.	*Macmillan*	0	2	6
Leger, History of Austro-Hungary (*trans.*)	*Longmans*	0	10	6

c. FRANCE

1. ELEMENTARY.

		£	s.	d.
Jervis, Student's History of France.	*Murray*	0	7	6
Yonge, Miss, History of France.	*Macmillan*	0	3	6
Gardiner, Mrs., French Revolution.	*Longmans*	0	2	6
Browning, Oscar, Modern France.	*Longmans*	0	1	0

2. ADVANCED.

		£	s.	d.
Kitchin, History of France to 1789. 3 vols.	*Clarendon Press*	1	11	6
Guizot, Popular History of France (*trans.*) 8 vols.	*Low*	4	4	0
Stephen, Sir J., Lectures on the History of France. 2 vols.	*Longmans*		O. P.	
Poole, R. L., Dispersion of the Huguenots.	*Macmillan*	0	6	0
Morley, John, Rousseau. 2 vols.	*Macmillan*	0	10	0
,, ,, Voltaire.	*Macmillan*	0	5	0
De Tocqueville, France before the Revolution (*trans.*)	*Murray*	0	14	0
Carlyle, History of the French Revolution. 3 vols.	*Chapman, Hall*	0	3	0
Mignet, History of the French Revolution (*trans.*)	*Bell*	0	3	6
Burke, Reflections on the French Revolution.	*Clarendon Press*	0	5	0
Stephens, Morse, The French Revolution. Vol. I.	*Longmans*	0	18	0
Thiers, History of Consulate and Empire (*trans.*)	*Unwin*	0	6	0
Lanfrey, History of Napoleon. 4 vols.	*Macmillan*		O. P.	

d. GERMANY

1. ELEMENTARY.

		£	s.	d.
Sime, History of Germany.	*Macmillan*	0	3	0
Baring Gould, Germany.	*Unwin*	0	5	0
Lewis, History of Germany.	*Harper (New York)*	0	8	6

History—Germany, continued

2. ADVANCED.

	£	s.	d.
Mullinger, The Schools of Charles the Great. *Longmans*	0	7	6
Ranke, History of the Reformation in Germany (*trans.*) 3 vols. *Longmans*	2	8	0
Robertson, W., Charles V. (edited by Prescott). *Routledge*	0	5	0
Ranke, History of Prussia. 3 vols. *Murray*	1	10	0
Tuttle, History of Prussia to 1740. *Boston*	0	7	6
Carlyle, History of Frederick the Great. 10 vols. *Chapman, Hall*	0	10	0
Broglie, Frederick II. and Maria Theresa. 2 vols. *Low*	1	10	0
Metternich, Memoirs, 1773-1815. 5 vols. *Bentley*	3	12	0
Seeley, Life and Times of Stein. 3 vols. *Cambridge Press*	1	10	0
Lowe, Bismarck. 2 vols. *Cassell*	0	10	6

(*See also Bryce, Gardiner, etc., under Europe.*)

e. ITALY

1. ELEMENTARY.

	£	s.	d.
Sismondi, Italian Republics. *Longmans*		O.	P.
Balzani, Early Chronicles of Italy. *S.P.C.K.*	0	4	0
Hunt, History of Italy. *Macmillan*	0	3	6
Probyn, Italy, 1815-1878. *Cassell*	0	7	6

2. ADVANCED.

	£	s.	d.
Hodgkin, Italy and her Invaders (A.D. 376-533). 4 vols. *Clarendon Press*	3	8	0
Napier, Florentine History. 6 vols. *Moxon*		O.	P.
Villari, Savonarola. 2 vols. *Unwin*	1	1	0
" Machiavelli. 4 vols. *Kegan Paul*	2	8	0
Reumont, Von, Lorenzo de Medici. *Smith, Elder*	1	10	0
Symonds, Age of the Despots. *Smith, Elder*	0	16	0
Gallenga, History of Piedmont. 3 vols. *Chapman, Hall*	1	4	0
Bent, Garibaldi. *Longmans*	0	4	6
Mazade, De, Life of Count Cavour. *Chapman, Hall*		O.	P.
Dicey, E., Victor Emmanuel. *M. Ward*	0	2	6
Godkin, Victor Emmanuel. *Macmillan*	0	6	0

f. NETHERLANDS

1. ELEMENTARY.

	£	s.	d.
Rogers, J. E. T., Holland. *Unwin*	0	5	0
Young, A., History of the Netherlands. *Boston*	0	7	6

History—Netherlands, continued

2. ADVANCED.

		£	s.	d.
Hutton, J., James and Philip van Artevelde.	*Murray*	0	10	6
Motley, Rise of the Dutch Republic.	*Routledge*	0	3	6
„ United Netherlands. 4 vols.	*Murray*	1	4	0
„ John of Barneveldt. 2 vols.	*Murray*	0	12	0

g. RUSSIA

		£	s.	d.
Rambaud, History of Russia. 2 vols.	*Low*	1	18	0
Schuyler, Peter the Great. 2 vols.	*Low*	1	12	0
Wallace, D. M., Russia.	*Cassell*	0	10	6
Holland, Treaty Relations of Russia and Turkey.	*Macmillan*	0	2	0

h. SCANDINAVIA

1. ELEMENTARY.

		£	s.	d.
Otté, Miss, Scandinavian History.	*Macmillan*	0	6	0

2. ADVANCED.

		£	s.	d.
Carlyle, Early Kings of Norway.	*Chapman, Hall*	0	1	0
Geijer, History of the Swedes.	*Whittaker*	0	8	6
Fletcher, Gustavus Adolphus.	*Unwin*	0	5	0
Voltaire, Charles XII.	*Black*	0	3	6

i. SPAIN AND PORTUGAL

1. ELEMENTARY.

		£	s.	d.
Yonge, Miss, Christians and Moors in Spain.	*Macmillan*	0	4	6
Hale, Spain.	*Unwin*	0	5	0
Articles in Encyclopædia Britannica.	*Black*			

2. ADVANCED.

		£	s.	d.
Lane-Poole, S., Moors in Spain.	*Unwin*	0	5	0
Prescott, Ferdinand and Isabella.	*Routledge*	0	5	0
„ Philip II.	*Routledge*	0	5	0
Ranke, Ottoman and Spanish Empires.	*Routledge*	0	3	0
Coxe, Bourbon Kings of Spain. 5 vols.		O. P.		
Napier, Sir W. F., Peninsular War. 3 vols.	*Routledge*	0	10	6

k. SWITZERLAND

		£	s.	d.
Hug and Stead, Switzerland.	*Unwin*	0	5	0
Adams and Cunningham, The Swiss Confederation.	*Macmillan*	0	14	0

History, continued

l. TURKEY AND GREECE

1. ELEMENTARY.

		£	s.	d.
Lane-Poole, S., Turkey.	*Unwin*	0	5	0
Freeman, Ottoman Power in Europe.	*Macmillan*	0	7	6
Creasy, Ottoman Turks.	*Bentley*	0	6	0

2. ADVANCED.

Finlay, History of Greece. 7 vols.	*Clarendon Press*	3	10	0
Ranke, Servia and Servian Revolution.	*Bell*	0	3	6

2. BRITISH COLONIES AND INDIA

a. COLONIES

1. GENERAL AND INTRODUCTORY.

Ransome, Our Colonies and India. How we got them, and why we keep them.	*Cassell*	0	1	0
Payne, History of European Colonies.	*Macmillan*	0	4	6
Cotton, Colonies and Dependencies.	*Macmillan*	0	3	6
England and her Colonies. (The five best Essays on Imperial Federation.)	*Sonnenschein*	0	1	0
Seeley, Our Colonial Expansion (extracts).	*Macmillan*	0	1	0
Dilke, Greater Britain.	*Macmillan*	0	6	0
„ Problems of Greater Britain.	*Macmillan*	0	12	6
Lucas, Introduction to a Historical Geography of the British Colonies and other volumes.	*Clarendon Press*	0	4	6
Maps, Wall Map of British Empire.	*Stanford*	0	13	0
„ British Colonial Pocket Atlas.	*J. Walker & Co.*	0	2	6
Statistical Abstract (Colonies).	*Eyre, Spottiswoode*	0	1	0

2. AUSTRALASIA.

Westgarth, Half a Century of Australian Progress.	*Low*	0	12	0
Ranken, The Dominion of Australia.	*Chapman, Hall*	0	12	0
Rusden, A History of Australia. 3 vols.	*Chapman, Hall*	2	10	0
„ A History of New Zealand. 3 vols.	*Chapman, Hall*	2	10	0
Wallace, A. R., Australasia (a compendium of Modern Geography).	*Stanford*	1	1	0
Hogan, Irish in Australia.	*Ward, Downey*	0	2	6
Froude, Oceana.	*Longmans*	0	2	6

(See also the *Year-books, etc., of different Colonies,* to be obtained through the Agents-General, Victoria St., Westminster.)

History—British Colonies and India, continued

3. THE DOMINION OF CANADA.

	£	s.	d.
Greswell, History of Canada. *Clarendon Press*	0	7	6
Marshall, The Canadian Dominion. *Longmans*	0	12	6
Macmullen, The History of Canada. *Low*	0	16	0
Kingsford, The History of Canada. 3 vols. *Trübner*	2	5	0
Parkman, Montcalm and Wolfe. 2 vols. *Macmillan*. Each	0	12	6
Munro, J. E. C., Constitution of Canada. *Cambridge Press*	0	10	6

(*Refer also to Bourinot's Works and Morgan's Annual Register.*)

b. INDIA

1. ELEMENTARY.

	£	s.	d.
Hunter, A Brief History of the Indian People. *Trübner*	0	3	6
Wheeler, College History of India. *Macmillan*	0	3	6
„ Short History of India. *Macmillan*	0	12	0
Müller, Max, India. What can it teach us? *Longmans*	0	12	6
Keene, Sketch of the History of Hindostan. *Allen*	0	18	0
Owen, S., India on the Eve of the British Conquest. *Allen*	0	8	0
Stanhope, British India, from its origin to 1783. *Murray*	0	3	6
Marshman, History of British India (abridged). *Blackwood*	0	6	6
Trotter, India under Victoria. 2 vols. *Allen*	1	10	0
Rulers of India Series. *Clarendon Press*. Each	0	2	6

2. ADVANCED.

	£	s.	d.
Elphinstone, History of India (edited by Cowell), Hindoo and Mahometan Period. *Murray*	0	18	0
Mill, James, History of India (edited by Wilson) 9 vols. *Allen*	2	10	0
Wilks, Sketches of the History of Mysore. 3 vols.		O. P.	
Kaye, War in Afghanistan. 3 vols. *Allen*	1	6	0
„ History of the Indian Mutiny (continued by Malleson), 6 vols. *Allen*	1	16	0
Napier, Conquest of Scinde. *Westerton*	0	12	0
„ Administration of Scinde. *Westerton*	0	12	0
Arnold, Administration of Lord Dalhousie. *Saunders*	1	10	0
Holmes, History of the Indian Mutiny. *Allen*	0	7	6

3. BOOKS OF REFERENCE.

	£	s.	d.
Hunter, Imperial Gazetteer of India. 14 vols. *Trübner*	3	3	0
Wellesley, Despatches. Selections (edited by S. T. Owen). *Clarendon Press*	1	4	0
Statistical Abstract (British India). *Eyre, Spottiswoode*	0	1	0

History, continued

3. AMERICA

a. UNITED STATES

1. ELEMENTARY.

		£	s.	d.
Doyle, History of America. *Macmillan*		0	4	6
Higginson, Young Folks' History of the United States. *Low*		0	6	0
Lodge, H. C., A Short History of the English Colonies in America. *Low*		0	15	0
Johnston, A., American Politics. *Scribner*		0	5	0

2. ADVANCED.

	£	s.	d.
Higginson, A Larger History of the United States. *Low*	0	14	0
Bancroft, History of America. 6 vols. *Low*	3	13	6
Doyle, English in America. 3 vols. *Longmans*	2	14	0
Palfrey, History of New England. *New York*	1	4	0
Arnold, History of Rhode Island. 2 vols. *New York*	1	4	0
Brodhead, History of the State of New York. 2 vols. *New York*	1	4	0
Cairnes, The Slave Power. *Macmillan*	0	10	6
Curtis, Life of Daniel Webster. 2 vols. *New York*	1	4	0
Franklin, Benj., Autobiography. *Bell*	0	1	0
Lodge, H. C., Studies in History. *Boston*	0	6	0
Marshall, Life of Washington. 2 vols. *Philadelphia*	1	4	0
Sparkes, American Biography. 10 vols. *New York*. Each	0	6	0
" American Statesmen Series. *Houghton, Mifflin.* Each	0	6	0
" American Commonwealth Series *Houghton, Mifflin.* Each	0	6	0

3. CONSTITUTIONAL AND GENERAL.

	£	s.	d.
Johnston, A., The United States, its History and Constitution. *Blackie*	0	4	6
Curtis, History of the Constitution of the United States. 2 vols. *New York*	1	4	0
De Tocqueville, Democracy in America. 2 vols. *Longmans*	0	16	0
Bryce, The American Commonwealth. 2 vols. *Macmillan*	1	5	0

4. REFERENCE.

Holmes, American Annals. 2 vols. *Cambridge, Mass.* O. P.

b. SOUTH AMERICA, MEXICO, ETC.

	£	s.	d.
Prescott, History of the Conquest of Peru. *Routledge*	0	5	0
" History of the Conquest of Mexico. *Routledge*	0	5	0

(*See also Biography.*)

LANGUAGES

BOOKS FOR BEGINNERS

I. GREEK

[NOTES AND SUGGESTIONS.—*If the student wants to learn Greek or Latin for reading only, not to write, he should begin reading at once, with grammar and vocabulary, taking the books at the head of the lists first. As soon as he can read at all easily, he should read no more books specially written for beginners, but plunge into Homer, Xenophon, Livy, and Ovid. Then he can take the other reading books, beginning with those that have a vocabulary, and going on to those that have to be read with a dictionary.*]

	£	s.	d.
Abbott and Mansfield, Greek Accidence Primer. *Longmans*	0	2	6
Heatley, Graecula. *Longmans*	0	1	6
Morice, Stories in Attic Greek. *Longmans*	0	3	6
Percival, Primer of Attic Greek. *Longmans*	0	3	6
Jerram, Reddenda Minora. *Clarendon Press*	0	1	6
Jerram and Phillpotts, Easy Selections from Xenophon. *Clarendon Press*	0	3	6
Colson, First Greek Reader. *Macmillan*	0	3	0
Phillpotts, Xenophon, Selections. *Clarendon Press*	0	3	6
Merry, Homer's Odyssey. 2 vols. *Clarendon Press.* Each	0	5	0
Monro, Homer's Iliad. 2 vols. *Clarendon Press.* Each	0	6	0
Sidgwick, Scenes from Greek Plays. 12 Plays. *Longmans.* Each	0	1	6
Moore, A., Easy Selections from Thucydides. *Longmans*	0	3	6

II. LATIN

(*For Notes and Suggestions see Greek above.*)

	£	s.	d.
Allen, J. B., Elementary Grammar. *Clarendon Press*	0	2	6
Bennet, Easy Latin Stories. *Longmans*	0	2	6
,, Second Latin Reading Book. *Longmans*	0	2	6
Heatley and Kingdon, Gradatim. *Longmans*	0	1	6

Languages—Books for Beginners—Latin, continued

		£	s.	d.
Ritchie, Fabulae Faciles.	*Longmans*	0	2	0
Macaulay, G. C., Hannibalian War.	*Macmillan*	0	1	6
Taylor, R. W., Stories from Ovid.	*Longmans*	0	3	6
Jerram, Anglice Reddenda (Latin and Greek).	*Clarendon Press*	0	2	6
Walford, Selections from Cicero.	*Clarendon Press*	0	4	6
Moberly, Cæsar, Part I. Gallic War.	*Clarendon Press*	0	4	6
,, ,, Part II. Civil War.	*Clarendon Press*	0	3	6

III. FRENCH

[NOTES AND SUGGESTIONS.—*The student is recommended to get some lessons in French pronunciation as soon as possible. This cannot be learned from books. For those who wish simply to be able to read French, it will be sufficient to work through the First French Course, and then through the First Reader and Second Course, taking the two last together. The other reading books on the list may then be taken in their order. For those who desire to acquire the art of writing French, a Composition Book has been added. For commercial purposes the two last books on the list will be found very useful.*]

Chardenal, First French Course.	*Hachette*	0	1	6
,, Second French Course.	*Hachette*	0	2	0
,, Key to First and Second Course.	*Hachette*	0	3	6
Cassal and **Karcher**, First French Reader.	*Trübner*	0	2	6
,, ,, Junior Course of French Composition.	*Longmans*	0	3	6
,, ,, Key to above.	*Longmans*	0	5	0
Chardenal, Practical French Conversation.	*Longmans*	0	1	6
Sharp, Fezensac, Campagne de Russie.	*Longmans*	0	2	6
Mme. **de Witt**, Derrière les Haies.	*Hachette*	0	2	0
Pétilleau, Labiche, " Le Voyage de Monsieur Perrichon."	*Hachette*	0	1	0
Testard, About, " Le Roi des Montagnes."	*Hachette*	0	2	0
Masson, La Lyre Française.	*Macmillan*	0	4	6
Perini, Questions and Rules in French Grammar and Idioms.	*Hachette*	0	2	0
Jeffcott and **Tossell**, French Newspaper Reader.	*Hachette*	0	2	6
Ragon, French Commercial Correspondence.	*Hachette*	0	3	6

IV. GERMAN

[NOTES AND SUGGESTIONS.—*To get an accurate idea of German pronunciation it is necessary to have one or two short lessons. The intelligent student will afterwards find little difficulty in mastering the following course without assistance. As soon after beginning the " First German Book" as possible, Wittich's German Tales should be commenced. These the reader should write out in English. By the time he has finished the " First German Book" he should begin to turn back into German the tale*

Languages—Books for Beginners—German, continued

he translated the previous day, compare it with the original, and correct it. The "Newspaper Reading Book" and the "Manual of Correspondence" are intended for those who may be acquiring German for commercial purposes.]

	£	s.	d.
Otto, E., First German Book, revised by Lange. *Nutt*	0	2	0
Wittich, German Tales for Beginners. *Williams, Norgate*	0	4	0
Otto, E., German Conversation Grammar. *Nutt*	0	5	0
Buchheim, Modern German Reader, Pt. I. *Clarendon Press*	0	2	6
Townson, Second German Reader. *Longmans*	0	2	6
Homan, Deutsche Märchen. *Hachette*	0	2	0
Meissner, Practical Lessons in German Conversation. *Hachette*	0	2	0
Rühle, German Examination Papers (Composition, etc.) *Nutt*	0	4	0
„ Key to German Examination Papers. *Nutt*	0	2	6
Hoffmann, Heute Mir. Morgen Dir. *Longmans*	0	3	6
Jeffcott and **Tossel**, German Newspaper Reading-Book. *Hachette*	0	3	0
Lévy, Manual of German Correspondence. *Hachette*	0	2	0
„ Manual of German Correspondence (in German Handwriting) *Hachette*	0	3	6
Buchheim, Deutsches Theater. 3 parts. *Williams, Norgate.* Each	0	2	6
„ Deutsche Lyrik. *Macmillan*	0	4	6
Schiller, Selections from Lyrical Poems. *Macmillan*	0	2	6

LITERATURE

[NOTES AND SUGGESTIONS.—*The various headings treated under this general class of "Literature" are by no means exhaustive. For History and Biography and kindred subjects see under History and Biography; for Philosophy see under Philosophy. The number of fairly good editions of some novels and many poetical works is so large that the reader cannot go far wrong. Those only have been mentioned which are fairly good and moderately cheap. The separate works actually named, as under Scott and Dickens, indicate those which are best worth reading first. The names of the host of novels of the second and third order can easily be ascertained from larger catalogues.*]

Literature consists of all the books—and they are not so many—where moral truth and human passion are touched with a certain largeness, sanity, and attraction of form. My notion of the literary student is one who through books explores the strange voyages of man's moral reason, the impulses of the human heart, the chances and changes that have overtaken human ideals of virtue and happiness, of conduct and manners, and the shifting fortunes of great conceptions of truth and virtue.

JOHN MORLEY.

I. INTRODUCTORY (*Historical and Critical*)

GREEK.

		£	s.	d.
Jebb, Primer of Greek Literature.	*Macmillan*	0	1	0
Abbott, E., Hellenica: Essays by various authors.	*Longmans*	0	16	0
Jevons, F. B., History of Greek Literature.	*Griffin*	0	8	6
Mahaffy, History of Greek Literature. 2 vols.	*Longmans.* Each	0	9	0
Symonds, Studies of the Greek Poets.	*Smith, Elder*	0	10	6

LATIN.

		£	s.	d.
Cruttwell, History of Roman Literature.	*Griffin*	0	8	6
Sellar, Roman Poets of the Republic.	*Clarendon Press*	0	14	0

Literature—Introductory, continued

ENGLISH.

	£	s.	d
Abbott and Seeley, English Lessons for English people. *Seeley*	0	4	6
Brooke, Stopford, Primer of English Literature. *Macmillan*	0	1	0
Craik, Manual of English Literature. *Griffin*	0	7	6
Arnold, T., Manual of English Literature. *Longmans*	0	7	6
Morley, H., First Sketch of English Literature. *Cassell*	0	7	6
Reed, English Literature from Chaucer to Tennyson. *Shaw*	0	3	0
Brink, Ten, History of Early English Literature (*trans.*) *Bell*	0	3	6
Morley, H., English Writers. 10 vols. (6 published). *Cassell.* Each	0	5	0

AMERICAN.

	£	s.	d
Nichol, American Literature. *Black*	0	15	0
Tyler, M., History of American Literature. *Putnams*	0	12	0

FRENCH.

	£	s.	d
Saintsbury, Primer of French Literature. *Clarendon Press*	0	2	0
,, Short History of French Literature. *Clarendon Press*	0	10	6

GERMAN.

	£	s.	d
Gostwick and R. Harrison, Outlines of German Literature. *Williams, Norgate*	0	10	0
Scherer, History of German Literature [*Trans.*] 2 vols. *Clarendon Press*	1	1	0

GENERAL.

	£	s.	d
Classical Writers. *Macmillan.* Each	0	1	6
Ancient Classics for English Readers. *Blackwood.* Each	0	2	6
English Men of Letters Series. *Macmillan.* Each	0	1	6
In paper covers	0	1	0
Foreign Classics for English Readers. *Blackwood.* Each	0	2	6

(*For some of the Men and Women of Letters see Biography (Men and Women of Letters), and for a few books of Literary Criticism see Essays, Lectures, and Studies.*)

Literature, continued

II. POETRY

The crown of literature is poetry.
MATTHEW ARNOLD.

1. COLLECTIONS OF POEMS

I give you the end of a golden string,
Only wind it into a ball;
It will lead you in at Heaven's gate,
Built in Jerusalem's wall.—BLAKE.

		£	s.	d.
Palgrave, F. T., Golden Treasury of Songs and Lyrics.	*Macmillan*	0	4	6
Trench, A Household Book of English Poetry.	*Kegan Paul*	0	5	6
Locker-Lampson, Lyra Elegantiarum.	*Ward, Lock*	0	2	0
Woods, Miss, A First School Poetry Book.	*Macmillan*	0	2	6
" Second and Third School Poetry Books.	*Macmillan.* Each	0	4	6
Ward, T. H., English Poets. 4 vols.	*Macmillan.* Each	0	7	6
Poems of the Inner Life.	*Low*	0	5	0
Palgrave, F. T., Treasury of Sacred Song.	*Clarendon Press*	0	4	6
Allingham, Ballad Book.	*Macmillan*	0	4	6
Bullen, Lyrics from Elizabethan Song Books.	*Nimmo*	0	5	0
Lamb, Specimens of English Dramatic Poetry.	*Bell*	0	3	6
Percy, Reliques of Ancient English Poetry.	*Warne*	0	2	0
Sparling, Irish Minstrelsy.	*W. Scott*	0	1	0
Aitken, Scottish Song.	*Macmillan*	0	4	6
Rossetti, W. M., Selected American Poems.	*Ward, Lock*	0	3	6

2. BEST CHEAP EDITIONS OF ENGLISH POETS

By nothing is England so glorious as by her poetry.
MATTHEW ARNOLD.

The immortal and universal poets of our race are to be read and re-read till their music and their spirit are a part of our nature; they are to be thought over and digested till we live in the world they created for us; they are to be read devoutly, as devout men read their Bible and fortify their hearts with psalms.
FREDERIC HARRISON.

Arnold, E., Light of Asia	*Trübner*	0	3	6
Arnold, M., Poetical Works.	*Macmillan*	0	7	6
" Selections.	*Macmillan*	0	4	6
Aytoun, Lays of the Scottish Cavaliers.	*Blackwood*	0	3	6
Barnes, Poems of Rural Life.	*Kegan Paul*	0	6	0

Literature—Poetry, continued

		£	s.	d.
Beaumont and Fletcher, Plays. 2 vols. *Vizetelly.* Each		0	2	6
Beowulf, Poems (trans. Lumsden). *Kegan Paul*		0	5	0
Blake, Poetical Works, with Life. *Bell*		0	2	6
„ Selections. *W. Scott*		0	1	0
Browning, E. B., Poetical Works. 5 vols. *Smith, Elder*		1	10	0
„ Selections. 2 vols. (Sep. 3s. 6d.) *Smith, Elder*		0	7	0
„ Selections. *Smith, Elder*		0	1	0
Browning, R., Poetical Works. 16 vols. (Sep. 5s.) *Smith, Elder*		4	0	0
„ Selections. 2 vols. (Sep. 3s. 6d.) *Smith, Elder*		0	7	0
„ Selections. *Smith, Elder*		0	1	0
Burns, Poetical Works. *Macmillan*		0	3	6
„ Selections. 2 vols. (Sep. 1s.) *W. Scott*		0	2	0
Butler, Hudibras. 2 vols. *Bell*		0	3	0
Byron, Poetical Works. *Murray*		0	3	6
„ Selections (M. Arnold). *Macmillan*		0	4	6
Calverley, Verses and Fly Leaves. *Bell*		0	7	6
Campbell, Poetical Works. *Bell*		0	2	6
„ Selections. *W. Scott*		0	1	0
Chaucer, Poetical Works. 4 vols. (Sep. 3s. 6d.) *Bell*		0	14	0
„ Canterbury Tales (Selected). 3 vols. (Sep. 2s. 6d., 4s. 6d., 4s. 6d.) *Clarendon Press*		0	11	6
„ Selections. *W. Scott*		0	1	0
Clough, Poems. *Macmillan*		0	7	6
Coleridge, Poetical Works. *Ward, Lock*		0	3	6
„ Selections. *W. Scott*		0	1	0
Collins, Poetical Works. *Bell*		0	1	6
Crabbe, Poetical Works. *James Blackwood*		0	2	6
Cowper, Poetical Works. *Macmillan*		0	3	6
„ Selections. *Macmillan*		0	4	6
Dryden, Poetical Works. *Macmillan*		0	3	6
Ford and Massinger, Plays. *Vizetelly*		0	2	6
Gay, Fables. *Kegan Paul*		0	6	0
Goldsmith, Poetical Works. *Bell*		0	1	6
Gray, Poems. *Bell*		0	1	6
Herbert, G., Poetical Works. *Bell*		0	5	0
„ „ *Nisbet*		0	1	0
Herrick, Selections. *Macmillan*		0	4	6
„ „ *W. Scott*		0	1	0
Hood, Poetical Works. 2 vols. (Sep. 3s. 6d.) *Ward, Lock*		0	7	0
Ingelow, Poetical Works. 3 vols. *Longmans*		0	17	0
„ Selections. *Longmans*		0	2	6
Jonson, Ben, Works. 3 vols. *Chatto.* Each		0	6	0
Keats, Poetical Works. *Reeves, Turner*		0	8	0
„ „ „ *Bell*		0	2	6
„ Selections. *W. Scott*		0	1	0
Kingsley, C., Poems. *Macmillan*		0	1	6

Literature—Poetry, continued

		£	s.	d.
Kingsley, C., Poems (Selections).	*Macmillan*	0	1	6
Langland, Vision of Piers the Plowman.	*Clarendon Press*	0	4	6
Longfellow, Poems.	*Ward, Lock*	0	3	6
„ Selections.	*W. Scott*	0	1	0
Lowell, Poems.	*Macmillan*	0	4	6
Macaulay, Lays of Ancient Rome.	*Longmans*	0	1	0
Marlowe, Plays.	*Chatto*	0	6	0
„ Selections.	*W. Scott*	0	1	0
Marvel, Poems and Satires.	*Ward, Lock*	0	3	6
Milton, Poetical Works. 3 vols.	*Macmillan*	0	15	0
„ „	*Macmillan*	0	3	6
„ Paradise Lost.	*W. Scott*	0	1	0
Moore, Poems.	*Ward, Lock*	0	3	6
Morris, Lewis, Works.	*Kegan Paul*	0	6	0
Morris, W., Earthly Paradise.	*Reeves, Turner*	0	7	6
„ Sigurd.	*Reeves, Turner*	0	6	0
„ Life and Death of Jason.	*Reeves, Turner*	0	8	0
Poe, E. A., Poems.	*Low*	0	2	0
„ Selections.	*W Scott*	0	1	0
Pope, Poetical Works.	*Macmillan*	0	3	6
„ Selections.	*W. Scott*	0	1	0
Praed, Poems. 2 vols.	*Ward, Lock*	1	1	0
„ Selections.	*W. Scott*	0	1	0
Ramsay, Poems.	*W. Scott*	0	1	0
Rejected Addresses.	*Routledge*	0	1	0
Rossetti, Christina, Poems.	*Macmillan*	0	7	6
Rossetti, D. G., Poems.	*Ellis*	0	6	0
Scott, Walter, Poems.	*Macmillan*	0	3	6
„ „ „	*Cassell*	0	1	0
Shakespeare, Works. 10 vols. (Sep. 2s. 6d.)	*Bell*	1	5	0
„ „	*Cassell*	0	3	6
„ „	*Macmillan*	0	3	6
„ Twenty-three Plays.	*Arnold.* Each	0	1	6
„ Songs and Sonnets.	*Macmillan*	0	4	6
Shelley, Poetical Works. 2 vols.	*Reeves, Turner*	0	16	0
„ „	*Macmillan*	0	7	6
„ „	*Warne*	0	3	6
„ Selections.	*Macmillan*	0	4	6
„ „	*W. Scott*	0	1	0
Sheridan, Plays.	*Routledge*	0	1	6
Southey, Poetical Works.	*Longmans*	0	14	0
„ Selections.	*W. Scott*	0	1	0
Spenser, Poetical Works.	*Macmillan*	0	3	6
„ Selections.	*W. Scott*	0	1	0
Swinburne, Songs before Sunrise.	*Chatto*	0	10	6
„ Atalanta in Calydon.	*Chatto*	0	6	0

Literature—Poetry, continued

		£	s.	d.
Swinburne, Selections from Poems.	Chatto	0	6	0
Taylor, Sir H., Philip von Artevelde.	Kegan Paul	0	3	6
Tennyson, Works.	Macmillan	0	7	6
,, Lyrical Poems.	Macmillan	0	4	6
Thomson, The City of Dreadful Night.	Reeves, Turner	0	5	0
Thomson, James, Poems.	Routledge	0	2	0
Vaughan, Poems.	Bell	0	1	6
Whitman, Walt, Poems (Selected).	Chatto	0	6	0
,, ,, Selections.	W. Scott	0	1	0
Whittier, Poems.	Macmillan	0	4	6
Wordsworth, Poems (ed. J. Morley).	Macmillan	0	7	6
,, Selections. (M. Arnold.)	Macmillan	0	4	6
,, ,, (Prof. Knight.)	Kegan Paul	0	4	6
,, ,,	W. Scott	0	1	0

3. TRANSLATIONS OF ANCIENT AND MODERN FOREIGN POETS

		£	s.	d.
Aeschylus: in verse by Morshead (House of Atreus).	Simpkin	0	5	0
Aristophanes: in verse by Frere. (4 Plays.)	Routledge	0	1	0
Dante: in verse by Plumptre. 2 vols.	Isbister	2	2	0
,, ,, Cary.	Bell	0	3	6
,, ,, Longfellow.	Routledge	0	3	6
,, in prose by J. A. Carlyle. (Inferno.)	Bell	0	5	0
,, ,, A. J. Butler. (Purgatorio and Paradiso). Macmillan. Each		0	12	6
Goethe: Faust, Bayard Taylor.	Ward, Lock	0	2	0
,, ,, Anster.	Routledge	0	1	6
Homer: Iliad and Odyssey. Pope. Routledge. Each		0	3	6
,, Iliad. Chapman.	Routledge	0	1	0
,, Iliad. Lord Derby. 2 vols.	Murray	0	10	0
,, Iliad, in prose by Lang, Leaf, and E. Myers.	Macmillan	0	12	6
,, Odyssey, in prose by Butcher and Lang.	Macmillan	0	6	0
Horace: Conington. 2 vols.	Bell	0	12	0
Lucretius: Munro.	Bell	0	6	0
Omar Khayyám: The Rubaiyat. Fitzgerald.	Quaritch	0	10	6
Pindar: in prose by Myers.	Macmillan	0	5	0
Schiller: Wallenstein.	Bell	0	3	6
Sophocles: in verse by Whitelaw.	Longmans	0	8	6
,, Campbell.	Kegan Paul	0	7	6
Theocritus, Bion, and Moschus: in prose by Lang	Macmillan	0	6	0
Virgil: Æneid in verse, by Dryden.	Routledge	0	1	0
,, Æneid in prose, by Mackail.	Macmillan	0	7	6
,, Georgics in verse, by Rhoades.	Kegan Paul	0	5	0

Literature, continued

III. FICTION

1. NOVELS AND TALES

[NOTES AND SUGGESTIONS.—*Some other Novels which do not appear in this list will be found under Historical Novels and Tales and under Children's Books. The separate books actually named as under Scott and Dickens indicate those which are best worth reading first.*]

"What are you reading, Miss —?" "Oh! it's only a novel!" replies the young lady; while she lays down her book with affected indifference, or momentary shame. "It is only *Cecilia*, or *Camilla*, or *Belinda*"; or, in short, only some work in which the greatest powers of the mind are displayed; in which the most thorough knowledge of human nature, the happiest delineation of its varieties, the liveliest effusions of wit and humour, are conveyed to the world in the best chosen language.—JANE AUSTEN: *Northanger Abbey*.

a. ENGLISH.

		£	s.	d.
Ainsworth, Tower of London.	*Routledge*	0	2	0
,, Lancashire Witches, and others.	*Routledge*	0	2	0
Austen, Jane, 5 vols. (Sep. 2s.)	*Routledge*	0	10	0
Pride and Prejudice. Sense and Sensibility. Emma. Northanger Abbey and Mansfield Park. Persuasion.				
Beaconsfield,	*Longmans*. Each	0	1	6
Coningsby. Sybil. Vivian Grey. Lothair. Tancred.				
Besant, W., All Sorts and Conditions of Men.	*Chatto*	0	2	6
,, Children of Gibeon.	*Chatto*	0	2	6
Besant, W., and Rice. Ready Money Mortiboy.	*Chatto*	0	2	6
,, ,, Monks of Thelema.	*Chatto*	0	2	6
,, ,, The Golden Butterfly, and others.	*Chatto*	0	2	6
Black, A Princess of Thule.	*Macmillan*	0	6	0
,, Macleod of Dare, and others.	*Macmillan*	0	6	0
Blackmore, Lorna Doone.	*Low*	0	2	6
,, The Maid of Sker, and others.	*Blackwood*	0	6	0
Borrow, Lavengro.	*Murray*	0	2	6
,, Romany Rye.	*Murray*	0	2	6
Brontë, Charlotte, 4 vols.	*Smith, Elder.* Each	0	2	6
Jane Eyre. Shirley. Villette. The Professor. } Also at		0	1	6
Brontë, Emily, Wuthering Heights.	*Smith, Elder*	0	2	6
Burnett, F. H., Through one Administration.	*Warne*	0	2	0
Burney, F., Evelina.	*Ward, Lock*	0	2	0
Collins, W., The Moonstone.	*Chatto*	0	2	6

Literature—Fiction, continued

		£	s.	d.
Collins, W., The Woman in White, and others. *Chatto*		0	2	6
Craik, Mrs., John Halifax, Gentleman, and others. *Hurst, Blackett*		0	5	0
Crawford, F. M., Mr. Isaacs. *Macmillan*		0	3	6
,, Dr. Claudius. *Macmillan*		0	3	6
Dickens, 32 vols. *Chapman, Hall.* Each		0	1	6
A Tale of Two Cities. Martin Chuzzlewit (2 vols.)				
Bleak House (2 vols.) Nicholas Nickleby (2 vols.)				
David Copperfield (2 vols.) Old Curiosity Shop (2 vols.)				
Dombey and Son (2 vols.) Pickwick Papers (2 vols.)				
and others.				
Edgeworth, The Absentee, Stories of Ireland, and others. *Routledge.* Each		0	1	6
Eliot, George, Adam Bede. *Blackwood*		0	3	6
,, Daniel Deronda. *Blackwood*		0	7	6
,, Felix Holt. *Blackwood*		0	3	6
,, Middlemarch. *Blackwood*		0	7	6
,, Romola. *Blackwood*		0	3	6
,, Scenes of Clerical Life. *Blackwood*		0	3	0
,, Silas Marner. *Blackwood*		0	2	6
,, The Mill on the Floss. *Blackwood*		0	3	6
Fielding, Tom Jones. 2 vols. *Low*		0	4	0
,, Amelia, and others. *Routledge*		0	3	6
Gaskell, Mrs., 7 vols. *Smith, Elder.* Each		0	2	6
Cranford. Ruth.				
North and South. Sylvia's Lovers. Also each		0	1	6
Mary Barton. Wives and Daughters.				
Goldsmith, Vicar of Wakefield. *Macmillan*		0	1	0
Gould, Baring, Mehalah. *Smith, Elder*		0	2	6
,, Red Spider, and others. *Chatto*		0	3	6
Hardy, Far from the Madding Crowd. *Low*		0	2	6
,, The Woodlanders, and others. *Macmillan*		0	3	6
Kingsley, C., 6 vols. *Macmillan.* Each		0	3	6
Alton Locke. Two Years Ago. Also each		0	0	6
Hypatia. Westward Ho! and others.				
Kingsley, H., Ravenshoe, and others. *Ward, Lock*		0	2	6
Laffan, Flitters, Tatters, and the Counsellor. *Macmillan*		0	2	0
Lever, Harry Lorrequer. *Routledge*		0	2	0
,, Charles O'Malley, and others. *Routledge*		0	2	0
Lover, Handy Andy. *Cassell*		0	1	0
Lytton, *Routledge.* Each		0	3	6
Kenelm Chillingly. The Last Days of Pompeii.				
My Novel (2 vols.) The Caxtons, and others.				
Marryat, Midshipman Easy. *Routledge*		0	3	6
,, Peter Simple, and others. *Routledge*		0	3	6

Literature—Fiction, continued

		£	s.	d.
Meredith, 9 vols. *Chapman, Hall.* Each		0	3	6
Beauchamp's Career. Rhoda Fleming.				
Diana of the Crossways. The Egoist.				
Evan Harrington. The Ordeal of Richard Feverel, and others.				
Oliphant, Mrs., A Beleaguered City, and others. *Macmillan*		0	6	0
„ Salem Chapel. *Blackwood*		0	2	6
Reade, C. *Chatto.* Each		0	3	6
Hard Cash. The Cloister and the Hearth.				
It is Never too Late to Mend. Peg Woffington, and others.				
Richardson, Clarissa Harlowe. *Routledge*		0	2	0
Schreiner, O., The Story of an African Farm. *Chapman, Hall*		0	1	6
Scott, Sir W., 25 vols. *Black.* Each		0	1	6
Guy Mannering. The Antiquary.				
Ivanhoe. The Bride of Lammermoor.				
Kenilworth. The Fortunes of Nigel.				
Old Mortality. The Heart of Midlothian.				
Quentin Durward. The Legend of Montrose.				
Redgauntlet. Waverley.				
Rob Roy. Woodstock, and others.				
Shorthouse, John Inglesant. *Macmillan*		0	6	0
Smollett, Roderick Random. *Routledge*		0	3	6
„ Humphrey Clinker. *Routledge*		0	3	6
Sterne, Tristram Shandy. *Routledge*		0	1	0
Stevenson, R. L., The Strange Case of Dr. Jekyll and Mr. Hyde. *Longmans*		0	1	6
„ „ Treasure Island. *Cassell*		0	5	0
„ „ Kidnapped. *Cassell*		0	5	0
„ „ The Master of Ballantrae. *Cassell*		0	5	0
Thackeray, Miss, Miss Angel. *Smith, Elder*		0	6	0
„ „ The Village on the Cliff. *Smith, Elder*		0	6	0
„ „ Old Kensington, and others. *Smith, Elder*		0	6	0
Thackeray, W. M., Works, 26 vols. *Smith, Elder.* Each		0	3	6
„ „ Works, 27 vols. *Smith, Elder.* Each		0	1	6
Barry Lyndon. The Newcomes (2 vols.)				
Esmond. The Virginians (2 vols.)				
Pendennis (2 vols.) Vanity Fair (2 vols.), and others.				
Trollope, A., Barchester Towers. *Longmans*		0	1	6
„ Framley Parsonage. *Smith, Elder*		0	2	6
„ Last Chronicle of Barset, 2 vols. *Chapman, Hall*		0	12	0
„ Orley Farm, and others. *Ward, Lock*		0	2	6
„ Phineas Finn. *Ward, Lock*		0	2	6
Woods, Mrs., A Village Tragedy. *Bentley*		0	3	6

Literature—Fiction, continued

b. AMERICAN.

		£	s.	d.
Cable, Old Creole Days.	*Douglas*	0	1	0
Harte, Bret, Selected Works.	*Chatto*	0	7	6
Hawthorne, N., House of the Seven Gables.	*Paterson*	0	2	0
,, The Scarlet Letter.	*Paterson*	0	2	0
,, The Blithedale Romance.	*Paterson*	0	2	0
,, Transformation, and others.	*Smith, Elder*	0	2	6
Holmes, A Mortal Antipathy.	*Paterson*	0	2	0
,, Elsie Venner.	*Paterson*	0	2	0
,, The Guardian Angel, and others.	*Low*	0	1	0
Howells, A Chance Acquaintance.	*Douglas*	0	1	0
,, A Foregone Conclusion.	*Douglas*	0	1	0
,, The Rise of Silas Lapham. 2 vols.	*Douglas*	0	2	0
,, The Undiscovered Country, and others.	*Douglas*	0	1	0
James, H., Roderick Hudson. 2 vols.	*Macmillan*	0	4	0
,, The American. 2 vols.	*Macmillan*	0	4	0
,, The Europeans.	*Macmillan*	0	2	0
,, The Portrait of a Lady. 3 vols.	*Macmillan*	0	6	0
Poe, E. A., Tales of Mystery.	*Ward, Lock*	0	2	0
Stowe, Mrs. Beecher, Uncle Tom's Cabin.	*Routledge*	0	1	0
,, ,, The Minister's Wooing.	*Low*	0	1	0

c. FOREIGN (Translations.)

		£	s.	d.
Auerbach, On the Heights. 3 vols. And others.	*Low*	0	6	0
Balzac, Eugénie Grandet.	*Routledge*	0	3	6
,, Père Goriot.	*Routledge*	0	3	6
Björnsen, Fisher Maiden.	*Bickers*	0	2	6
,, Synnöve Solbakken, and others.	*Bickers*	0	2	6
Cervantes, Don Quixote.	*Routledge*	0	2	0
Dostoieffsky, Crime and Punishment.	*Vizetelly*	0	2	0
,, Injury and Insult.	*Vizetelly*	0	5	0
Dumas, A. père, Chicot the Jester.	*Routledge*	0	2	0
,, ,, Monte Cristo.	*Routledge*	0	2	0
,, ,, Three Musketeers.	*Routledge*	0	2	0
,, ,, Twenty Years After.	*Routledge*	0	2	0
,, ,, Vicomte de Bragelonne, and others.	*Routledge*	0	2	0
Fouqué, Tales.	*Low*	0	2	0
Goethe, Wilhelm Meister. 3 vols.	*Chapman, Hall*	0	3	0
Hillern, The Vulture Maiden.	*Low*	0	2	0
Hugo, Les Misérables.	*Routledge*	0	2	0
,, Notre Dame.	*Routledge*	0	2	0
,, Ninety-Three.	*Routledge*	0	2	0
,, Toilers of the Sea.	*Routledge*	0	2	0

Literature—Fiction, continued

		£	s.	d.
Lesage, Gil Blas.	*Bell*	0	6	0
Manzoni, Promessi Sposi.	*Ward, Lock*	0	2	0
Prevost, Manon Lescaut.	*Routledge*	0	1	0
Rabelais, Gargantua and Pantagruel. 2 vols.	*Routledge*	0	2	0
Sand, G., Consuelo.	*Weldon*	0	2	0
„ La Petite Fadette.	*Weldon*	0	2	0
„ Mauprat.	*Weldon*	0	2	0
Sue, Mysteries of Paris.	*Routledge*	0	2	0
„ Wandering Jew.	*Routledge*	0	2	0
Tolstoi, Anna Karenina. 2 vols.	*Walter Scott*	0	5	0
„ War and Peace. 4 vols., and others.	*Walter Scott*	0	10	0
Turgenieff, 5 vols.	*Ward, Lock.* Each	0	2	6
Dimitri Roudine. Smoke.				
Fathers and Sons. Virgin Soil.				
Liza, and others.				
Voltaire, Candide.	*Routledge*	0	1	0

2. HISTORICAL NOVELS AND TALES

[NOTES AND SUGGESTIONS.—*The amount of actual history contained in a historical tale may range from a slight sketch of some notable character, or a narrative of obscure local incidents, to a careful study of events of world-wide importance; some are concerned with the facts of social or domestic life; others with the fate of kingdoms or nations. Their truthfulness to the facts dealt with must also be expected to vary indefinitely with the purpose and ability of the writer, and the exigencies of his tale. The one advantage common, in a greater or less degree, to all worthy books of the kind, is that of helping us to realise vividly the characters, surroundings, and events of other times than our own. Not to replace, but to stimulate and enliven the pursuit of serious historical study, is the object of Historical Novels; and to do it by giving us that insight into the human interest of bygone events which many of us find it hard to discover for ourselves in the annals of history. Our best writers have shown how possible it is to do this, and at the same time to fulfil those demands upon the writers of ordinary fiction which require their books to be, in George Eliot's phrase, "The cup of self-forgetting excitement to the busy who can snatch an hour of entertainment."*]

			£	s.	d.
1st cent.	**Lytton**, Last Days of Pompeii.	*Routledge*	0	3	6
„	**Whyte-Melville**, The Gladiators.	*Longmans*	0	1	0
3d cent.	**Pater**, Marius the Epicurean. 2 vols.	*Macmillan*	0	12	0
4th cent.	**Ebers**, Homo Sum. (Monks in Arabia.) 2 vols.	*Low*	0	4	0
5th cent.	**Kingsley, C.**, Hypatia. (Christians and Neo-Platonists in Alexandria.)	*Macmillan*	0	3	6
6th cent.	**Ebers**, An Egyptian Princess. 2 vols.	*Low*	0	4	0
11th cent.	**Kingsley, C.**, Hereward the Wake.	*Macmillan*	0	3	6
„	**Lytton**, Harold. (Norman Conquest.)	*Routledge*	0	3	6
„	**Scott, W.**, Count Robert of Paris. (First Crusade.)	*Black*	0	1	6

Literature—Historical Novels and Tales, continued

			£	s.	d.
12th cent.	Scott, W., Ivanhoe. ⎱ ⎰ (Third Crusade.) ⎱ *Black*		0	1	6
,,	,, The Talisman.	*Black*	0	1	6
,,	,, The Betrothed.	*Black*	0	1	6
14th cent.	Yonge, C., The Lances of Lynwood. (Black Prince.) *Macmillan*		0	2	6
,,	Lytton, Rienzi. (Last Roman Tribune.) *Routledge*		0	3	6
15th cent.	Scott, W., Quentin Durward. (Louis XI. of France.) *Black*		0	1	6
,,	,, Fair Maid of Perth. (Scottish Clans.) *Black*		0	1	6
,,	,, Anne of Geierstein. (Wars of the Roses.) *Black*		0	1	6
,,	Lytton, The Last of the Barons. (Edward IV.) *Routledge*		0	3	6
,,	Reade, The Cloister and the Hearth. (European Social Life.) *Chatto*		0	3	6
,,	Eliot, G., Romola. (Florence, Savonarola.) *Blackwood*		0	3	6
,,	Yonge, C., The Dove in the Eagle's Nest. (German Social Life.) *Macmillan*		0	3	6
16th cent.	Scott, W., The Monastery. (Mary Queen of Scots.) *Black*		0	1	6
,,	,, The Abbot. (Mary Queen of Scots.) *Black*		0	1	6
,,	Ainsworth, The Tower of London. (Lady Jane Grey.) *Routledge*		0	2	0
,,	Scott, W., Kenilworth. (Elizabeth and Leicester.) *Black*		0	1	6
,,	Kingsley, C., Westward Ho! (Buccaneers, Armada.) *Macmillan*		0	3	6
,,	Black, Judith Shakespeare. *Macmillan*		0	6	0
,,	Yonge, The Chaplet of Pearls. (St. Bartholomew.) *Macmillan*		0	3	6
17th cent.	Scott, W., The Fortunes of Nigel. (James I.) *Black*		0	1	6
,,	,, Woodstock. (Commonwealth and Charles II.) *Black*		0	1	6
,,	,, Peveril of the Peak. (Charles II.) *Black*		0	1	6
,,	,, Old Mortality. (Covenanters.) *Black*		0	1	6
,,	,, The Legend of Montrose. (Covenanters.) *Black*		0	1	6
,,	Church, A. J., With the King at Oxford. *Seeley*		0	5	0
,,	Manzoni, The Betrothed. (Milan.) *Ward, Lock*		0	2	0
,,	Lyall, E., In the Golden Days. (Charles II.) *Hurst, Blackett*		0	6	0
,,	Besant, For Faith and Freedom. (Monmouth's Rebellion.) *Chatto*		0	3	6
,,	Blackmore, Lorna Doone. (Exmoor.) *Low*		0	2	6
18th cent.	Thackeray, Esmond. (Queen Anne.) *Smith, Elder*		0	3	6

Literature—Historical Novels and Tales, continued

		£	s.	d.
18th cent. Scott, W., Waverley. (Jacobite Conspiracies.)	*Black*	0	1	6
„ „ Rob Roy. (Jacobite Conspiracies.)	*Black*	0	1	6
„ „ Redgauntlet. (Jacobite Conspiracies.)	*Black*	0	1	6
„ „ Heart of Midlothian. (Porteous Riots.)	*Black*	0	1	6
„ Besant, W., Dorothy Forster. (Derwentwater's Rebellion.)	*Chatto*	0	2	6
„ „ The Chaplain of the Fleet. (Social Life.)	*Chatto*	0	2	6
„ Thackeray, The Virginians. (America, George II and George III.) 2 vols.	*Smith, Elder*	0	7	0
„ Cooper, The Spy. (American War.)	*Routledge*	0	1	0
„ Thackeray, Miss, Miss Angel. (Reynolds.)	*Smith, Elder*	0	6	0

FRENCH REVOLUTION—

Dickens, A Tale of Two Cities.	*Chapman, Hall*	0	1	6
Hugo, Victor, Ninety-three. [*trans.*]	*Routledge*	0	2	0
Kingsley, H., Mademoiselle Mathilde.	*Bradbury*	0	2	6
Roberts, Miss, Atelier du Lys.	*Longmans*	0	2	6
„ On the Edge of the Storm.	*Warne*	0	3	6
Erckmann-Chatrian, The Blockade of Phalsburg.	*Ward, Lock*	0	2	6

NAPOLEON—

Tolstoi, War and Peace. [*trans.*] 4 vols.	*Walter Scott*	0	10	0
Erckmann-Chatrian, The Conscript. [*trans.*]	*Ward, Lock*	0	2	6
„ Waterloo. [*trans.*]	*Ward, Lock*	0	2	6

[*For a much fuller list see "A Descriptive Catalogue of Historical Novels and Tales," by H. Courthope Bowen. Stanford, 1s. 6d.*]

IV. ESSAYS, LECTURES, AND STUDIES

Education begins the gentleman, but reading, good company, and reflection must finish him.—JOHN LOCKE.

1. ENGLISH.

Addison, Selections (ed. T. Arnold).	*Clarendon Press*	0	4	6
„ „ (ed. J. R. Green.)	*Macmillan*	0	4	6
Arnold, M., Essays in Criticism.	*Macmillan*	0	9	0
„ Culture and Anarchy.	*Smith, Elder*	0	2	6
„ Mixed Essays.	*Smith, Elder*	0	9	0
Bacon, Essays.	*Macmillan*	0	4	6
„ Advancement of Learning.	*Clarendon Press*	0	4	6

Literature—Essays, Lectures, and Studies, continued

		£ s. d.
Bagehot, Literary Studies. 2 vols.	*Longmans*	0 8 0
,, Biographical Studies.	*Longmans*	0 12 0
Birrell, Obiter Dicta. Two Series. 5s. and 6s.	*Stock*	0 11 0
Brown, Dr. John, Horæ Subsecivæ. 3 vols. *Douglas*. Each		0 7 6
Carlyle, Sartor Resartus.	*Chapman, Hall*	0 1 0
,, Past and Present.	*Chapman, Hall*	0 1 0
,, On Heroes and Hero-Worship.	*Chapman, Hall*	0 1 0
,, Life of Sterling.	*Chapman, Hall*	0 1 0
,, Miscellaneous Essays. 7 vols. *Chapman, Hall*. Each		0 1 0
,, Latter Day Pamphlets.	*Chapman, Hall*	0 1 0
Church, R. W., Dante, and other Essays.	*Macmillan*	0 5 0
Coleridge, Biographia Literaria.	*Bell*	0 3 6
,, Lectures on Shakespeare.	*Bell*	0 3 6
Cowley, Essays.	*Cambridge Press*	0 4 0
De Quincey, Works. 14 vols. *Black*. Each		0 3 6
,, Selections.	*W. Scott*	0 1 0
Dobson, Austin, Eighteenth Century Essays.	*Kegan Paul*	0 6 0
Dowden, Shakespeare, his Mind and Art.	*Kegan Paul*	0 12 0
Dryden, Select Essays.	*Macmillan*	0 2 6
Froude, Short Studies on Great Subjects. 4 vols.	*Longmans*	1 4 0
Hamerton, The Intellectual Life.	*Macmillan*	0 10 6
,, Human Intercourse.	*Macmillan*	0 8 6
Harrison, F., The Choice of Books.	*Macmillan*	0 6 0
Hazlitt, Essays.	*W. Scott*	0 1 0
,, Selections (ed. Ireland).	*Warne*	0 3 6
Helps, Friends in Council. 2 series. *Smith, Elder*. Each		0 7 6
Hudson, Life, Art, and Characters of Shakespeare. 2 vols.	*Arnold*	0 16 0
Hutton, R. H., Literary Essays.	*Macmillan*	0 6 0
Huxley, Critiques and Addresses.	*Macmillan*	0 10 6
Kingsley, C., Prose Idylls.	*Macmillan*	0 3 6
Lamb, Works and Letters. 6 vols. *Macmillan*. Each		0 5 0
,, Elia.	*Routledge*	0 1 0
Landor, Selections.	*Macmillan*	0 4 6
Macaulay, Essays.	*Longmans*	0 2 6
,, Miscellaneous Writings.	*Longmans*	0 2 6
Mazzini, Essays.	*W. Scott*	0 1 0
Müller, Max, Lectures on the Science of Language. 2 vols.	*Longmans*	0 16 0
Morley, J., Compromise.	*Macmillan*	0 5 0
,, Miscellanies. 3 vols. *Macmillan*. Each		0 5 0
,, Studies in Literature.	*Macmillan*	0 5 0
Morris, W., Hopes and Fears for Art.	*Reeves, Turner*	0 4 6
Myers, F., Essays. 2 vols. *Macmillan*. Each		0 4 6
Pater, Marius the Epicurean. 2 vols.	*Macmillan*	0 12 0
,, The Renaissance.	*Macmillan*	0 10 6

Literature—Essays, Lectures, and Studies, continued

		£	s.	d.
Robertson, F. W., Lectures, Addresses, etc. *Kegan Paul*		0	5	0
Ruskin, Frondes Agrestes. *George Allen*		0	3	0
,, Sesame and Lilies. *George Allen*		0	5	0
,, Crown of Wild Olive (and others). *George Allen*		0	5	0
Seeley, Lectures and Essays. *Macmillan*		0	10	6
Shairp, Studies in Poetry and Philosophy. *Douglas*		0	7	6
Smith, Sydney, Essays. *Routledge*		0	2	0
Steele, Selections. *Clarendon Press*		0	5	0
Stephen, L., Hours in a Library. 3 vols. *Smith, Elder.* Each		0	9	0
Stevenson, Familiar Studies of Men and Books. *Chatto*		0	6	0
,, Memories and Portraits. *Chatto*		0	6	0
,, Virginibus Puerisque. *Chatto*		0	6	0
Swift, Works, Selections. *Nimmo*		0	5	0
,, Selections. *W. Scott*		0	1	0
Swinburne, Essays and Studies. *Chatto*		0	12	0
Symonds, Studies of the Greek Poets. *Smith, Elder*		0	10	6
Thackeray, The Four Georges and English Humourists. *Smith, Elder*		0	3	6
,, Roundabout Papers, and others. *Smith, Elder*		0	3	6
Thring, Addresses. *Unwin*		0	5	0

2. AMERICAN.

	£	s.	d.
Emerson, Works. 6 vols. *Macmillan.* Each	0	5	0
,, Selections. *W. Scott*	0	1	0
Holmes, The Autocrat of the Breakfast Table. *Paterson*	0	2	0
,, The Professor at the Breakfast Table. *Paterson*	0	2	0
Lowell, My Study Windows. *Low*	0	1	0
,, Essays and Addresses. 6 vols. *Macmillan.* Each	0	6	0
Thoreau, Walden. *W. Scott*	0	1	0
Whitman, Specimen Days. *W. Scott*	0	1	0

V. SOME FAMOUS BOOKS

Hundreds of people can talk for one who can think, but thousands can think for one who can see. To see clearly is poetry, prophecy, and religion—all in one.—RUSKIN.

	£	s.	d.
Æsop's Fables. *Bell*	0	1	0
Plato, Trial and Death of Socrates. *Macmillan*	0	4	6
Epictetus, Selections. *Bell*	0	5	0
Plutarch, Lives. *Scott*	0	1	0
Marcus Aurelius, Selections. *W. Scott*	0	1	0
Chronicle of the Cid. *Routledge*	0	1	0
Arabian Nights. *W. Scott*	0	1	0
The Imitation of Christ. *Kegan Paul*	0	1	0
Malory, Morte D'Arthur. *Macmillan*	0	3	6

Literature—Some Famous Books, continued

		£	s.	d.
Machiavelli, The Prince.	Routledge	0	1	0
Luther, Table Talk.	Low	0	3	6
Erasmus, Praise of Folly.	Reeves, Turner	0	12	0
More, Utopia. (Ideal Commonwealths.)	Routledge	0	1	0
Sidney, Arcadia.	Low	0	6	0
Montaigne, Essays.	Low	0	2	6
Hooker, Ecclesiastical Polity, Book I.	Clarendon Press	0	2	0
Milton, Areopagitica.	Arber	0	0	6
,, Selected Prose Works.	Kegan Paul	0	6	0
Pascal, Thoughts.	Low	0	3	6
Bunyan, The Pilgrim's Progress.	Macmillan	0	4	6
La Rochefoucauld, Maxims.	Whittingham	0	1	0
Walton, The Complete Angler.	Warne	0	2	0
Le Sage, Gil Blas.	Warne	0	2	0
Browne, Religio Medici.	W. Scott	0	1	0
Defoe, Robinson Crusoe.	Macmillan	0	4	6
,, History of the Plague.	Routledge	0	1	0
Swift, Gulliver's Travels.	Routledge	0	2	0
Spectator, The.	Routledge	0	3	6
Lessing, Laokoon.	Bell	0	1	6
Letters of Junius.	Routledge	0	3	6
Chesterfield, Letters.	Low	0	2	6
Johnson, Rasselas.	Low	0	2	6
Burke, Selections. 3 vols.	Clarendon Press	0	14	6
,, Thoughts on Present Discontent.	Cassell	0	0	3
Goethe and Schiller, Correspondence. 2 vols.	Bell	0	7	0
Goethe, Conversations with Eckermann.	Bell	0	3	6
Heine, Prose Writings.	W. Scott	0	1	0

(*For complete editions of the works of several of the authors above mentioned see larger catalogues. See also in connection with this group, besides the books under the head of Poetry, Fiction, Essays, etc., Boswell (Biography), Plato and Aristotle (Philosophy), Herodotus, Thucydides, Gibbon (History), Adam Smith (Political Economy), Darwin (Science), and others.*)

PHILOSOPHY

[NOTES AND SUGGESTIONS.—It is impossible for a mere list of books to give the guidance which, in nearly all cases, must be needful for the prosperous study of philosophy. The difficulties are so great, the divergence on fundamental principles is so serious, that it is to be feared any who tried to gain a knowledge of Ethics or Metaphysics only by steadily reading through the books recommended would be likely to end in confusion instead of a clear grasp of the subject. No one must suppose that the following list is considered an adequate substitute for personal guidance.

Two rules should be kept in mind by the student: (1) Philosophers are always thinking of facts, and usually very familiar facts. The student should check his reading by his own experience of men and things. In reading a philosopher of a past age he should ask himself, " What does this correspond to, and how must it be modified at the present time." Remember also that a philosopher even when erroneous may be imperfectly and mistakenly representing a truth. (2) Read great philosophers themselves, and only use books about them afterwards, or with them as a help. The history of philosophy can never be a substitute for philosophy; but it is useful for understanding minor thinkers whom there is no time to study, and to show the connection between great thinkers (see especially Schwegler). But one great philosopher studied carefully is worth any amount of miscellaneous knowledge about philosophy.

The best preparation for philosophy is to have read reflective works in general literature, history, science, poetry. A student will do well to read by way of introduction some of the works under V. 1. Most, however, will probably find it useful to proceed as soon as possible to Ethics.]

> Who would lose,
> Though full of pain, this intellectual being,
> Those thoughts that wander through eternity?—*Milton.*

> Sure, He that made us with such large discourse,
> Looking before and after, gave us not
> That capability and god-like reason
> To fust in us unused.—*Shakespeare.*

I. METAPHYSICS
[See also V.]

		£	s.	d.
Descartes, Discourse on Method and Meditations (*trans.* Veitch).	*Blackwood*	0	6	6
Spinoza, Chief Works (*trans.*) 2 vols.	*Bell*	0	10	0
Locke, Essay on the Human Understanding.	*Ward, Lock*	0	3	6

Philosophy—Metaphysics, continued

		£	s.	d.
Berkeley, Works (especially "Three Dialogues"). 4 vols. *Clarendon Press*		2	18	0
Hume, Inquiry on the Human Understanding, in Essays. *Ward, Lock*		0	3	6
„ Treatise of Human Nature (ed. Selby-Bigge). *Clarendon Press*		0	9	0
Mill, J. S., Examination of Hamilton's Philosophy. *Longmans*		0	16	0
Lewes, Problems of Life and Mind, 1st and 2d series. *Trübner.* Each		0	16	0
Spencer, H., First Principles. (See also under V.) *Williams, Norgate*		0	16	0
„ „ 3rd Series. 2 vols. *Trübner*		1	2	6
Kant, Selections by Watson. *Maclehose*		0	7	6
„ Critique of Pure Reason (*trans.* Meiklejohn). *Bell*		0	5	0
Stirling, Text-Book to Kant. *Edinburgh*			O. P.	
Caird, E., Philosophy of Immanuel Kant. *Maclehose*		1	12	0
Adamson, Philosophy of Kant. *Douglas*		0	6	0
Fichte, Popular Works (*trans.* Smith). 2 vols. *Trübner*		1	1	0
Hegel. (See under III. V. and VI.)				
Lotze, Metaphysic (*trans.*) 2 vols. *Clarendon Press*		0	12	0
„ Mikrokosmus (*trans.*) 2 vols. *T. and T. Clark*		1	16	0
Green, T. H., Introduction to Hume in Vol. I. of Collected Works. (See also under II.) *Longmans*		0	16	0
Grote, John, Exploratio Philosophica. *Deighton, Bell*		0	6	0

II. ETHICS

1. INTRODUCTORY.

		£	s.	d.
Butler, Sermons. *Bell*		0	3	6
Mill, J. S., Utilitarianism. *Longmans*		0	5	0
Fowler, T., Progressive Morality. *Macmillan*		0	5	0
Calderwood, Handbook of Moral Philosophy. *Macmillan*		0	6	0

2. SYSTEMATIC WORKS.

		£	s.	d.
Green, T. H., Prolegomena to Ethics. *Clarendon Press*		0	12	6
Martineau, Dr., Types of Ethical Theory. 2 vols. *Clarendon Press*		0	15	0
Sidgwick, H., Methods of Ethics. *Macmillan*		0	14	0
Spencer, H., Data of Ethics. *Williams, Norgate*		0	8	0
Stephen, Leslie, Science of Ethics. *Smith, Elder*		0	16	0
Wilson and T. Fowler, Principles of Morals. 2 vols. *Clarendon Press*		0	14	0
Hume, Essays: Enquiry concerning Morals. *Ward, Lock*		0	3	6
Kant, Theory of Ethics (*trans.* Abbott). *Longmans*		0	10	6
Aristotle, Ethics (*trans.* Peters). *Kegan Paul*		0	6	0
Grote, John, A Treatise on the Moral Ideals. *Deighton, Bell*		0	12	0

Philosophy—Ethics, continued

3. HISTORY OF ETHICS.

	£	s.	d.
Sidgwick, H., Outlines of the History of Ethics. *Macmillan*	0	3	6

III. LOGIC

1. ELEMENTARY.

		£	s.	d.
Jevons, Elementary Lessons in Logic.	*Macmillan*	0	3	6
Fowler, T., Deductive Logic.	*Clarendon Press*	0	3	6
„ Inductive Logic.	*Clarendon Press*	0	6	0
Keynes, Formal Logic.	*Macmillan*	0	10	6

2. ADVANCED.

		£	s.	d.
Mill, J. S., System of Logic.	*Longmans*	0	5	0
Jevons, Principles of Science.	*Macmillan*	0	12	6
Bacon, Novum Organum (*trans.* Kitchin).	*Clarendon Press*	0	9	6
Lotze, Logic (*trans.*) 2 vols.	*Clarendon Press*	0	12	0
Bradley, H., Principles of Logic.	*Kegan Paul*	0	16	0
Bosanquet, Logic or the Morphology of Knowledge.	*Clarendon Press*	1	1	0
Venn, Empirical or Inductive Logic.	*Macmillan*	0	18	0
Hegel, Logic (*trans.* Wallace).	*Clarendon Press*	0	14	0

IV. PSYCHOLOGY

1. ELEMENTARY.

		£	s.	d.
Sully, Outlines of Psychology.	*Longmans*	0	12	6
„ The Teacher's Handbook of Psychology.	*Longmans*	0	6	6
Murray, Handbook of Psychology.	*Alex. Gardner*	0	7	6
Lotze, Outlines of Psychology (*trans.* Ladd).	*Chicago*	0	5	0
Kirchner, Psychology.	*Sonnenschein*	0	4	6

2. ADVANCED.

		£	s.	d.
Ward, Article "Psychology" in Ency. Brit., Part 77 separately.	*Black*	0	7	6
Lewes, The Study of Psychology.	*Trübner*	0	7	6
„ The Physical Basis of Mind.	*Trübner*	0	16	0
Bain, The Senses and the Intellect.	*Longmans*	0	15	0
„ The Emotions and the Will.	*Longmans*	0	15	0
Spencer, H., Principles of Psychology. 2 vols.	*Williams, Norgate*	1	16	0

V. MISCELLANEOUS BOOKS

1. INTRODUCTORY.

		£	s.	d.
Ferrier, Lectures on Early Greek Philosophy.	*Blackwood*	0	10	6
Plato, The Republic (*trans.* Davies and Vaughan).	*Macmillan*	0	4	6

Philosophy—Miscellaneous, continued

	£	s.	d.
Plato. The Republic (*trans.* Jowett with Introduction). *Clarendon Press*	0	12	6
[Other dialogues translated with introductions by Jowett. See especially Gorgias, Phaedo, Symposium, Phaedrus, Theaetetus.]			
Berkeley, Selections by Fraser. *Clarendon Press*	0	7	6
Clifford, Lectures and Essays. *Macmillan*	0	8	6
Green, T. H., Collected Works, vol. III., with Memoir. *Longmans*	0	16	0

2. BOOKS ON MISCELLANEOUS SUBJECTS.

	£	s.	d.
Hegel, Philosophy of History (*trans.*) *Bell*	0	5	0
,, Introduction to Philosophy of Fine Art (*trans.* Bosanquet). *Kegan Paul*	0	5	0
Allen, Grant, Physiological Æsthetics. *King*	O. P.		
Mill, J. S., Three Essays on Religion. *Longmans*	0	5	0
Martineau, Dr., A Study of Religion. 2 vols. *Clarendon Press*	1	4	0
Pfleiderer, Philosophy of Religion (*trans.*) 4 vols. *Williams, Norgate*	2	2	0
Caird, J., Introduction to Philosophy of Religion. *Maclehose*	0	10	6

VI. HISTORY OF PHILOSOPHY

1. ELEMENTARY AND SPECIAL.

	£	s.	d.
Zeller. Outlines of Greek Philosophy (*trans.* Alleyne and Abbott). *Longmans*	0	10	6
Seth, Scottish Philosophy. *Blackwood*	0	5	0
Philosophical Classics for English Readers :—Descartes, Butler, Berkeley, Fichte, Kant, Hegel, Leibnitz, Hobbes, Hume, Spinoza, Bacon, Locke. *Blackwood.* Each	0	2	6
Stephen, L., History of English Thought in 18th century. 2 vols. *Smith, Elder*	1	8	0

2. SYSTEMATIC.

	£	s.	d.
Schwegler, History of Philosophy (*trans.* Stirling). *Oliver, Boyd*	0	6	0
Ueberweg, History of Philosophy (*trans.*) 2 vols. *Hodder*	1	19	0
Erdmann, History of Philosophy (*trans.*) 3 vols. *Sonnenschein*	2	2	0

(*The last two give references to the literature of philosophy.*)

POLITICAL AND SOCIAL ECONOMY

[NOTES AND SUGGESTIONS.—*There are very great difficulties in the way of any attempt to provide a good list of books on Political and Social Economy. There has been a great deal of writing of general treatises,—some very good,—and comparatively little writing of first-rate books on special subjects in English. Probably in the next few years much will be done to improve this state of things. At present many of the best sources of information are either foreign works or else scattered papers in Reviews or Scientific Journals or Pamphlets, copies of which cannot be procured. Political partisanship, again, affects the value of many books by capable men. This list is in many ways very incomplete, but it may be hoped that the publications of each succeeding year will, to some extent, remedy this defect.*

Students who are beginning the subject might read Jevons' Primer and then take a Textbook, like Walker's First Lessons in Political Economy or Marshall's Economics of Industry, and read it carefully through, referring under the various heads to some of the books mentioned in this list.]

The stock of materials by which any nation is rendered flourishing and prosperous are its industry, its knowledge or skill, its morals, its execution of justice, its courage, and the national union in directing these powers to one point, and making them all centre in the public benefit. Other than these I do not know, and scarcely can conceive, any means by which a community may flourish.—BURKE.

I. GENERAL

1. ECONOMIC THEORY

ELEMENTARY.

		£	s.	d.
Jevons, Primer of Political Economy.	*Macmillan*	0	1	0
Symes, Political Economy.	*Longmans*	0	2	6
Marshall, A., and M. P., Economics of Industry.	*Macmillan*	0	2	6
Walker, Political Economy.	*Macmillan*	0	12	6
„ „ (Abridged).	*Macmillan*	0	6	6
„ First Lessons in Political Economy.	*Macmillan*	0	5	0

ADVANCED.

		£	s.	d.
Wicksteed, Alphabet of Economic Science.	*Macmillan*	0	2	6
Marshall, A., Principles of Economics. Vol. I.	*Macmillan*	0	12	6
Sidgwick, H., Principles of Political Economy.	*Macmillan*	0	16	0
Jevons, Theory of Political Economy.	*Macmillan*	0	10	6
Böhm Bauwerk, Capital and Interest.	*Macmillan*	0	14	0
Cairnes, Leading Principles of Political Economy.	*Macmillan*	0	14	0

Political and Social Economy, continued

2. STANDARD WORKS

		£	s.	d.
Smith, Adam, Wealth of Nations (Nicholson's Edition).	*Nelson*	0	4	0
Malthus, The Principle of Population.	*Reeves and Turner*	0	8	0
Bonar, Malthus and his Work.	*Macmillan*	0	12	6
Ricardo, Works (M'Culloch's Edition).	*Murray*	0	16	0
Mill, J. S., Political Economy.	*Longmans*	0	5	0
Roscher, Principles of Political Economy. 2 vols. (Chicago)	*Callaghan*	1	12	0
Cairnes, Essays on Political Economy.	*Macmillan*	0	10	6
Jevons, Works.	*Macmillan*	Various		

3. ECONOMIC AND COMMERCIAL HISTORY

		£	s.	d.
Ashley, Economic History.	*Longmans*	0	5	0
Cunningham, W., Growth of English Industry and Commerce.	*Cambridge Press*	0	16	0
Levi, History of British Commerce, 1763-1878.	*Murray*	0	18	0
Rogers, J. E. T., Economic Interpretation of History.	*Unwin*	0	16	0
„ Six Centuries of Work and Wages.	*Sonnenschein*	0	10	6
„ „ (Abridged. 1 vol.)		0	3	6
Toynbee, The Industrial Revolution.	*Longmans*	0	10	6
Wells, Recent Economic Changes.	*Appleton, New York*	0	10	6

(*See also under Special Subjects.*)

4. METHOD AND HISTORY OF ECONOMIC SCIENCE

		£	s.	d.
Cossa, Guide to the Study of Political Economy.	*Macmillan*	0	4	6
Ingram, A History of Political Economy.	*Black*	0	6	0
Blanqui, History of Political Economy.	*Bell*	0	12	0
Cairnes, Logical Method of Political Economy.	*Macmillan*	0	6	0
Keynes, The Scope and Method of Political Economy.	*Macmillan*	0	7	0
Leslie, Cliffe, Essays in Political and Moral Philosophy.	*Longmans*	0	10	6
Bagehot, Economic Studies.	*Longmans*	0	10	6
(Part has been republished under title, The Postulates of English Political Economy).				
Marshall, A., The Present Position of Economics.	*Macmillan*	0	2	0
Sidgwick, H., The Scope and Method of Economic Science.	*Macmillan*	0	2	6

II. ORGANISATION OF INDUSTRY

1. DIVISION OF LABOUR AND MODERN PRODUCTION

		£	s.	d.
Babbage, Economy of Machines and Manufactures.	*Murray*	O. P.		
Young, Labor in Europe and America. 1876.	*Washington Government Printing Office*	0	10	6

Political and Social Economy, continued

		£	s.	d.
Nicholson, The Effects of Machinery on Wages.	*Bell*	0	2	6
Hearn, Plutology.	*Longmans*		O. P.	

2. FACTORY SYSTEM

Taylor, Cooke, Introduction to the History of the Factory System. *Bentley*		0	16	0
Von Plener, The English Factory System. *Chapman, Hall*		0	3	0
Physical and Moral Condition of Children, etc., employed in Manufactures: Abstract of Reports of Commissioners, 1843. *Parker*			O. P.	
Pidgeon, Old-World Questions and New-World Answers. 1884. *Warne*		0	7	6

3. GUILDS

Brentano, The History of Gilds and The Origin of Trade Unions. 1870. *Trübner*		0	3	6
Bain, Ebenezer, Merchant and Craft Gilds. (Aberdeen.) *Edmond, Spark*		0	7	6
Smith, Toulmin, English Gilds: their Ordinances. *Early English Text Society*		1	1	0
Gross, The Gild Merchant. 2 vols. *Clarendon Press*		1	4	0

4. TRADES UNIONS AND STRIKES

Howell, Conflicts of Capital and Labour. *Macmillan*		0	7	6
Trades Societies and Strikes: Report of the Committee of Social Science Association, 1860. *Parker*			O. P.	
Reports of the Labour Correspondent of the Board of Trade. *Eyre, Spottiswoode*			Various.	
Reports of the Principal Trades Unions				
Paris, Comte de, Trades Unions of England. *Smith, Elder*		0	7	6
Smith, Llewellyn, and Nash, The Story of the Dockers' Strike *Unwin*		0	1	0

5. THE WAGES QUESTION

Walker, The Wages Question. *Macmillan*		0	14	0
Brassey, Foreign Work and English Wages. *Longmans*		0	10	6
Levi, Leone, Wages and Earnings of the Working Classes. *Murray*		0	3	6
Fawcett, The Economic Position of the British Labourer. *Macmillan*		0	5	0

Political and Social Economy, continued

6. CONCILIATION AND ADJUSTMENT OF WAGES

		£	s.	d.
Price, Industrial Peace.	*Macmillan*	0	6	0
Munro, Sliding Scales in the Coal Industry.	*Heywood*	0	1	0
,, ,, ,, Iron Industry.	*Heywood*	0	1	0
Crompton, Industrial Conciliation.	*King*	0	2	6

7. PROFIT-SHARING

		£	s.	d.
Gilman, Profit-Sharing between Employer and Employed.	*Macmillan*	0	7	6
Taylor, Sedley, Profit-Sharing between Capital and Labour.	*Kegan Paul*	0	2	6

8. CO-OPERATION

		£	s.	d.
Acland and Jones, Working Men Co-operators.	*Cassell*	0	1	0
Hughes and Neale, A Manual for Co-operators.	*Co-operative Union, Manchester*	0	1	0
Holyoake, History of Co-operation. 2 vols.	*Trübner*	0	14	0
Adams, History of Co-operation in the United States.	*Macmillan*	0	15	0
Co-operative Life: A Series of Lectures.	*Co-operative Printing Society, London*	0	1	6
The Co-operative Wholesale Society's Annual.	*Manchester*	Various.		
Statistical Report, Annual. *Co-operative Union, Manchester*		0	1	0

III. LAND, AGRICULTURE, AND MINING

1. LAND TENURE

		£	s.	d.
Systems of Land Tenure in Various Countries.	*Cassell*	0	3	6
Pollock, The Land Laws.	*Macmillan*	0	3	6
Brodrick, English Land and Landlords.	*Cassell*	0	12	6
Leslie, Cliffe, Land Systems of England and Scotland.	*Longmans*	0	12	0

2. LAND TRANSFER

		£	s.	d.
Land Transfer. Published by order of the Bar Committee.	*Butterworths*	0	1	0
Brickdale, Registration of Title to Land.	*Stanford*	0	5	0
Kay, J., Free Trade in Land. Preface by John Bright.	*Cassell*	0	1	6

Political and Social Economy—Land, etc., continued

3. RENT AND TENANCY

		£	s.	d.
Walker, Land and its Rent.	*Macmillan*	0	3	6
Nicholson, Tenants' Gain not Landlords' Loss.	*Douglas*	0	5	0
Prothero, Pioneers and Progress of English Farming.	*Longmans*	0	5	0
Lloyd, Science of Agriculture.	*Longmans*	0	12	0
Caird, The Landed Interest.	*Cassell*	0	5	0
Town Holdings: Parliamentary Reports and Evidence.	*Eyre, Spottiswoode*	Various		

4. COMMONS AND ENCLOSURES

		£	s.	d.
Six Essays on Commons Preservation.	*Sampson Low*	0	14	0
Elton, Charles, Observations on the Bill for the Improvement and Regulation of Commons.	*Wildy and Sons*	0	6	0

5. ALLOTMENTS AND COTTAGE FARMING

		£	s.	d.
Onslow, Lord, Landlords and Allotments.	*Longmans*	0	2	0
Hall, The Law of Allotments.	*Longmans*	0	7	6
Stubbs, The Land and the Labourers.	*Sonnenschein*	0	1	0
Small Holdings: Parliamentary Reports and Evidence.	*Eyre, Spottiswoode*	0	4	8

6. MINING AND ROYALTIES

		£	s.	d.
Sorley, Mining Royalties.	*Clarendon Press*	0	1	6
Price, West Barbary, Work and Wages in the Cornish Mines (Statistical Society's Journal, Vol. 51, Pt. 3).	*Stanford*	0	5	0
Jevons, The Coal Question.	*Macmillan*	0	10	6

7. VILLAGE COMMUNITIES

		£	s.	d.
Nassé, Agricultural Community of the Middle Ages.	*Macmillan*	0	5	0
Seebohm, The English Village Community.	*Longmans*	0	16	0
Maine, Village Communities.	*Murray*	0	9	0

IV. CONDITION OF THE PEOPLE

1. GENERAL

Eden, State of the Poor. 3 vols.		O. P.
Porter, Progress of the Nation.		O. P.
Ludlow and Lloyd Jones, Progress of the Working Classes, 1832-67.	*Strahan*	O. P.

Political and Social Economy, continued

	£	s.	d.
Engels, The Condition of the Working Classes in 1844 (*trans*). *New York, J. W. Lovell*	0	5	0
Giffen, Progress of the Working Classes [and in his Essays in Finance]. *Bell*		O. P.	
Booth, Charles, Labour and Life of the People (Vol. I. East London). *Williams, Norgate*	0	10	6
Booth, Charles, Occupations of the People—Tower Hamlets. *Stanford*		O. P.	
Hill, Octavia, Homes of the London Poor. *Macmillan*	0	1	0
Graham, W., The Social Problem. *Kegan Paul*	0	14	0
Foxwell and Others, The Claims of Labour. *Edinburgh Co-operative Printing Society*	0	1	0
Booth, General, In Darkest England. *Salvation Army Offices*	0	3	6

2. POPULATION AND VITAL STATISTICS

	£	s.	d.
Malthus, Essay on Population. *Ward, Lock*	0	5	0
Newsholme, The Elements of Vital Statistics. *Sonnenschein*	0	7	6
Farr, Vital Statistics. *Stanford*	1	10	0
Longstaff, Studies in Statistics. *Stanford*	1	1	0

3. THRIFT AND TEMPERANCE

	£	s.	d.
Blackley, Collected Essays on the Prevention of Pauperism. *Kegan Paul*	0	1	0
Baernreither, English Associations of Working Men. *Sonnenschein*	1	1	0
Wilkinson, The Friendly Society Movement. *Longmans*	0	2	6
Lewins, A History of Banks for Savings. *Low*	0	15	0
Intemperance, Report of Lords' Committee on. 2 vols. *Eyre, Spottiswoode*		O. P.	
Richardson, Dr., Alcohol (Cantor Lectures). *Macmillan*	0	1	0
,, Total Abstinence. *Macmillan*	0	3	6

4. POOR LAW AND PAUPERISM

	£	s.	d.
Fowle, The Poor Law (English Citizen Series). *Macmillan*	0	3	6
Aschrott, The English Poor Law System. *Knight and Co.*	0	9	0
Turner, Ribton, A History of Vagrants and Vagrancy, and Beggars and Begging. *Chapman, Hall*	1	1	0
Report on the Elberfeld Poor Law System. *Eyre, Spottiswoode*	0	0	9
Poor Law Relief (Lords' Committee Evidence). *Eyre, Spottiswoode*	0	7	10

(*See also under* " General Condition," " Pauperism," *etc.*)

Political and Social Economy, continued

5. CHARITIES

a. ORGANISATION.

		£	s.	d.
Loch, Charities Register and Digest. *C.O.S., 15 Buckingham Street, W.C.*		0	10	6
Hornsby and Wright, Thoughts and Experiences of a Charity Organisationist. *Hunt*		0	3	6
Loch, Charity Organisation. *Sonnenschein*		0	2	6
Chalmers, The Christian and Civic Economy of Large Towns (in Life and Works, also separate).		O. P.		

b. ENDOWMENTS.

	£	s.	d.
Charity Commission Acts (edited Mitcheson). *Stevens*	0	18	0
Hobhouse, Lord, The Dead Hand. *Chatto*	0	5	0
Kenny, Courtney, Endowed Charities. *Reeves, Turner*	0	7	6

V. CURRENCY, BANKING, AND TRADE

1. MONEY, CREDIT, AND BANKING

	£	s.	d.
Jevons, Money. *Kegan Paul*	0	5	0
Walker, Money, Trade, and Industry. *Macmillan*	0	7	6
Nicholson, Money and Monetary Problems. *Blackwood*	0	10	6
Bagehot, Lombard Street. *Kegan Paul*	0	7	6
Gilbart, On Banking (ed. Michie). 2 vols. *Bell*	0	10	0
Rae, The Country Banker. *Murray*	0	7	6
Crump, Manual of Banking. *Longmans*	0	12	0

ADVANCED.

	£	s.	d.
Walker, Money. *Macmillan*	0	16	0
Graham, History of the One Pound Note in Scotland, etc. *Simpkin, Marshall*	0	7	6
Barbour, Theory of Bimetallism. *Cassell*	0	6	0
Howell, Synopsis of the Report of Gold and Silver Commission. *Heywood*	0	1	0
Rogers, J. E. T., First Nine Years of the Bank of England. *Clarendon Press*	0	8	6
Journal of the Institute of Bankers. *Per No.*	0	1	6

Political and Social Economy—Currency, etc., continued

2. SPECULATION, MARKETS, AND EXCHANGES

		£	s.	d.
Giffen, Stock Exchange Securities.	*Bell*	0	8	6
Crump, Theory of Stock Exchange Speculation.	*Longmans*	0	10	6
Melsheimer and Lawrence, The Law and Customs of the Stock Exchange.	*Henry Sweet*	0	5	0
The Rationale of Market Fluctuations.	*Effingham Wilson*	0	7	6
Mathieson's Highest and Lowest Prices (Annual).	*Mathieson*	0	2	6
The Economist, Weekly.	*Per No.*	0	0	8
The Statist, Weekly.	*Per No.*	0	0	6

3. PRICES

		£	s.	d.
Foxwell, Employment and Prices (in Claims of Labour), 1886.	*Edinburgh Co-operative Printing Society*	0	1	0
Jevons, Investigations in Currency and Finance.	*Macmillan*	1	1	0
Giffen, Essays in Finance. 2 vols. (Vol. I. 10s. 6d., Vol. II. 14s.)	*Bell*	1	4	6
Tooke and Newmarch, History of Prices. 6 vols.	O. P.			
Rogers, Thorold, History of Agriculture and Prices. 6 vols.	*Clarendon Press*	7	2	0

4. FOREIGN TRADE AND FOREIGN EXCHANGES

		£	s.	d.
Goschen, Foreign Exchanges.	*Wilson*	0	5	0
Seyd, Bullion and Foreign Exchanges.	*Wilson*	1	0	0
Bastable, Theory of International Trade.	*Simpkin*	0	3	6
Phear, Foreign Trade.	*Macmillan*	0	2	6
Giffen, Use of Export and Import Statistics (in Essays in Finance, Vol. II.)	*Bell*	0	14	0
Dymes, The Trade of the United Kingdom with the World, 1889.	*Stock*	0	3	6
The Year-Book of Commerce.	*Cassell*	0	5	0

VI. FINANCIAL POLICY

1. TAXATION

M'Culloch, On Taxation and Funding.	*Black*	O. P.
Baxter, Dudley, The Taxation of the United Kingdom.	*Macmillan*	O. P.

Political and Social Economy—Financial, continued

		£	s.	d.
Noble, The Queen's Taxes.	*Longmans*		o.	p.
Wright and Hobhouse, An Outline of Local Government and Taxation.	*P.S. King*		o.	p.
Goschen, Local Taxation.	*Macmillan*	o	5	o
Local Government and Taxation in the United Kingdom (Cobden Club).	*Cassell*	o	5	o
Dowell, History of Taxes and Taxation. 4 vols.	*Longmans*	2	2	o
Cossa, Taxation in its Principles and Methods.	*Putnam*	o	3	6

2. NATIONAL FINANCE

		£	s.	d.
Northcote, Stafford, Financial Policy 1862.	*Saunders, Otley*		o.	p.
Gladstone, Financial Statements of 1853, 1860-1863, etc.	*Murray*		o.	p.
Baxter, Dudley, National Income.	*Macmillan*		o.	p.
Buxton, S., Finance and Politics.	*Murray*	1	6	o
Giffen, Growth of Capital.	*Bell*	o	7	6

3. NATIONAL DEBTS

		£	s.	d.
Wilson, A. J., The National Budget, National Debts, etc.	*Macmillan*	o	3	6
Baxter, Dudley, National Debts.	*Bush*	o	4	6
Adams, Public Debts.	*New York, Appleton*	o	12	6

VII. FREE TRADE AND PROTECTION

1. PROTECTION TO TRADE

		£	s.	d.
Fawcett, Free Trade and Protection.	*Macmillan*	o	2	6
Smith, Adam, Wealth of Nations (book iv.)	*Nelson*	o	4	o
List, National System of Political Economy.	*Routledge*	o	5	o
Baden-Powell, State Aid and State Interference.	*Chapman, Hall*	o	9	o
Sumner, History of American Protection.	*New York*	o	5	o
Taussig, The Tariff History of the United States.	*Putnam*	o	6	6
Rawson, Synopsis of the Tariffs and Trade of the British Empire.	*Imperial Federation League*	o	2	6
Farrer, Free Trade v. Fair Trade.	*Cassell*	o	5	o
MacNeill, English Interference with Irish Industries.	*Cassell*	o	1	o

2. PROTECTION TO LABOUR

		£	s.	d.
Seward, Chinese Immigration, and its Social and Economical Aspects.	*San Francisco, Bosqui and Co.*	o	12	6
Immigration of Foreigners, Report of Parliamentary Committee on.	*Eyre, Spottiswoode*	o	3	6

Political and Social Economy, continued

VIII. PRIVATE ENTERPRISE AND PUBLIC CONTROL

1. INDIVIDUALISM

		£	s.	d.
Spencer, H., The Man v. the State.	*Williams, Norgate*	0	1	0
Sumner, What Social Classes owe to each other.	*Trübner*	0	3	6
Donisthorpe, Individualism: a System of Politics.	*Macmillan*	0	14	0
Bastiat, Harmonies of Political Economy.	*Simpkin, Marshall*	0	7	6
Mackay, A History of the English Poor.	*Murray*	0	7	6
„ A Plea for Liberty (Essays by various writers).	*Murray*	0	12	0

2. SOCIALISM

a. HISTORICAL, DESCRIPTIVE, AND CRITICAL.

Rae, Contemporary Socialism.	*Isbister*	0	7	6
Laveleye, Socialism of To-day.	*Simpkin*	0	6	0
Ely, French and German Socialism.	*Trübner*	0	3	6
Schaeffle, Quintessence of Socialism.	*Sonnenschein*	0	2	6
Nordhoff, Communistic Societies of the United States.	*Murray*	0	15	0
Noyes, History of American Socialism.	*Lippincott*	0	15	0
Lloyd-Jones, Life of Robert Owen.	*Sonnenschein*	0	6	0
Smith, Llewellyn, Economic Aspects of State Socialism.	*Simpkin, Marshall*	0	3	6

b. EXPOSITORY AND PROPAGANDIST.*

Marx, Capital. Cheap edition.	*Sonnenschein*	0	10	6
Gronlund, The Co-operative Commonwealth.	*Sonnenschein*	0	2	6
Webb, S., Socialism in England.	*Sonnenschein*	0	2	6
Bax, Belfort, Essays in Socialism.	*Sonnenschein*	0	2	6
Fabian Essays in Socialism.	*Scott*	0	1	0
Bellamy, Looking Backward.	*Reeves*	0	1	0
George, Henry, Progress and Poverty.	*Kegan Paul*	0	2	6
Hyndman, Historical Basis of Socialism in England.	*Kegan Paul*	0	8	6
Morris, W., Signs of Change.	*Reeves, Turner*	0	4	6

* *The books in this list are of very different degrees of merit, some of them being from the economical point of view of very small value; but the English Socialistic Movement at the present time is many-sided, and it is necessary, in order to understand it, to be acquainted with the views of Socialists of various schools.*

Political and Social Economy, continued

3. THE PROVINCE AND POLICY OF STATE INTERVENTION

a. GENERAL.

		£	s.	d.
Mill, J. S., Liberty.	*Longmans*	0	1	4
Jevons, Methods of Social Reform.	*Macmillan*	0	10	6
Cunningham, W., Politics and Economics.	*Kegan Paul*	0	5	0
Sidgwick, H., Principles of Political Economy. (Book III.)	*Macmillan*	0	16	0
Green, T. H. Liberal Legislation and Freedom of Contract in Vol. III. of Works.	*Longmans*	0	16	0

b. REGULATION OF INDUSTRY.

Jevons, The State in Relation to Labour.	*Macmillan*	0	3	6
Von Plener, The English Factory Legislation.	*Chapman, Hall*	0	3	0
Redgrave, The Factory and Workshop Act 1879. 2d edition.	*Shaw*	0	5	0

c. REGULATION OF TRADE AND MARKETS, ETC.

Farrer, The State in Relation to Trade.	*Macmillan*	0	3	6

d. COMMUNICATION.

Adams, C., Railroads and Railroad Questions	*Putnam*	0	5	0
Hadley, Railroad Transportation. 1885.	*Putnam*	0	6	0
Grierson, Railway Rates: English and Foreign.	*Stanford*	0	5	0
Jeans, Railway Problems.	*Longmans*	0	12	6

IX. LITERARY WORKS DEALING WITH ECONOMIC PROBLEMS

Carlyle, Past and Present.	*Chapman, Hall*	0	1	0
,, Chartism (Critical Essays, Vol. VI.)	*Chapman, Hall*	0	1	0
Cobbett, Rural Rides. 2 vols.	*Reeves, Turner*	0	12	6
Ruskin, Unto this Last.	*George Allen*	0	3	0
,, Crown of Wild Olive.	*George Allen*	0	5	0
,, Munera Pulveris.	*George Allen*	0	5	0
Kingsley, C., Alton Locke.	*Macmillan*	0	3	6
,, Yeast.	*Macmillan*	0	3	6
Tolstoi, What must we do then?	*W. Scott*	0	2	6
Young, A., Travels in France.	*Bell*	0	3	6

Political and Social Economy, continued

X. WORKS OF REFERENCE AND PERIODICAL LITERATURE

	£	s.	d.
Palgrave, R. H., Inglis, Dictionary of Political Economy (in preparation—to be issued in quarterly parts). *Macmillan.* Each	0	3	6
M'Culloch, Literature of Political Economy.	O. P.		
Macpherson, Annals of Commerce. 4 vols.	O. P.		
Eden, Sir F. M., State of the Poor. 3 vols.	O. P.		
Ruding, Annals of the Coinage. 3 vols.	O. P.		
Tooke and Newmarch, History of Prices. 6 vols.	O. P.		
Rogers, J. E. T., History of Agriculture and Prices. 6 vols. *Clarendon Press*	7	2	0
M'Culloch's Dictionary of Commerce (Reid's edition). *Longmans*	3	3	0
Journal of the Royal Statistical Society. *Stanford.* Yearly	1	0	0
Political Science Quarterly. *Clarendon Press.* Yearly	0	13	0
Quarterly Journal of Economics. *Macmillan.* Yearly	0	10	0
Annual Review of the Economist. 340 *Strand.*	0	1	4
Board of Trade Journal. *Eyre, Spottiswoode.* Monthly	0	0	6
Reports of the Labour Correspondent of the Board of Trade. *Eyre, Spottiswoode*	Various.		
Publications of the American Economic Association.			
The Economist. Weekly	0	0	8
The Statist. Weekly	0	0	6

(*For Statistical Abstracts (Eyre, Spottiswoode), see Government Publications.*)

POLITICAL SCIENCE

[NOTES AND SUGGESTIONS.—*It is well to begin the study of this subject with books about our own constitution, and then to take those of a more general and less immediately practical kind. Many of the books in this list can be used for reference, without being read through. The student of this subject is advised to consult the books given under "Constitutional History" (under History), for political questions can only be properly studied in connection with history.*]

Come, let us talk a little of the affairs of the nation, or some such subject that we can all of us understand. SQUIRE WESTERN.

Let any one take to pieces the brains of any twenty persons he knows well, and think how little accurate knowledge, how little definite opinion, how little settled notion of state policy, there is in any of them. We all want more knowledge. The lukewarm politician wants knowledge to give him interest. The violent partisan wants knowledge to give him moderation. The corrupt voter wants knowledge to awaken his responsibility. If constituencies knew more, members would have to know more, and the standard of intelligence of the House of Commons would be raised. BAGEHOT.

I. SOCIOLOGY

1. ELEMENTARY

		£	s.	d.
Spencer, H., Study of Sociology.	*Kegan Paul*	0	5	0
Tylor, Anthropology.	*Macmillan*	0	7	6

2. ADVANCED

		£	s.	d.
Bagehot, Physics and Politics.	*Kegan Paul*	0	5	0
Letourneau, Sociology (*trans.*)	*Chapman, Hall*	0	10	0
Lubbock, Origin of Civilisation.	*Longmans*	0	18	0
Maine, Ancient Law.	*Murray*	0	9	0
,, Early History of Institutions.	*Murray*	0	9	0
,, Early Law and Custom.	*Murray*	0	9	0
,, Village Communities.	*Murray*	0	9	0
Tylor, Primitive Culture. 2 vols.	*Murray*	1	4	0

Political Science—Sociology, continued

3. REFERENCE

		£	s.	d
M'Lennan, Studies in Ancient History.	*Macmillan*	0	16	0
Morgan, Ancient Society.	*Macmillan*		O. P.	
Spencer, H., Principles of Sociology. 2 vols.	*Williams, Norgate*	2	2	0
,, Descriptive Sociology (parts 1 to 8 inclusive).	*Williams, Norgate*	7	15	0

II. POLITICS

1. GENERAL POLITICAL SCIENCE

a. ELEMENTARY.

Raleigh, Elementary Politics.	*Clarendon Press*	0	1	0
Kinnear, Principles of Civil Government.	*Smith, Elder*	0	7	6

b. ADVANCED.

Amos, Sheldon, The Science of Politics.	*Kegan Paul*	0	5	0
Bluntschli, Theory of the State (*trans.*)	*Clarendon Press*	0	12	6
Freeman, Comparative Politics.	*Macmillan*	0	14	0
Green, T. H., Lecture on Political Obligation, in Philosophical Works. Vol. II.	*Longmans*	0	16	0
Lewis, Sir G. C., Use and Abuse of Political Terms.	*Thornton, Oxford*	0	6	0
Woolsey, Political Science. 2 vols.	*Sampson Low*	1	10	0

2. SPECIAL POLITICAL QUESTIONS

Mill, J. S., Liberty.	*Longmans*	0	1	4
,, Representative Government.	*Longmans*	0	2	0
,, Subjection of Women.	*Longmans*		O. P.	
Spencer, H., The Man *versus* the State.	*Williams, Norgate*	0	1	0
Stephen, Sir J. Fitzjames, Liberty, Equality, Fraternity.	*Smith, Elder*	0	14	0

3. FAMOUS OLDER BOOKS OF POLITICAL THEORY

Plato, The Republic (*trans.* by Jowett).	*Clarendon Press*	0	12	6
,, ,, (,, Davies and Vaughan) (Golden Treasury Series).	*Macmillan*	0	4	6

Political Science—Politics, continued

		£	s.	d.
Aristotle, The Politics (*trans.* by Jowett). 2 vols. *Clarendon Press*		1	1	0
„ „ (*trans.* by Welldon). *Macmillan*		0	10	6
„ Essays on the Politics, by Lang. *Longmans*		0	2	6
Dante, On Monarchy (*trans.* by Church). *Macmillan*		0	4	6
Machiavelli, The Prince, *trans.* *Routledge*		0	1	0
„ Essay on, by Macaulay. *Longmans*		0	0	6
More, Sir T., Utopia, in "Ideal Commonwealths." *Routledge*		0	1	0
Harrington, Oceana. *Routledge*		0	1	0
Hobbes, Leviathan. *Routledge*		0	1	0
Locke, Civil Government. *Routledge*		0	1	0
Milton, Areopagitica. *Arber*		0	1	6
Montesquieu, Spirit of Laws (*trans.*) 2 vols. *Bell*		0	7	0
Rousseau, J. Morley. 2 vols. *Macmillan*		0	10	0
Burke, Select Works (ed. Payne). 3 vols. *Clarendon Press*		0	14	6
„ J. Morley. *Macmillan*		0	1	0
Bentham, A Fragment on Government. *Clarendon Press*		0	7	6
Comte, Positive Polity (*trans.*) 4 vols. *Longmans*		4	0	0
„ The Social Philosophy of, by Caird. *Maclehose*		0	5	0
Mazzini, Essays. *W. Scott*		0	1	0
„ Life and Writings. 6 vols. *Smith, Elder.* Each		0	4	6

4. ENGLISH CONSTITUTION AND PRACTICAL WORKS

(See also books on "*English Constitutional History*," p. 46).

1. ELEMENTARY.

		£	s.	d.
Escott, England, its People, Polity, etc. *Chapman, Hall*		0	8	0
Fonblanque, How we are Governed. *Warne*		0	1	6
Rogers, J. E. T., The British Citizen. *S.P.C.K.*		0	1	0

2. ADVANCED.

		£	s.	d.
Anson, Law and Custom of the Constitution. Part I. Parliament. *Clarendon Press*		0	10	6
Bagehot, The English Constitution. *Kegan Paul*		0	7	6
Blackstone, The Students' Blackstone (edited by Kerr). *Clowes*		0	7	6
Dicey, The Law of the Constitution. *Macmillan*		0	12	6
Hearn, The Government of England. *Longmans*		0	16	0

Political Science—Politics, continued

3. REFERENCE.

	£	s.	d.
Buxton, S., Handbook to Political Questions of the Day. *Murray*	0	7	6
" (edited by), The Imperial Parliament Series. *Sonnenschein.* Each	0	1	0
Probyn (edited by), Local Government and Taxation in the United Kingdom (Cobden Club). *Cassell*	0	5	0
The English Citizen Series. *Macmillan.* Each	0	3	6
Parliamentary Atlas and Handbook of England and Wales. *Stanford*	1	8	0

(*See also Government Publications and Political Economy.*)

5. BRITISH COLONIES

(*See also books on "History of the Colonies."*)

	£	s.	d.
Acton, Our Colonial Empire. *Cassell*	0	1	0
Cotton and Payne, India and Colonies. *Macmillan*	0	3	6
The Colonial Year-Book (Annual). *Low*	0	6	0

6. AMERICAN CONSTITUTION

(*See also books on "History of America."*)

	£	s.	d.
Macy, Our Government (Elementary). *Boston*	0	1	6
Bryce, The American Commonwealth. 2 vols. *Macmillan*	1	5	0
De Tocqueville, Democracy in America (*trans.* Reeve). 2 vols. *Longmans*	0	16	0
The Federalist. *Unwin*	0	10	6
Bannatyne, Republican Institutions of the United States. *Blackwood*	0	7	6

7. VARIOUS CONSTITUTIONS OF THE WORLD

	£	s.	d.
Sergeant, L., The Government Handbook. *Unwin*	0	10	6
The Statesman's Year-Book. *Macmillan*	0	10	6

SCIENCE

[NOTES AND SUGGESTIONS.—*No works introductory to the whole range of scientific study have been included in the following list. The best introduction to the study of a group of sciences, and indeed to the study of science generally, is a sound grasp and appreciation of the fundamental principles of some special branch. In the attainment of such preliminary knowledge the student will insensibly acquire something of that fair and open mind, unbiassed by preconceptions, seeking only unmixed truth for its own sake, which is characteristic of the genuine scientific investigator.*

In scientific study books must be regarded merely as aids to observation and reflection. They furnish the scientific student with a knowledge of what has been observed, or discovered by experiment, and with excellent expositions of modern scientific theories. But let the student take no statement on trust which he has the means of verifying, and pass over finally no point of theory which does not commend itself to his judgment and intelligence. He should not, however, allow a difficulty to be a bar to further progress. His best course, if the difficulty does not disappear after careful consideration, is to make a note of it, and pass on. Frequently, some further remark of the author will throw light on the meaning which formerly seemed obscure, and the difficulty when returned to will vanish.

In the experimental sciences practical laboratory work is of the greatest importance for making the knowledge of the student real and living; but even in these sciences the man whose eyes are open to the phenomena of nature finds all around him illustrations of scientific principles, and food for the profoundest reflection. The motions of the stars, the rise and fall of the tide, the changes of the seasons, summer's sun and winter's snow and ice, bird and beast and plant, all teach him their lessons, and furnish him with a continual delight which the man whose eyes are shut to natural things knows nothing of.

The student will do well to limit the choice of subjects of study at first to one or two at most, and then enlarge the range of his reading, as his stock of ideas and power of working increase. But ever let his aim be to become no student of mere "paper science," but one whose knowledge is a real living part of himself, and whose books are his servants and friends, not the controllers of his scientific faith and conscience.]

"It won't do. I went into science a great deal myself at one time; but I saw it would not do. It leads to everything; you can let nothing alone."—MR. BROOKE in *Middlemarch*.

> There rolls the deep where grew the tree:
> O Earth, what changes hast thou seen!
> There, where the long street roars, hath been
> The stillness of the central sea.—*In Memoriam*.

I. MATHEMATICS

[NOTES AND SUGGESTIONS.—*It is almost essential that the student of this subject should obtain some personal help and superintendence in his work. If unable*

Science—Mathematics, continued

[to do so, he is recommended to procure the key in the case of those books which are marked K in the following list. In no case, however, should the key be consulted, until the problem whose solution is sought has been attempted by the student. The Elementary Books on Mixed Mathematics do not require a knowledge of pure mathematics beyond that supplied by the Elementary Books of that branch.]

1. PURE MATHEMATICS

ELEMENTARY.

		£	s.	d.
Smith, Barnard, Arithmetic (K. 8s. 6d.)	*Macmillan*	0	4	6
Hall and Knight, Elementary Algebra. (With answers, 4s. 6d.)	*Macmillan*	0	3	6
Todhunter, Elements of Euclid.	*Macmillan*	0	3	6
Wilson, J. M., Elementary Geometry. Books I.-V.	*Macmillan*	0	4	6
Lock, Trigonometry for Beginners. (K. 8s. 6d.)	*Macmillan*	0	4	6
Smith, Hamblin, Elementary Trigonometry. (K. 7s. 6d.)	*Longmans*	0	4	6

ADVANCED.

ALGEBRA, ETC.

		£	s.	d.
Hall and Knight, Higher Algebra. (K. 10s. 6d.)	*Macmillan*	0	7	6
Todhunter, Higher Algebra. (K. 10s. 6d.)	*Macmillan*	0	7	6
Chrystal, Algebra. Part I.	*Black*	0	10	6
Salmon, Modern Higher Algebra.	*Hodges, Figgis*	0	10	6
Muir, Thomas, Treatise on the Theory of Determinants.	*Macmillan*	0	7	6
Todhunter, Theory of Equations.	*Macmillan*	0	7	6
Burnside and Panton, Theory of Equations.	*Hodges, Figgis*	0	12	6
Whitworth, Choice and Chance. (On Probability.)	*Bell*	0	6	0

TRIGONOMETRY.

		£	s.	d.
Todhunter, Plane Trigonometry. (K. 10s. 6d.)	*Macmillan*	0	5	0
Lock, Higher Trigonometry.	*Macmillan*	0	4	6
Todhunter, Spherical Trigonometry.	*Macmillan*	0	4	6

PURE GEOMETRY.

		£	s.	d.
A. I. G. T., A Syllabus of Modern Plane Geometry.	*Macmillan*	0	1	0
Casey, Sequel to Euclid.	*Hodges, Figgis*	0	3	6
Cockshott and Walters, Geometrical Treatise on Conics.	*Macmillan*	0	5	0

Science—Pure Mathematics, continued

		£	s.	d.
Besant, Geometrical Conic Sections. (K. 4s.) *Bell*		0	4	6
Cremona, Luigi, Elements of Projective Geometry (*trans.* by C. Leudesdorf). *Clarendon Press*		0	12	6
Cremona, Luigi, Elementary Geometry of Conics. *Bell*		0	4	6

ANALYTICAL GEOMETRY.

		£	s.	d.
Smith, C., Conic Sections. (K. 10s. 6d.) *Macmillan*		0	7	6
Salmon, Conic Sections. *Longmans*		0	12	0
„ Higher Plane Curves. *Hodges, Figgis*		0	12	0
Smith, C., Elementary Solid Geometry. *Macmillan*		0	9	6
Salmon, Solid Geometry. *Hodges, Figgis*		0	15	0

CALCULUS, ETC.

		£	s.	d.
Edwards, Differential Calculus. *Macmillan*		0	10	6
Todhunter, Differential Calculus. (K. 10s. 6d.) *Macmillan*		0	10	6
Williamson, Differential Calculus. *Longmans*		0	10	6
Rice and Johnson, Elementary Treatise on the Differential Calculus. *Macmillan*		0	18	0
or abridged		0	9	0
Todhunter, Integral Calculus. (K. 10s. 6d.) *Macmillan*		0	10	6
Greenhill, Differential and Integral Calculus with Applications. *Macmillan*		0	7	6
Forsyth, Differential Equations. *Macmillan*		0	14	0
Boole, Finite Differences. *Macmillan*		0	10	6
Cayley, Elliptic Functions. *Bell*		0	15	0
Kelland and Tait, Introduction to Quaternions. *Macmillan*		0	7	6

2. MIXED MATHEMATICS.

ELEMENTARY.

		£	s.	d.
Smith, Hamblin, Elementary Statics. *Longmans*		0	3	0
Garnett, Elementary Dynamics. *Bell*		0	6	0
Robinson, Elements of Dynamics. *Longmans*		0	6	0
Sanderson, Hydrostatics for Beginners. *Macmillan*		0	4	6
Todhunter, Mechanics for Beginners. *Macmillan*		0	4	6

ADVANCED.

MECHANICS.

		£	s.	d.
Minchin, Statics. Vol. I. Equilibrium of Coplanar Forces. *Clarendon Press*		0	9	0
„ Vol. II. Statics. *Clarendon Press*		0	14	0
„ Uniplanar Kinematics of Solids and Fluids. *Clarendon Press*		0	7	6

Science—Mixed Mathematics, continued

		£	s.	d.
Loney, Elementary Dynamics. *Cambridge Press*		0	7	6
Tait and Steele, Dynamics of a Particle. *Macmillan*		0	12	0
Routh, Rigid Dynamics. Vol. I. Elementary. *Macmillan*		0	14	0
„ Vol. II. Advanced. *Macmillan*		0	14	0

HYDROMECHANICS.

Besant, Hydromechanics. Vol. I. Hydrostatics. *Bell*	0	5	0
„ Vol. II. Hydrodynamics. Not published yet.			
Basset, Hydrodynamics. 2 vols. Vol. I. *Bell*	0	10	6
„ „ Vol. II. *Bell*	0	12	6

OPTICS.

Airy, Undulatory Theory of Optics. *Macmillan*	O. P.		
Lloyd, Elementary Treatise on the Wave Theory of Light. *Longmans*	0	10	6
Parkinson, A Treatise on Optics. *Macmillan*	0	10	6

ACOUSTICS.

Rayleigh, The Theory of Sound. 3 vols. (Vol. III. not yet published.) *Macmillan*. Each	0	12	6
Donkin, Theoretical Acoustics. *Clarendon Press*	0	7	6

THERMODYNAMICS.

Baynes, Lessons on Thermodynamics. *Clarendon Press*	0	7	6
Tait, Sketch of Thermodynamics. *Douglas*	0	5	0
Thomson, Sir W., Mathematical and Physical Papers. Vol. I. *Cambridge Press*	0	18	0

ELECTRICITY AND MAGNETISM.

Maxwell, Clerk, Elementary Treatise on Electricity. *Clarendon Press*	0	7	6
Maxwell, Clerk, Treatise on Electricity and Magnetism. 2 vols. *Clarendon Press*	1	11	6

ASTRONOMY.

Bain, Introduction to Plane Astronomy. *Bell*	0	4	0
Chauvenet, Spherical and Practical Astronomy. 2 vols. *Lippincott*	1	11	6
Godfray, A Treatise on Astronomy. *Macmillan*	0	12	6
Cheyne, Elementary Treatise on the Planetary Theory. *Macmillan*	0	7	6
Godfray „ „ Lunar Theory. *Macmillan*	0	5	6

Science—Mathematics, continued

3. HISTORIES AND MISCELLANEOUS.

		£ s. d.
Ball, Short History of Mathematics.	*Macmillan*	0 10 6
Todhunter, History of the Mathematical Theory of Probability.	*Macmillan*	O. P.
De Morgan, Arithmetical Books from the Invention of Printing to 1847.	*Layton*	0 5 0
Newton, I., "Principia," ed. Thomson and Blackburn.	*Maclehose*	1 11 6
" " (parts), ed. Evans and Bain.	*Bell*	0 4 0
Thomson, Sir W., and Tait, Treatise on Natural Philosophy. Part I. 16s. Part II. 18s.	*Cambridge Press*	1 14 0
Clifford, Mathematical Papers, ed. Tucker.	*Macmillan*	1 10 0
Wolstenholme, Mathematical Problems (Pure and Mixed).	*Macmillan*	0 18 0
Abbott, E. A., Flatland : a Romance.	*Seeley*	0 4 6

II. PHYSICS

[NOTES AND SUGGESTIONS.—*A knowledge of the Elements of Algebra and of the Geometry of the Straight Line and Circle is highly desirable before beginning the study of these subjects. The student should begin with Mechanics, and should gain an elementary knowledge of branches* 3, 4, 5, 6 *before passing to a more detailed study of any one of them. He should supplement his reading, when possible, by work in a Physical Laboratory, also by attendance at Experimental Lectures on the subject. For the higher branches of Physics, a knowledge of Analytical Geometry and of the Differential and Integral Calculus is necessary. For the more Mathematical treatises, the list given under the head "Mixed Mathematics" should also be consulted.*]

1. GENERAL PHYSICS

1. ELEMENTARY.

Stewart, Balfour, Primer of Physics.	*Macmillan*	0 1 0
" Elementary Lessons in Physics.	*Macmillan*	0 4 6
Ganot, Natural Philosophy for General Readers.	*Longmans*	0 7 6
Deschanel, Natural Philosophy (*trans.*) 4 parts.	*Blackie.* Each	0 4 6

2. ADVANCED.

Daniell, Text-Book of the Principles of Physics.	*Macmillan*	1 1 0
Tait, Properties of Matter.	*Black*	0 7 6

Science—Physics, continued

3. REFERENCE.

		£	s.	d.
Thomson, Sir W., Popular Addresses and Lectures. Vol. I.	*Macmillan*	0	6	0
Everett, Units and Physical Constants.	*Macmillan*	0	5	0

2. MECHANICS

1. ELEMENTARY.

Blaikie, The Elements of Dynamics.	*Simpkin*	0	3	6
Lodge, O. J., Mechanics.	*Chambers*	0	3	0
Ball, Experimental Mechanics.	*Macmillan*	0	6	0

2. ADVANCED.

Maxwell, Clerk, Matter and Motion.	*S.P.C.K.*	0	1	0
Rankine, Applied Mechanics.	*Griffin*	0	12	6

3. REFERENCE.

Thomson, Sir W., and Tait, Treatise on Natural Philosophy. 2 vols.	*Cambridge Press*	1	14	0

(*See also under "Mixed Mathematics."*)

3. SOUND

1. ELEMENTARY.

Mayer, Sound.	*Macmillan*	0	3	6
Stone, Elementary Lessons on Sound.	*Macmillan*	0	3	6
Tyndall, Sound.	*Longmans*	0	10	6
Taylor, S., Sound and Music.	*Macmillan*	0	8	6

2. ADVANCED.

Donkin, Theoretical Acoustics.	*Clarendon Press*	0	7	6
Helmholtz, Sensations of Tone (*trans.* Ellis).	*Longmans*	1	8	0
Blaserna, Theory of Sound in Relation to Music.	*Kegan Paul*	0	5	0

3. REFERENCE.

Rayleigh, Theory of Sound. 3 vols. (Vol. III. not yet published.)	*Macmillan*. Each	0	12	6

Science—Physics, continued

4. HEAT

1. ELEMENTARY.

		£	s.	d.
Baynes, The Book of Heat.	*Stewart*	0	1	0
Garnett, Elementary Treatise on Heat.	*Bell*	0	4	0
Stewart, B., Elementary Treatise on Heat.	*Clarendon Press*	0	7	6
Tait, Heat.	*Macmillan*	0	6	0
Tyndall, Heat as a Mode of Motion.	*Longmans*	0	12	0

2. ADVANCED.

Maxwell, Clerk, Theory of Heat.	*Longmans*	0	3	6
Baynes, Thermodynamics.	*Clarendon Press*	0	7	6
Shann, Heat in Relation to Steam.	*Macmillan*	0	4	6

3. REFERENCE.

Fourier, Analytical Theory of Heat (*trans.* Freeman).	*Cambridge Press*	0	16	0

5. LIGHT

1. ELEMENTARY.

Aldis, Geometrical Optics.	*Bell*	0	4	0
Lloyd, Wave Theory of Light.	*Longmans*	0	10	6
Stokes, Sir G., "Burnett Lectures" on Light.	*Macmillan*	0	7	6
Spottiswoode, Polarisation of Light.	*Macmillan*	0	3	6
Glazebrook, Physical Optics.	*Longmans*	0	6	0
Wright, Light : a Course of Experiments.	*Macmillan*	0	7	6
Rood, Ogden, Modern Chromatics.	*Kegan Paul*	0	5	0

2. ADVANCED.

Parkinson, Optics.	*Macmillan*	0	10	6
Heath, Geometrical Optics.	*Cambridge Press*	0	12	6
Airy, Undulatory Theory of Optics.	*Macmillan*		O. P.	
Aldis, Fresnel's Theory of Double Refraction.	*Bell*	0	2	0
Pendlebury, Lenses and Systems of Lenses.	*Bell*	0	5	0

3. REFERENCE.

Glazebrook, Report on Physical Optics, in British Association Report for 1885.	*Murray*	1	4	0

Science—Physics, continued

6. ELECTRICITY AND MAGNETISM

I. THEORETICAL

1. ELEMENTARY.

		£	s.	d.
Thompson, S. P., Elementary Lessons in Electricity and Magnetism.	*Macmillan*	0	4	6
Larden, Electricity.	*Longmans*	0	6	0

2. ADVANCED.

		£	s.	d.
Maxwell, Clerk, Elementary Treatise on Electricity.	*Clarendon Press*	0	7	6
Mascart and Joubert, Electricity and Magnetism (*trans.* Atkinson). 2 vols.	*De La Rue*	1	1	0
Gray, A., Absolute Measurements. Vol. I.	*Macmillan*	0	12	6

3. REFERENCE.

		£	s.	d.
Maxwell, Clerk, Electricity and Magnetism. 2 vols.	*Clarendon Press*	1	11	6
Thomson, Sir W., Papers on Electrostatics and Magnetism.	*Macmillan*	0	18	0
Thomson, Sir W., Report on Electrical Theories (British Association Report 1885).	*Murray*	1	4	0

II. APPLIED

		£	s.	d.
Ayrton, Practical Electricity.	*Cassell*	0	7	6
Thompson, S. P., Dynamo-Electric Machinery.	*Spon*	0	16	0
Gordon, J., Practical Treatise on Electric Lighting.	*Sampson Low*	0	18	0
Urbanitzky, Electricity in the Service of Man.	*Cassell*	0	9	0
Fleming, Alternating Currents.	*"Electrician" Office*	0	7	6
Martin and Wetzler, Electrical Motors.	*Spon*	0	12	6

7. THE THEORY OF ENERGY

		£	s.	d.
Stewart, Balfour, The Conservation of Energy.	*Kegan Paul*	0	5	0
Holmholtz, The Conservation of Force (Scientific Memoirs, ed. Tyndall and Francis).	*Taylor, Francis*	0	3	0
Helmholtz, Popular Lectures on Scientific Subjects. 2 vols.	*Longmans.* Each	0	7	6

Science—Physics, continued

	£	s.	d.
Tait, Recent Advances in Physical Science. *Macmillan*	0	9	0
Thomson, J. J., Applications of Dynamics to Physics and Chemistry. *Macmillan*	0	7	6

8. MISCELLANEOUS

Tyndall, Fragments of Science. 2 vols. *Longmans*	0	16	0

9. METHOD

Jevons, Principles of Science. *Macmillan*	0	12	6

III. CHEMISTRY

[NOTES AND SUGGESTIONS.—*The student of Chemistry, after having read the primers, should try to gain admission into a good laboratory, and should, if possible, attend a full course of Experimental Lectures on Inorganic Chemistry. Before beginning the study of Organic Chemistry, he should attend, if possible, a course of Elementary Lectures on the general features of that branch, as without help it is most difficult to begin the study of Organic Chemistry. The progress of the science is so rapid that it is necessary to obtain the latest editions of modern works.*]

1. GENERAL

1. ELEMENTARY.

	£	s.	d.
Odling, Chemistry Primer. *Ward, Lock*	0	0	6
Roscoe, Primer of Chemistry. *Macmillan*	0	1	0
,, Lessons in Elementary Chemistry. *Macmillan*	0	4	6
Tilden, Practical Chemistry. *Longmans*	0	1	6
Würtz, Elements of Modern Chemistry. *Lippincott*	0	10	6
Remsen, Inorganic Chemistry. *Macmillan*	0	6	6

2. ADVANCED.

	£	s.	d.
Roscoe and Schorlemmer, C., Treatise on Chemistry. Vols. I.-III. in 8 Parts. *Macmillan*	7	16	0
Miller, Elements of Chemistry. 3 vols. *Longmans*	3	11	6
Watts, Inorganic Chemistry (ed. Tilden). *Churchill*	0	8	6
Clowes, Practical Chemistry. *Churchill*	0	7	6
Thorpe, Quantitative Chemical Analysis. *Longmans*	0	4	6
Fresenius, Quantitative Analysis. *Churchill*	0	15	0

Science—Chemistry, continued

		£	s.	d.
Fresenius, Qualitative Analysis.	*Churchill*	0	15	0
Bernthsen, Organic Chemistry.	*Blackie*	0	9	0
Armstrong, Organic Chemistry.	*Longmans*	0	3	6
Meyer, Modern Theories of Chemistry.	*Longmans*	0	18	0
Ostwald, Outlines of General Chemistry.	*Macmillan*	0	10	0
Tilden, Introduction to Chemical Philosophy.	*Longmans*	0	4	6
Wurtz, The Atomic Theory.	*Kegan Paul*	0	5	0
Cooke, Josiah P., The New Chemistry.	*Kegan Paul*	0	5	0
Richter, Chemistry of the Carbon Compounds.	*Philadelphia*	0	12	6

3. REFERENCE.

Gmelin, Handbook of Chemistry (*trans.* H. Watts). 19 vols.
            Cavendish Society 10 3 0
Watts, Dictionary of Chemistry. 9 vols. *Longmans* 15 2 6
 (New edition now appearing, ed. Morley and Muir. 4 vols., each £2, 2s.)
Carnelley, Physico-Chemical Constants. 2 vols. *Harrison* 4 4 0
Journal of the Chemical Society.
        Gurney, Jackson. Yearly 1 10 0

2. APPLIED

(*It is impossible to give a satisfactory list of works on Applied Chemistry without including foreign books. For the great number of technical books under this head larger catalogues must be consulted.*)

Thorpe's Dictionary of Applied Chemistry. Vol. I.
              Longmans 2 2 0

Allen, Commercial Organic Analysis. 3 vols.	*Churchill*	1	12	0
Lunge, Coal-Tar and Ammonia.	*Gurney, Jackson*	1	11	6
„ Sulphuric Acid and Alkali. 3 vols.	*Gurney, Jackson*	4	16	0
Hummel, Dyeing.	*Cassell*	0	5	0
Benedikt and Knecht, Coal-Tar Colours.	*Bell*	0	5	0
Phillips, Metallurgy.	*Griffin*	1	16	0
Percy, Metallurgy. 3 vols. (Fuel, Lead, Silver.)				
	Murray. Each	1	10	0
Procter, H. R., Tanning.	*Spon*	0	10	6
Abney, Photography.	*Longmans*	0	3	6
Roscoe, Spectrum Analysis.	*Macmillan*	1	1	0
Winkler and Lunge, Gas Analysis.	*Gurney, Jackson*	0	7	0
Wagner, Handbook of Chemical Technology.	*Churchill*	1	5	0
Journal of the Society of Chemical Industry. Yearly		1	10	0

Science, continued

IV. BIOLOGY

[NOTES AND SUGGESTIONS.—*In this as in other branches of Science, the more carefully the study is followed up in the laboratory or out of doors, the more real and living will the knowledge of the subject become.*]

1. ZOOLOGY

a. ZOOLOGY (General)

ELEMENTARY.

		£	s.	d.
Huxley and Martin, Elementary Practical Biology. *Macmillan*		0	10	6
Nicholson, The Study of Biology. *Blackwood*		0	5	0
Macalister, Zoology of Invertebrate Animals, and of Vertebrate Animals. *Longmans.* Each		0	1	6

ADVANCED.

		£	s.	d.
Mivart, The Cat. *Murray*		1	10	0
Marshall, Milnes, The Frog. *Smith, Elder*		0	3	6
Lankester, Notes on Embryology and Classification. *Churchill*			O. P.	
Claus and Sedgwick, An Elementary Text-Book of Zoology. 2 vols. (Vol. I., Protozoa to Insects, £1, 1s.; Vol. II., Mollusca to Man, 16s.) *Sonnenschein*		1	17	0
Macalister, Introduction to Morphology and Systematic Zoology of Invertebrates. *Hodges*		0	10	6
,, Do. of Vertebrates. *Hodges*		0	10	6
Foster and Balfour, Elements of Embryology (ed. Sedgwick). *Macmillan*		0	10	6
Rolleston, Forms of Animal Life. *Clarendon Press*		1	16	0
Marshall, Milnes, Practical Zoology (a Laboratory Handbook). *Smith, Elder*		0	10	6
Huxley, Manual of the Anatomy of Vertebrated Animals. *Churchill*		0	12	0
,, ,, Invertebrated. *Churchill*		0	16	0

b. EVOLUTION

		£	s.	d.
Darwin, C., The Origin of Species. *Murray*		0	6	0
,, Descent of Man. *Murray*		0	7	6
Lankester, Degeneration—Chapter in Darwinism. *Macmillan*		0	2	6
Mivart, Contemporary Evolution. *Kegan Paul*		0	7	6

Science—Biology—Evolution, continued

		£	s.	d.
Romanes, Scientific Evidences of Organic Evolution.	Macmillan	0	2	6
Wallace, A. R., Darwinism.	Macmillan	0	9	0
Weismann, Studies in the Theory of Descent. 2 vols.	Low	2	0	0
Allen, Grant, The Evolutionist at Large.	Chatto	0	6	0

c. ANATOMY AND PHYSIOLOGY

ELEMENTARY.

Foster, Physiology Science Primer.	Macmillan	0	1	0
Huxley, Elementary Lessons in Physiology.	Macmillan	0	4	6
Yeo, Manual of Physiology.	Churchill	0	14	0
Kirke, Handbook of Physiology.	Murray	0	14	0
Heath, Practical Anatomy.	Churchill	0	15	0

ADVANCED.

Foster, Text-book of Physiology.	Macmillan	1	1	0
M'Kendrick, Text-Book of Physiology. Vol. I.—General.	Maclehose	0	16	0
,, ,, Vol. II—Special.	Maclehose	1	4	0
Quain, Anatomy with Histology.	Longmans	1	16	0

For an extensive Bibliography of the subject, see the end of
Landois's Text-Book of Physiology, translated, with additions, by W. Stirling.   *Griffin*   1   14   0

SPECIAL.

Gamgee, Physiological Chemistry of the Animal Body. Vol. I.	Macmillan	0	18	0
Rosenthal, The General Physiology of Muscles and Nerves.	Kegan Paul	0	5	0
Marckwald, Respiration (*trans.* by M'Kendrick).	Blackie	0	10	0
Stirling, W., Physiology.	Griffin	0	8	6

d. NATURAL HISTORY

1. ELEMENTARY.

Huxley, Introduction to Classification of Animals.	Churchill	O. P.		
Nicholson, H. A., Introductory Text-Book of Zoology.	Blackwood	0	3	0
Buckley, Arabella, Life and Her Children.	Stanford	0	6	0

Science—Biology—Natural History, continued

2. GENERAL MANUALS.

	£	s.	d.
Nicholson, H. A., Manual of Zoology (*illus.*) *Blackwood*	0	18	0
Coues and Kingsley, Standard Natural History (by leading American Scientific writers—*illus.*) 6 vols. *Boston*	5	5	0
Wood, J. G., Natural History (*illus.*) 3 vols. 14s. each. *Routledge*	2	2	0
Cassell, New Natural History (ed. by E. M. Duncan). 6 vols. *Cassell.* Each	0	9	0
Gosse, Manual of Marine Zoology. Parts I. and II. *Gurney, Jackson.* Each	0	7	6
„ A Year on the Shore. *Daldy*	0	9	0
Taylor, J. E., The Aquarium : its Inhabitants, Structure, and Management (*illus.*) *Allen*	0	3	6

3. MICROSCOPE.

	£	s.	d.
Carpenter, The Microscope and its Revelations. (Reprinting, probable price not less than £1, 1s.) *Churchill*			

4. SPECIAL.

	£	s.	d.
Romanes, Jellyfish, Starfish, and Sea Urchins. *Kegan Paul*	0	5	0
Darwin, C., Vegetable Mould and Earth-Worms. *Murray*	0	6	0
Huxley, The Crayfish. *Kegan Paul*	0	5	0
Staveley, British Spiders. *Lovell Reeve*	0	10	6

5. INSECTS.

	£	s.	d.
Lubbock, Origin and Metamorphoses of Insects *Macmillan*	0	3	6
Wood, J. G., Insects at Home. *Longmans*	0	10	6
„ Insects Abroad. *Longmans*	0	10	6
Staveley, British Insects: Form, Structure, Habits. *Lovell Reeve*	0	14	0
Kirby, W. E., Handbook of Entomology. *Sonnenschein*	0	15	0
Figuier, Insect World *Cassell*	0	3	6
Kirby, British Butterflies, Moths, and Beetles (*illus.*) *Sonnenschein*	0	1	0
Coleman, British Butterflies. *Routledge*	0	1	0
„ „ Coloured Plates. *Routledge*	0	3	6
Wood, J. G., British Moths. *Routledge*	0	1	0
„ „ „ Coloured Plates. *Routledge*	0	3	6
Newman, E., British Butterflies. *Allen*	0	7	6
„ British Moths (*illus.*) *Allen*	1	0	0
Or, both vols.	1	5	0
Stainton, Manual of British Butterflies and Moths. (Vol. I. 4s. 6d., Vol. II. 5s. 6d.) *Gurney, Jackson*	0	10	0

Science—Biology—Natural History, continued

		£	s.	d.
Rye, Beetles. *Lovell Reeve*		0	10	6
Wood, J. G., Common British Beetles. *Routledge*		0	3	6
Lubbock, Ants, Bees, and Wasps. *Kegan Paul*		0	5	0
White, W. F., Ants and Their Ways. *Religious Tract Society*		0	5	0

6. FISHES.

Couch, History of the Fishes of the British Islands. 4 vols. *Bell* 2 12 0

Yarrell, History of British Fishes. 2 vols. £3 : 3s. 1st supplement, 7s. 6d. ; 2d supplement 5s. *Gurney, Jackson* 3 15 6

7. REPTILES.

Bell, History of British Reptiles. *Gurney, Jackson* 0 12 0

8. BIRDS.

Morris, F. O., Nests and Eggs of British Birds. 3 vols. *Bell* O. P.
Johns, British Birds in Their Haunts. *S. P. C. K.* 0 6 0
„ Birds, Nests, and Eggs. *S. P. C. K.* 0 3 0
Morris, History of British Birds. 6 vols. *Nimmo* 6 6 0
Seebohm, A History of British Birds. 3 vols. *Dulau* 6 6 0
Yarrell, British Birds. 4 vols. *Gurney, Jackson* 4 0 0

9. MAMMALS.

Bell, History of British Quadrupeds. *Gurney, Jackson* 1 6 0
Schmidt, The Mammalia. *Kegan Paul* 0 5 0

10. FAMOUS OLD BOOKS.

White, Gilbert, Natural History of Selborne (ed. by Harting, with illus. by Bewick). *Sonnenschein* 0 7 6
Walton, Izaak, Complete Angler. *Bell* 0 5 0

11. MISCELLANEOUS.

Jefferies, Wood Magic. *Cassell* 0 6 0
Knight, F., By Leafy Ways. *Elliot Stock* 0 5 0
Fowler, Warde, A Year with the Birds. *Macmillan* 0 3 6
Batty, Practical Taxidermy. *New York* 0 6 0
Wood, The Field Naturalist's Handbook. *Cassell* 0 5 0
Natural History Handbooks for Collectors (various Authors). 8 vols. *Sonnenschein.* Each 0 1 0

Science—Biology, continued

2. BOTANY

[NOTES AND SUGGESTIONS.—*The study of this subject should be, from the first, practical. The student should begin by obtaining, with the assistance of the elementary books, a thorough acquaintance, based on the examination of specimens, of the plants growing in his neighbourhood. Having obtained this, he may then proceed to study the anatomy and physiology of plants with the assistance of the microscope and of the books on practical study. Should he ultimately devote himself to the study of one particular group of plants, he will find references to the special literature of the groups in the reference books mentioned below.*]

1. ELEMENTARY.

		£	s.	d.
Kitchener, A Year's Botany.	*Longmans*	0	5	0
Hooker, Primer of Botany.	*Macmillan*	0	1	0
Oliver, Elementary Lessons in Botany.	*Macmillan*	0	4	6

BRITISH FLORA

Hayward, The Botanist's Pocket-Book.	*Bell*	0	4	6
Hooker, Student's Flora of the British Islands.	*Macmillan*	0	10	6
Bentham, British Flora.	*Lovell Reeve*	0	10	6
,, Illustrations of British Flora.	*Lovell Reeve*	0	10	6

PRACTICAL STUDY (Microscope)

Strasburger and Hillhouse, Practical Botany.	*Sonnenschein*	0	9	0
Bower, Course of Practical Instruction in Botany (Parts I. and II. in one vol.)	*Macmillan*	0	10	6

2. ADVANCED.

Prantl, and Vines, Text-Book of Botany.	*Sonnenschein*	0	9	0
Thome and Bennett, Structural and Physiological Botany.	*Longmans*	0	6	0
Gray, Asa, Structural Botany.	*Macmillan*	0	10	6

SPECIAL

Darwin, C., Variation of Animals and Plants under Domestication. 2 vols.	*Murray*	0	15	0
,, Fertilisation of Orchids.	*Murray*	0	7	6
,, Insectivorous Plants (*illus*).	*Murray*	0	9	0

Science—Biology—Botany, continued

		£	s.	d.
Darwin, C., Movements and Habits of Climbing Plants (*illus.*) Murray		0	6	0
,, Effects of Cross and Self-Fertilisation. Murray		0	9	0
,, Different forms of Flowers. Murray		0	7	6
De Candolle, Origin of Cultivated Plants. Kegan Paul		0	5	0
Dawson, Geological History of Plants. Kegan Paul		0	5	0
Henslow, Floral Structures. Kegan Paul		0	5	0

3. REFERENCE.

	£	s.	d.
Goebel, Outlines of Classification. *Clarendon Press*	1	1	0
De Bary, Comparative Anatomy of Plants. *Clarendon Press*	1	2	6
,, Fungi. *Clarendon Press*	1	2	6
Sachs, Lectures on Physiology of Plants. *Clarendon Press*	1	11	6
Vines, Lectures on Physiology of Plants. *Cambridge Press*	1	1	0

3. ANTHROPOLOGY

[NOTES AND SUGGESTIONS.—*The reader is recommended to gain from one of the introductory manuals a general view of the scope of the science of man, as he will then more easily find his way into the branches of the study most congenial to him. These lie in very different directions, including portions of subjects as different as anatomy, philology, and history. Any of these would give occupation for a life, but the attempt to become acquainted with such parts of them as bear most directly on man's life and thought is not only feasible, but advantageous in leading the student into lines of culture profitable for their own sake.*

History of Civilisation will be found under History (Europe). Travels must be referred to for Cook's Voyages, *&c. The books of Mariner, Catlin, Burton, Grey, Wallace, Ellis, Turner, St. John, Sibree, Im Thurn, and the like, are full of Anthropological knowledge. It is not desirable to mention here more abstruse works which the advanced student will find referred to in the course of his reading.*]

INTRODUCTORY.

	£	s.	d.
Tylor, Anthropology. *Macmillan*	0	7	6
Peschel, Races of Man. *Kegan Paul*	0	9	0
De Quatrefages, The Human Species. *Kegan Paul*	0	5	0

PHYSICAL.

	£	s.	d.
Topinard, Anthropology. *Chapman, Hall*	0	3	6

Science—Biology—Anthropology, continued

PREHISTORIC ARCHÆOLOGY, etc.

(See also Antiquities and Archæology.)

		£	s.	d.
Joly, Man before Metals.	*Kegan Paul*	0	5	0
Lubbock, Prehistoric Times.	*Williams, Norgate*	0	18	0
Evans, Ancient Stone Implements.	*Longmans*	1	8	0
Dawkins, Cave-Hunting.	*Macmillan*	1	1	0

CIVILISATION.

(See Civilisation, History of, under European History.)

Lubbock, Origin of Civilisation.	*Longmans*	0	18	0
Tylor, Early History of Mankind.	*Murray*	0	12	0
„ Primitive Culture. 2 vols.	*Murray*	1	4	0
Wood, J. G., Illustrated History of Man. 2 vols.	*Routledge*	1	8	0
Brown, Peoples of the World. 6 vols.	*Cassell.* Each	0	7	6

V. GEOLOGY

[NOTES AND SUGGESTIONS.—*The greater part of the study of Geology must be carried on in the open air. Some amount of reading is of course necessary at the first start, but as soon as a knowledge of the rudiments has been acquired, the beginner should procure the best description he can of the Geology of his own district, and compare its statements with what he sees in quarries, railway cuttings, beds of brooks, cliffs, or even ditches. He should always try to realise the connection between the physical features of the neighbourhood and its geological structure. For points of which he cannot find illustration round his own home, he should as far as possible fall back upon Museums. The student should not be content with the mere collection and naming of geological specimens, valuable as this may be—for the end of Geology is not a well-filled cabinet, but the deciphering of the records in which the early history of the earth is written.*

For local details, the memoirs and maps of the Geological Survey may be used. Catalogues can be obtained of Mr. E. Stanford, 26 and 27 Cockspur Street, S.W. Every Geological student ought to have the one-inch Geological Map of his neighbourhood, and the descriptive explanation of it, where this is published.]

1. GENERAL

1. **INTRODUCTORY.**

Geikie, A., Primers of Geology and Physical Geography.
Macmillan. Each 0 1 0

Science—Geology, continued

2. ELEMENTARY.

	£	s.	d.
Page and Lapworth, Introductory Text-Book of Geology. *Blackwood*	0	3	6
Jukes-Browne, Student's Handbook of Historical Geology. *Bell*	0	6	0
Geikie, A., Class-Book of Geology. *Macmillan*	0	4	6

3. ADVANCED.

Lyell, Student's Elements of Geology. *Murray*	0	9	0
Geikie, A., Text-Book of Geology. *Macmillan*	1	8	0
Green, A. H., Physical Geology. *Longmans*	1	1	0
Prestwich, Geology: Chemical, Physical, and Stratigraphical. 2 vols. *Clarendon Press*	3	1	0
Ramsay, Physical Geology and Geography of Great Britain. *Stanford*	0	15	0
Hull, Physical History of the British Isles. *Stanford*	0	12	6

2. PALÆONTOLOGY

1. ELEMENTARY.

Nicholson, H. A., Ancient Life-History of the Earth. *Blackwood*	0	10	6

2. ADVANCED.

Nicholson, H. A., and Lydekker, Palæontology. 2 vols. *Blackwood*	3	3	0

(*The best book is in German, by Zittel.*)

3. MINERALOGY

1. ELEMENTARY.

Rutley, Mineralogy (Murby's Science and Art Department Series of Text-Books). *Murby*	0	2	0
Dana, Manual of Mineralogy. *New York*	0	8	6

2. ADVANCED.

Bauerman, Systematic Mineralogy. *Longmans*	0	6	0
Dana, A System of Mineralogy. *New York*	2	2	0

Science, continued

VI. ASTRONOMY

1. POPULAR AND DESCRIPTIVE

		£	s.	d.
Airy, Lectures on Astronomy.	*Macmillan*	0	4	6
Ball, R., Starland.	*Cassell*	0	6	0
,, Elements of Astronomy.	*Longmans*	0	6	0
,, Story of the Heavens.	*Cassell*	0	12	6
Chambers, G. F., Astronomy. 3 vols.	*Clarendon Press*	2	16	0
Guillemin, The Heavens.	*Bentley*	0	12	0
Herschel, Outlines of Astronomy.	*Longmans*	0	12	0
Lardner and Dunkin, Handbook of Astronomy.	*Crosby, Lockwood*	0	9	6
Lockyer, Lessons in Astronomy.	*Macmillan*	0	5	6
Newcomb, Popular Astronomy.	*Macmillan*	0	18	0
Proctor, The Sun.	*Longmans*	0	14	0
,, The Moon.	*Longmans*	0	5	0
,, Saturn and its System.	*Chatto*	0	10	6
,, A New Star Atlas.	*Longmans*	0	5	0

2. MATHEMATICAL

(*See Mixed Mathematics—Astronomy.*)

3. HISTORICAL

Clerke, Agnes, History of Astronomy during the 19th Century.   *Black*   0   12   6

(*See also several good articles in the latest edition of the* Encyclopædia Britannica *for the whole subject of Astronomy and its History.*)

Of making many books there is no end; and much study is a weariness of the flesh.—ECCLESIASTES.

INDEX

[The names of all the subjects on which lists of books are given, and of all the authors, with the exception of a few authors of biographies, are included in the index. The names of the principal subjects are given in darker type for greater convenience. Whenever initials of authors are not likely, in the case of several authors of the same name, to be of much use, the subject on which the author writes has been given.]

ABBEY AND OVERTON, 45
Abbott, E. A. (Life of Bacon), 11
—— (Education), 30
—— (Mathematics), 98
Abbott, E., 41, 58
Abbott and Mansfield, 55
Abbott and Seeley, 59
Abney, 103
Accounts, Government, 37
Acland and Jones, 81
Acland and Ransome, 44
Acoustics, 97
Acton, 93
Acts of Parliament, 37, 38
Adam Smith, 79, 86
Adams (Co-operation), 81
Adams (Finance), 86
Adams, C. (Railroads), 88
Adams and Cunningham, 51
Adamson, 75
Addison, 70
—— life of, 11
Adventures (*see* **Children's Books**)
Æschylus, 63
Æsop, 72
Africa, Geography, 31-33
Africa, South (*see* **Colonies**)
Africa, Travels, 34, 35
Agassiz, Louis, 15
Agriculture, 81, 82
A. I. G. T., 95
Ainsworth, 64
—— 69
Airy, 97, 100, 112
Aitken, 60
Akerman, 3
Albert, Prince, 22

Albertinelli, 9
Alcott, 24
Aldis, 100
Algebra, 95
Allen, J. B. (Latin), 55
Allen (Chemistry), 103
Allen, Grant (Antiquities), 3
—— (Biology), 105
—— (Darwin's Life), 15
—— (Philosophy), 77
Allen, Romilly, 3
Allibone, xviii
Allingham, 60
Allotments, 82
Alps, 34
Althorp, 19
Amazons, 35
America, Constitution, 93
—— **Essays, etc.**, 72
—— **Fiction**, 67
—— **Geography**, 31-33
—— **History**, 54
—— **Literature**, 59
—— **Travels**, 35
American Commonwealth, 54
—— statesmen, 54
Amos, Sheldon, 91
Anatomy, 105
—— (Art), 8
Ancient Geography, 32
—— **History**, 39-42
—— **Society**, 90, 91
—— **Poetry**, 63
Andersen, Hans, 24
Anderson, 3
Andrea del Sarto, 9
Andrée's Atlas, 36
Angelico, Fra, 9
Anglo-Saxon Chronicle, 44

Animals, Zoology of, 104-107
Annals of the Disruption (Scotland), 48
Annual Register, xviii, 46
Anselm, 16
Anson, Sir W., 92
Anster, 63
Anthropology, 109, 110
Antiquities, 1-3
Aquarium, 106
Arabia, 34
Arabian nights, 24, 72
Ararat, 34
Archæology, 1-3
Archbishops of Canterbury, Lives of, 23
Architects (*see* Biography)
Architecture, 6, 7
Arctic Travels, 35
Aristophanes, 63
Aristotle, 75, 92
Arithmetic, 95
Armitage, 47
Armstrong, 103
Army (*see* **Soldiers**)
Arnold, Dr., 41
—— Life of, 22
Arnold, M. (Education), 29, 30
—— (Essays), 70
—— (Poetry), 60
Arnold, T. (Literature), 59
Arnold, E. (Poetry) 60
Arnold (India), 53
Arnold (Rhode Island), 54
Art, 4-8
Art, Decorative, 7
Artists (*see* **Biography**)
Ascham, 30

INDEX

Aschrott, 83
Ashley, 79
Asia, Central, 34
Asia, Geography, 31-33
Asia, Travels, 34
Astronomers, 15
Astronomy, 112
—— Children's, 26
—— Historical, 112
—— Mathematical, 97
—— Popular, 112
Assisi, Francis of, 16
Assyria, Antiquities, 1
Assyria, History, 39, 40
Athanasius, 16
Athens, History, 41
Atlas mountains, 34
Atlases, 36
Auerbach, 67
Augustine, 16
Austen, Jane, 64
—— Life of, 11
Austin, Stella, 24
Australasia, Geography, 31-33
Australia, History, 52
Austria, History, 49
Autobiographies (*see* **Biography**)
Ayrton, 101
Aytoun, 60

BABBAGE, 79
Babies, How to rear, 27
Bach, 15
Bacon, Lord (Essays), 70
—— (History), 45
—— (Philosophy), 76
—— Life of, 11
Baddeley and Ward, 36
Baden-Powell, 86
Bædeker (Guide-books), 35
Baernreither, 83
Bagehot (English Constitution), 46, 90
—— (Economics), 79, 84
—— (Essays), 71
—— (Politics), 92
Bagwell, 48
Bain, A. (Education), 30
—— (Philosophy), 76
Bain (Astronomy), 97
Bain, E. (Economics), 80
Baker, Sir S., 35
Balfour Stewart, 98, 100, 101
Balfour and Foster, 104
Ball (Mathematics), 98
Ball, R. (Astronomy), 112
Ball (Mechanics), 99

Ball, J. (Travels), 35
Ball, J., and Hooker, 34
Ballads (*see* **Poetry**)
Ballantyne, 24
Balzac, 67
Balzani, 50
Bancroft, 54
Bankers, Institute of, Journal, 84
Banking, 84, 85
Bannatyne, 93
Barbour, 84
Barents, 21
Baretti, xvii
Barnard Smith, 95
Barnes, 60
Barnett, Mrs., 28
Baronage, Official, 46
Barrett, Howard, 27
Bartholomew, xvii, 31
Bartolommeo, Fra, 9
Bary, De, 109
Basset, 97
Bastable, 85
Bastiat, 87
Bates, 35
Batty, 107
Batuta, Ibn, 21
Bauerman, 111
Bauwerk, 78
Bax, Belfort, 87
Baxter, Life of, 16
Baxter, Dudley, 85, 86
Bayard Taylor, 63
Baynes, 97, 100
Beaconsfield, Life of, 19
Beaconsfield, 64
Beaumont, 61
Becker, 2, 3
Bede, 16, 44
Beethoven, 15
Bell (Reptiles), 107
Bellamy, 87
Belt, 35
Benedikt and Knecht, 103
Bennet, 55
Bennett and Thomé, 108
Bent, 50
Bentham, J. (Political Science), 92
Bentham (Botany), 108
Bentley, 11
Beowulf, 61
Berghaus, 36
Berkeley, 75, 77
Bernard, 16
Bernthsen, 103
Besant, W. (novelist), 14, 64, 69, 70

Besant (Mathematics), 96, 97
Bewick, 107
Bible, The, 40
Bible-History, 40, 41
Bible, Men of the, 40
Bibliographer's Manual, xviii
Bibliography (*see* **Books of Reference**)
Bills, Parliamentary, 37, 38
Bimetallism, 84
Binns, 8
Biography, 9-23
—— Dictionaries of, xvii. 46
—— Essays in Ecclesiastical, 17
—— Industrial, 11
Biology, 104-111
Bion, 63
Birch, 40
Birds, 107
Birdwood, 2
Birrell, 71
Bishop's Little Daughter, The, 25
Bismarck, 19, 50
Bjornsen, 67
Black (novelist), 64, 69
Blackie, 12
Blackley, 83
Blackmore, 64, 69
Blackstone, 92
Blaikie, 99
Blake, Admiral, 18
Blake (poet), 61
—— Life of, 11
Blanford, 32
Blanqui, 79
Blaserna, 99
Blind, 12, 22
Blue-Books, 37, 38
Bluntschli, 91
Boase, 30
Böhm Bauwerk, 78
Bolingbroke, 19
Bonaparte, Napoleon, 19
Bonar, 79
Books of Reference, xvii, xviii
Books, Children's, 24-26
Books, Some Famous, 72, 73
Boole, 96
Booth, Chas., 83
Booth, General, 83
Borrow, 34, 64
Bosanquet, B., 76
Boswell, 13

INDEX

Botany, 108, 109
Botany, Children's, 26
Botanists, 15
Botticelli, 9
Bourinot, 53
Bower, 108
Boys' Books, 24-26
Brachet, xvii
Bradley, Herbert, 76
Bradley, T. (Drawing), 8
Brassey, 11, 80
Brazil, 35
Brentano, 80
Bret Harte, 67
Brewer, 45
Brewster, 15
Brickdale, 81
Bright, John, 19
Bright, J. F., 43
Bright, W., 44
Brink, Ten, 59
Britain, Early, 44
British Antiquities, 3
British Coins, 3
British Colonies, 52, 53
British Geography, 31-33
British History, 42-48
British Literature, 59
British Museum Catalogue of Oriental, Persian, and Indian Coins, 22
British Museum Guides, 6
British Poetry, 60-63
Brock, Carey, 24
Brodhead, 54
Brodrick, 30, 81
Broglie, 50
Brontë, Charlotte, 64
—— Life of, 11
Brontë, Emily, 64
—— Life of, 11
Brooke, Stopford, 13, 17, 59
Brougham, 19
Brown (Peoples of the World), 110
Brown, Dr. John, 71
Browne, 73
Browning, Mrs., 11, 61
Browning, Oscar, 49
Browning, Robert, 11, 61
Bruce (traveller), 21
Brugsch-Bey, 40
Bryan, 5
Bryce, James, 34, 42, 54, 93
Buchheim, 57
Buck, Mrs., 27

Buckland, F. T., 26
—— Life of, 15
Buckle, 11
Buckley, Arabella, 26, 105
Buckton, Mrs., 27, 28
Buddha, 16
Bullen, 60
Bunbury, 32
Bunyan, 73
—— Life of, 11
Burchett, 8
Burckhardt, 43
Burke (History), 49
—— Speeches, etc., 73, 92
—— Life of, 12
Burn, 3, 42
Burnaby, 34
Burnet, Bishop, 45
Burnett, Mrs. F. H., 24, 64
Burney, F., 64
Burns, R., 61
—— Life of, 12
Burnside and Panton, 95
Burton, J. H., 47
Burton, Sir R., 35
Butler, A. J., 1, 63
Butler, Bishop, 75
Butler, Samuel (poet), 61
Butler, W. F., (Travels), 35
Butcher, 63
Butterflies, 106
Buxton, S., 86, 93
Buxton, Sir T. F., 22
Byron, 61
—— Life of, 12

CABLE, 67
Cæsar (Languages), 56
—— Life of, 18
Caird, E. (Philosophy), 75
Caird, J., 77
Caird (Land), 82
Cairnes (Economics), 78, 79
Cairnes (History), 54
Calculus, 96
—— **Differential**, 96
—— **Integral**, 96
Caldecott, 26
Calderwood, 75
Calverley, 61
Calvin, 16
Cambridge (*see* **Universities**)
Campbell, Lord, 23
Campbell, L., 63
Campbell, T. (poet), 61
Canada, History, 53
Candolle, De, 109

Canning, 19
Capes, 42
Capital (Economics), 80, 81
Carlyle, J. A., 63
Carlyle, Thomas (Economics), 88
—— (Essays, etc.), 71
—— (John Knox), 16
—— (History), 45, 49, 50, 51
—— (Life of Frederick the Great), 20
—— (Life of Schiller), 14
—— Life of, 12
Carlyle, Mrs., 22
Carnelley, 103
Carpenter, 106
Carroll, 24
Carte, 48
Carthage, History, 39, 40
Cartier, Jacques, 21
Cary, 63
Casaubon, 12
Casey, 95
Cassal and Karcher, 56
Cassell, 106
Catalogue of Books, English, xviii
Catalogue of Current Literature, xviii
Caucasus, 34
Cavalcaselle and Crowe, 10
Cavendish, 45
Cavour, 50
Caxton, 11
Cayley, 96
Cedar Creek, 24
Cellini, Benvenuto, 9
Cervantes, 67
Ceylon, 34
Chaldea, Antiquities, 1
Chalmers (Economics), 84
—— Life of, 16
Chambers (Scotland), 47
—— (Health), 28
Chambers, R., Life of, 22
Chambers, G. F. (Astronomy), 112
Chambers's Encyclopædia, xvii
Channing, 16
Chapman (Homer), 63
Chardenal, 56
Charities, 84
Charity Commission, 30
Charity Commission Acts, 84
Charity Organisation, 84
Charles XII, 18

Charlesworth, Miss, 24
Charts, 36
Charts, Admiralty, 36
Chatrian-Erckmann, 70
Chaucer, 61
—— Life of, 12
Chauvenet, 97
Chemical Industry, Society of, 103
—— Society, Journal of, 103
Chemists, 15
Chemistry, 102, 103
—— **Applied**, 103
—— **Theory of**, 102, 103
Cherry Stones, The, 25
Chesneau, 5
Chesterfield, 73
Chevreul, 8
Cheyne, 97
Chief Justices, Lives of, 23
Children, Care of, 27
Children Employed in Manufactures, 80
—— of Blackberry Hollow, The, 25
Children's Books, 24-26
Children's Poetry, 25
Chipiez and Perrot, 1
Chisholm, 31, 33
Chopin, 15
Christian Leaders of Last Century, 17
Chronology, Dictionaries of, xvii
Chrysostom, 16
Chrystal, 95
Church, A. H., 8, 27
Church, A. J., 24, 69
Church, R. W., Dean (Biography), 11, 14, 16
—— (Essays), 71
—— (History), 42, 44
Church and Gilbert, 34
Church History, England, 43-46
—— **Europe**, 42, 43
Cicero, 56
Cid, 72
Civilisation, 110
—— **History of**, 43
Clarendon, 45
Clarendon, Life of, 12
Classical Dictionaries, 42
Classical Literature, 58, 59, 63, 72
Claude le Lorrain, 9
Claus and Sedgwick, 104
Clerke, Agnes, 112

Cliffe Leslie, 79, 81
Clifford, 77, 98
Clive, 18
Clough, 61
Clowes, 102
Clyde, 18
Cobbett, 88
Cobden, 19, 20
Cockshott and Walters, 95
Coins, Oriental, etc., 2
—— **British, etc.**, 3
Colbeck, 30
Colbeck, 46
Coleman, 106
Coleridge (Essays, etc.), 71
—— (Poetry), 61, 63
—— Life of, 12
Coligny, 20
Collignon, 2
Collingwood, 7
Collins (poet), 61
Collins (Bolingbroke), 19
Collins, Wilkie, 64, 65
Colonial Year-Book, 93
Colonies, British, 93
—— **History of**, 52, 53
—— **Travels**, 33-35
Colour, 8
Colson, 55
Columbus, 21
Colvin, 13
Commerce, Economics of, 79-81, 84-86
—— Year-Book of, 85
Commercial Geography, 33
Commissions, Reports of, 37, 38
Committee of Council on Education Report, 29
Common Objects of the Country, 26
Commons, 82
—— **Preservation**, 82
Compayré, 30
Comte, 92
Comte de Paris, 80
Conciliation (Economics), 81
Congreve, 12
Conic Sections, 95, 96
Conington, 63
Constable, 9
Constitutional History, England, 46
—— **United States**, 54
Conway, 5, 8
Cook, Capt., 18, 21, 33
Cook, E. T., 4

Cooke, J. P., 103
Cooke, Taylor, 80
Cookery, 27
Coombe, 28
Cooper (novelist), 24, 70
Cooper, Thomas, 22
Co-operation (Economics), 81
Co-operative Life, 81
—— Wholesale Society's Annual, 81
Copsley Annals, 24
Coptic Antiquities, 1
Cordery and Phillpotts, 44
Corfield, 28
Corneille, 12
Corporations (*see* **English History**)
Correggio, 9
Cory, 46
Cossa, 79, 86
Cotton, 52
Cotton and Payne, 93
Couch, 107
Coues and Kingsley, 106
County Councils Companion, xviii
Courthope, 14
Courtney, L., 10
Cowell, 53
Cowley, 71
Cowper (poet), 61
—— Life of, 12
Cox, G., 41
Coxe, 18, 49, 51
Crabbe, 61
—— Life of, 12
Craik, G. (Literature), 59
Craik, H. (Education), 29
Craik, Mrs., 65
Crane, 26
Crawford, F. M., 65
Creasy, 52
Creighton, M., 21, 41, 43, 44
Cremona, Luigi, 96
Crompton, 81
Cromwell, 20, 45
Cross, 12
Crowe and Cavalcaselle, 10
Crump, 84, 85
Crusades (*see* **History, Europe**)
Cruttwell, 58
Cunningham, 2
Cunningham and Adams, 51
Cunningham, W., 79, 88
Currency, 84, 85

Curtis, 54
Curtius, 41
Curzon, 34

DAKYNS, 41
Dalhousie, 20
Dampier, 18, 21
Dana, 111
Daniell, 98
Dante, 63, 92
—— Life of, 12
Darwin, Charles (Biology) 104, 106, 108, 109
—— (Travels) 33
—— Life of, 15
Darwin, Erasmus, 15
Darwinism, 104, 105
Dates, Dictionary of, 46
Davids, Rhys, 16
Davis, John (explorer), 21, 33
Davis, Thomas (Ireland), 22
Davy, Sir H., 15
Dawkins, 110
Dawson, 109
Day, Lewis, 7
De Bary, 109
De Beaumont, 49
De Candolle, 109
Decorative Art, 1
Defoe, 12, 24, 73
Delaroche, 10
Della Robbia, 9
Democracy, 91-93
De Morgan, 98
Denmark, Antiquities, 3
Dennis, H. J., 8
Denny, 11
De Quatrefages, 109
De Quincey, 12, 71
Derby, Lord (Homer), 63.
—— Life of, 20
Descartes, 74
Deschanel, 98
Desert of the Exodus, 34
De Tocqueville, 49, 54
Dicey, Albert, 92
Dicey, E., 40
Dick, Robert, 22
Dickens, 65, 70
—— Life of, 12
Dictionaries, xvii, xviii
Dictionary of Dates, 46
Dictionary of English History, 46
Diderot, 12
Dignities, Book of, 46
Dilke, Sir C., 34, 52
Discoverers (*see* **Biography**)

Dixon, 45
Dobson, Austin, 71
Dolomites, 34
Domestic Economy, 27, 28
Donatello, 9
Donisthorpe, 87
Donkin, 97, 99
Don Quixote, 67
Dora, Sister, 22
Dostoieffsky, 67
Dowden, 14, 71
Dowell, 86
Doyle (America), 54
Doyle (Baronage), 46
Drake, 18
Dramatic Poetry, 60-63
Drawing, Geometrical, 8
Drawing, Practice of, 7, 8
Drink Question, 83
Droysen's Historical Atlas, 36
Drummond, 35
Dryden (Essays), 71
Dryden (Poetry), 61, 63
—— Life of, 12
Dudley-Baxter, 85, 86
Dufferin, Lord, 35
Duffy, G., 22, 48
Dumas, A. père, 67
Duncan, 106
Duncker, 40
Dunckley, 20
Dunkin and Lardner, 112
Dürer, Albrecht, 9
Dutch Art, 5
Dwellings, Healthy, 28
Dyeing, 103
Dyer, 3, 42, 43
Dymes, 85
Dynamics, 96

EASTLAKE, 5
Ebers, 68
Ecclesiastical Biography, Essays in, 17
Ecclesiastical History, England, 43-46
—— **Europe**, 42, 43
—— **Scotland**, 47, 48
Economic Association (American), publications of, 89
Economics, Journals, and Dictionaries, 89
Economics, Quarterly Journal of, 89
Economist, Annual Review of the, 89

Economist, The, 89
Economists (*see* **Biography**).
Economy, Domestic, 27, 28
Economy, Political and Social, 78-89
Eden, Sir F. M., 82, 89
Edersheim, 40
Edgeworth, Miss, 12, 65
Education, 29, 30
—— Code, 29
—— **Elementary**, 29
—— **History**, 30
—— **Methods**, 30
—— **Secondary**, 30
—— **Technical**, 29
Edward I., 20
Edward, Thomas, 22
Edwards (Mathematics), 96
Eggs, Birds', 107
Egypt, Antiquities, 1
—— **History**, 40
Elberfeld Poor Laws, Report on, 83
Electricity, 97, 101
Elementary Education, 29
Eliot, George, 65, 69
—— Life of, 12
Elizabeth, Queen, 20
Elliott, Miss, 24
Elphinstone, 53
Elton, C., 82
Elwin, 14
Ely, 87
Embryology, 104
Emerson, 72
—— Life of, 12
Enclosures, 82
Encyclopædias, xvii
Encyclopædia Britannica, xvii
Encyclopædia, Chambers's, xvii
Encyclopædic Dictionary, xvii
Endowed Schools, 30
Endowments, 84
Energy, Theory of, 101
Engels, 83
Engineers, Lives of the, 11
England, Antiquities, 3
—— **Art**, 5
—— **Coins**, 3
—— **Constitution, Law of**, 92
—— **Fiction**, 64-70
—— **Geography**, 31-33
—— **History**, 43-46

INDEX

England, Literature, 59
—— Philosophy, 74-77
—— Poetry, 60-63
English Catalogue of Books, xviii
English Citizen Series, 93
English Dictionaries, xvii
Engraving, 8
Entomology, 106, 107
Epictetus, 72
Epochs of Modern History, 44
Equations, 95, 96
Erasmus, 73
—— Life of, 16
Erckmann-Chatrian, 70
Erdmann, 77
Erikson, Leif, 21
Escott, 92
Essays, Lectures, and Studies, 70-72
Etching, 8
Ethics, 75, 76
Euclid, 95
Europe, Geography, 31-33
—— **Travels**, 34
Evans, 3, 110
Evelyn, 45
Everett, 99
Evolution, 104, 105
Ewald, 40
Ewing, Mrs., 24
—— Life of, 12
Examinations, Local, 30
Exchanges, Foreign, 85

FABIAN ESSAYS, 87
Factories (Economics), 80-88
Fair Trade, 86
Fairy-book, Blue, 24
Fairy Tales, 24, 25
Faraday, 15
Farr, 83
Farrer, 86, 88
Faust, 63
Fawcett, 80, 86
—— Life of, 10
Fearon, 30
Federalist, The, 93
Fergusson, 2, 7
Ferrier, 76
Fichte, 75
Fiction, 64-70
Field, 8
Fielding, 65
—— Life of, 12
Figuier, 106
Finance, 84-86

Findlay, 32
Fine Arts, 4-8
Finlay, 52
Fishes, 107
Fitch, 30
Fitzgerald, 63
Fleming, 101
Flemish Art, 5
Fletcher (poet), 61
Fletcher (Gustavus Adolphus), 51
Flora, 108
Flower-garden, The, 28
Flowers (*see* Botany)
Fonblanque, 92
Food, 27
Forbes, 34
Force, Conservation of, 101
Ford, 61
Foreign Essays, etc., 72, 73
—— **Exchanges**, 85
—— **Fiction**, 67, 68
—— **Literature**, 59, 63, 67, 68, 73
—— **Trade**, 85
Foreigners, Immigration of, 86
Forster, W. E., 20
Forsyth, 96
Foster, 105
Foster and Balfour, 104
Fouqué, 67
Four Famous Soldiers, 19
Fourier, 100
Fowle, 83
Fowler, T., 13, 75, 76
Fowler, Warde, 107
Fowler and Wilson, 75
Fox, Caroline, 22
Fox, C. J., 20
Foxwell, 83, 85
Fra Angelico, 9
Fra Bartolommeo, 9
France, Art, 5
—— **History**, 49
—— **Literature**, 59
Francia, 9
Francis de Sales, 16
Francis of Assisi, 16
Francis Xavier, 16
Franklin, Benjamin, 54
Franklin, Sir John, 22, 35
Frederick the Great, 20
Free Libraries, xviii
Free Trade, 86
Freeman (Architecture), 7
—— (Biography), 21

Freeman, (Geography), 32
—— (History), 42, 43, 44, 46, 52
—— (Political Science), 91
Freeman and Hunt, 44
French (for beginners), 56
French Dictionaries, xvii
French Revolution, Tales, 70
Frere, 63
Fresenius, 102
Freshfield, 34
Freshfield and Wharton, 36
Friendly Societies, 83
Froude (Biography), 11, 17, 18, 19, 22
Froude (History), 45, 48, 52
Froude (Essays), 71
Fry, Elizabeth, 22
Fyffe, 41, 43

GAINSBOROUGH, 9
Gairdner, 20, 44
Galileo, 15
Gallenga, 50
Galton, 34, 35, 36
Gama, Vasco de, 22
Gambetta, 20
Gamgee, 105
Ganot, 98
Gardiner, 20, 43, 44, 45
Gardiner, Mrs., 49
Gardiner and Mullinger, 44
Gardening, 28
Gardner, 2
Garibaldi, 18, 50
Garnett, R., 96, 100
Gaskell, Mrs., 65
—— Life of, 11
Gatty, Mrs., 24
Gay, 61
Gazetteers, xvii
Geijer, 51
Geikie, A., (Geography), 30, 31, 32
—— (Geology), 110, 111
Geikie, C., 40
Geography, 31-36
—— **Ancient**, 42
—— **Commercial**, 33
—— **Historical**, 32, 33
Geography, Physical, 31, 32
Geography and Travels, 31-36
Geologists, 15
Geology, 110, 111
Geometrical Drawing, 8
Geometry, 95, 96

George, Henry, 87
German (for beginners), 56, 57
German Maps, 36
Germany, Art, 5
—— History, 49, 50
—— Literature, 59
Ghiberti, 9
Gibbon, 42
—— Life of, 12
Giberne, Agnes, 26
Giffen, 83, 85, 86
Gilbart, 84
Gilbert (Art), 5
Gilbert, J. T. (Ireland), 49
Gilbert and Church, 34
Gil Blas, 68, 73
Gilchrist, 11
Gill, 34
Gilman, 81
Giotto, 9
Girl's Books, 24-26
Gladstone, 86
—— Life of, 20
Glazebrook, 100
Gmelin, 103
Gneist, 46
Godfray, 97
Godkin, 50
Godwin, 12
Goebel, 109
Goethe, 63, 67, 73
—— Life of, 12, 13
Goldsmith, 61, 65
—— Life of, 13
Gordon, Gen., 18
Gordon, J., 101
Goschen, 85, 86
Gosse (Zoology), 106
Gostwick, 59
Gothic Architecture, 6, 7
Gould, Baring, 49, 65
Government Handbook, xviii
Government, Local, 86
—— Principles of, 91, 92
—— Publications, 37, 38
Graham, 83, 84
Grattan, 20
Graves, 5
Gray, A., 101
Gray, Asa, 108
Gray (poet), 61
—— Life of, 13
Greece, Antiquities, 2
Coins, 2
History, ancient, 4
—— History, modern, 52
—— Literature, 58

Greece, Philosophy, 74-77
—— Sculpture, 2, 6
Greek Dictionaries, xvii
Greek (for beginners), 55
Green, A. H. (Geology), 111
Green, J. R., 43, 44
Green, J. R. and A. S., 31
Green, T. H. 75, 77, 88, 91
Greenaway, K., 26
Greenhill, 96
Greenwell, 3
Greenwood, T., xviii
Greswell, 53
Greville, 46
Grierson, 88
Grimm, 24
Gronlund, 87
Grote, G., 41
—— Life of, 13
Grote, John, 75
Grove, Sir G., 31, 34
Grub, 48
Guide-books, 35, 36
Guilds (Economics), 80
Guillemard, 34
Guillemin, 112
Guizot, 43, 49
Gullick and Timbs, 7
Gulliver's Travels, 73
Gustavus Adolphus, 18

Hadley, 88
Hale, 51
Hall, S. (Allotments), 82
Hall and Knight, 95
Hallam, 42, 46
Halliwell-Phillipps, 14
Hals, 10
Hamblin Smith, 95
Hamerton, 8, 10, 71
Hampden, 20
Handel, 15
Handicrafts for Handy People, 28
Hannibalian War, 56
Hans Andersen, 24
Hans Brinker, 24
Hardy, 65
Hare, 35
Harrington, 92
Harrison, F., 20, 71
Harrison, J. E., 2, 41
Harrison, R., 59
Harting, 107
Hassall and Wakeman, 46
Hassencamp, 48
Hastings, Warren, 20

Häusser, 43
Havard, 5
Havelock, 18
Hawke, 18
Hawthorne, N., 24, 67
—— Life of, 13
Haydn, xvii, 46
Hayward (Botany), 108
Hazell's Annual, xviii
Hazlitt, 71
Health, 28
Health Lectures for the People, 28
Hearn, 46, 80, 92
Heat, 100
Heath (Anatomy), 105
Heath (Optics), 100
Heather, 8
Heatley, 55
Heatley and Kingdon, 55
Hebrews (*see* **Jewish History**)
Hegel, 75, 76, 77
Heine, 73
—— Life of, 13
Helmholtz, 99, 101
Helps, 21, 71
Henfrey, 3
Henry II., 20
Henry V., 18, 20
Henry VII., 20
Henslow, 26, 109
Henty, 24
Herbert, George, 61
Herodotus, 41
Heroes of Industry, 11
Herrick, 61
Herschel, 112
—— Life of, 15
Hicks, 2
Hickson, 48
Higginson, 54
Hildebrand, 3
Hill, Birkbeck, 13
Hill, Octavia, 83
Hill, Sir Rowland, 11
Hillern, 67
Hillhouse and Strasburger, 108
Himalayas, 34
Hinman, 32
Historians (*see* **Biography**)
Historic Towns, 44
Historical Geography, 32, 33
History (for subdivisions see Table of Contents), 39-54

History of Philosophy, 77
History, Philosophy of, 77
Hobbes, 92
Hobhouse, Lord, 84
Hobhouse and Wright, 86
Hodgkin, 50
Hoffmann, 57
Hogan, 52
Hogarth, 9
Holbein, 9
Hole, xvii
Holland (Russia), 51
Holmes (India), 53
Holmes (America), 54
Holmes, O. W., 67, 72
Holyoake, 81
Holland, Art, 5
—— **History,** 50, 51
Homan, 57
Home, The, 27, 28
Homer, 55, 63
Hood, 61
Hook, Dean, 23
—— Life of, 16
Hooker (Botany), 108
Hooker, Richard, 73
Hooker and Ball, 34
Hooker (Travels), 34
Horace, 63
Hornsby and Wright, 84
Horticulture (*see* **Gardening**)
Hosack, 47
Houghton, Lord, 22
Household, 27, 28
Howe, 18
Howell, G,, 80, 84
Howells, 67
Hudson, 14, 71
Hueffer, 16
Hug and Stead, 51
Hughes, T., 22, 25
Hughes and Neale, 81
Hugo, Victor, 67, 70
—— Life of, 13
Hull, 32, 111
Humboldt, 35
—— Life of, 15, 22
Hume, 75
—— Life of, 13
Hummel, 103
Hungary, History, 49
Hunt, 50
Hunt, W., and Freeman, 44
Hunter, W. W., 20, 31, 53
Husenbeth, 5
Hutchinson, Mrs., 45
Hutten, Ulrich von, 16
Hutton, J. (Netherlands), 51

Hutton, R. H., 14, 17, 71
Huxley (Life of Hume), 13
Huxley (Essays), 71
Huxley (Biology), 104, 105, 106
Huxley and Martin, 104
Hydrodynamics, 97
Hydromechanics, 97
Hydrostatics, 96
Hygiene, 28
Hyndman, 87

IDDESLEIGH, Lord, 20
Ihne, 41
Imitation of Christ, 72
Immigration of Foreigners, 86
Imperial Federation, 52
India, Antiquities, 2
—— **Geography,** 31-33
—— **History,** 53
Indian Officers, Lives of, 19
Individualism, 87
Industrial Biography, 11
Industry, Economics of, 78-81
—— Heroes of, 11
—— Men of Invention and, 11
—— **Leaders of** (*see* **Biography**)
Infants, Care of, 27
Ingelow, 61
Ingram, 79
Inner Life, Poems of, 60
Innes, 47
Insects, 106, 107
Inspectors, Instructions to, 29
Insurance, National, 83
Intemperance, 83
Invention and Industry, Men of, 11
Inventors (*see* **Biography**)
Investors, *Vade Mecum* for, 85
Ireland, Antiquities, 3
—— **Geography,** 31-33
—— **History,** 48, 49
—— **Poetry,** 60-63
Irish History, Two Centuries of, 49
Irving (Annals), xviii
Irving, Edward, 16
Irving, Washington, 21
Italian Dictionaries, xvii
Italy, Art, 5
—— **History,** 50
—— **Sculpture,** 6

Italy, (Travel), 35

JAMES, Henry, 67
James, H. A. (Drawing), 8
Jameson, Mrs., 5, 10
Jeans, 88
Jebb, 58
Jeffcott and Tossell, 57
Jefferies, 107
Jerome, 16
Jerram, 55, 56
Jerram and Phillpotts, 55
Jerrold (Gardening), 28
Jervis, 49
Jevons, F. B. (Greek Literature), 58
Jevons, W. S. (Philosophy), 76
—— (Political Economy), 78, 79, 82, 84, 88
—— (Science), 102
—— Life of, 10
Jewish History, 40, 41
Jewitt, Ll., 3
Johns, 107
Johnson, Dr., 14, 73
—— Life of, 13
Johnson and Rice, 96
Johnston, Alex. (America), 54
Johnston, Keith, 31
Joly, 110
Jones, Lloyd, 87
Jones, Owen, 7
Jones, B., and Acland, 81
Jonson, Ben, 61
Josephus, 41
Joubert and Mascart, 101
Journals (*see* **Biography**)
Jowett, 41, 91, 92
Judges of England, Lives of, 23
Jukes-Browne, 111
Junius, 73
Jusserand, 45
Justices, Lives of the Chief, 23

KALENDAR, The Royal, xviii
Kane, 49
Kant, 75
Karcher and Cassal, 55
Kay, J., 81
Kaye, 19, 53
Keary, Miss, 25
Keats, 61
—— Life of, 13
Keble, 16
Keene, 53
Kegan Paul, 12

INDEX

Kelland and Tait, 96
Kelly's Handbook, xviii
Kemble, Frances, 22
Kempis, 72
Ken, Bishop, 16
Kenny, Courtney, 84
Keynes, 76, 79
Khiva, 34
Kiepert, 32
Kindergarten, 30
King, 34
Kingdon and Heatley, 55
Kinglake, 34, 46
Kingsford, 52
Kingsley, C. (Health), 28
—— (Natural History), 26
—— (Novels), 65, 68, 69, 88
—— (Poems), 61, 62
—— (Prose Idylls), 71
—— (Stories), 25
—— Life of, 13
Kingsley, H., 65, 70
Kingsley and Coues, 106
Kingston, 25
Kinnear, 91
Kirby, W. E., 106
Kirchner, 76
Kirkes, 105
Kitchener, 26, 108
Kitchin, 49
Knechts and Benedikt, 103
Knight, F., 107
Knight and Hall, 95
Knox, John, 16
Kugler, 5

Labour (Economics), 79-81
Labour Correspondent of the Board of Trade, 80, 89
Labour Statistics, 38
Laffan, 65
Lamb, 25, 60, 71
—— Life of, 13
Land, 81, 82
Landois, 105
Landon, 30
Landor, 71
—— Life of, 13
Landscape, 5
Landseer, 9
Land-laws, 81, 82
Land-tenure, 81
Land-transfer, 81
Lane-Poole, 2, 15, 51, 52
Lanfrey, 18, 49
Lang, A., 24, 63
Langland, 62
Langmead, Taswell, 46

Languages (Books for Beginners), 55-57
Lankester, 104
Lapworth and Page, 111
Larden, 101
Lardner and Dunkin, 112
La Rochefoucauld, 73
Latimer, 16
Latin (for Beginners), 55, 56
Latin Dictionaries, xvii
Laurie, 30
Laveleye, 87
Lawless, Miss, 48
Lawrence (painter), 9
Lawrence, Henry, 22
Lawrence, Lord, 22
Lawrence and Melsheimer, 85
Layard, 40
Leaf, 63
Lear, 26
Lecky, 43, 45, 48, 49
Lectures, Essays, and Studies, 70-72
Legendary Art, 5
Leger, 49
Leonardo da Vinci, 8, 9
Lesage, 68, 73
Leslie, Cliffe, 79, 81
Lessing, 73
—— Life of, 13
Letourneau, 90
Letters (see **Biography**)
Letters, Men of (see **Biography**)
Letters, Women of (see **Biography**)
Lever, 65
Levi, Leone, 79, 80
Levy, 57
Lewes, 13, 75, 76
Lewins, 83
Lewis, Sir G. C., 91
Lewis (German History), 49
Lewis and Short, xvii
Libraries (see **Books of Reference**)
Liddell and Scott, xvii
Light, 97, 100
Lincoln, Abraham, 20
Lincoln (Cookery), 27
Linnæus, 15
Lippincott, xvii
List, 86
Liszt, 15
Literature (for subdivisions see Table of Contents), 58-73

Literature, Dictionaries, of, xvii
Literature, Periodical Index to, xviii
Lives of the Engineers, 11
—— of Indian Officers, 19
Livingstone, 34
—— Life of, 22
Lloyd (Agriculture), 82
Lloyd Jones, and Ludlow, 82
Lloyd (Mathematics), 97
Lloyd (Optics), 100
Local Examinations, 30
Local Government, 86
Local Government and Taxation in the United Kingdom, 86
Local Taxation, 85, 86
Loch, 84
Lock, 95
Locke, T. (Education), 30
—— (Philosophy), 74
—— (Political Science), 92
—— Life of, 13
Locker-Lampson, 60
Lockhart, 14
Lockyer, 112
Lodge, H. C., 54
Lodge, O. J., 99
Lodge, R., 42
Logic, 76
London Poor, 83, 84
Loney, 97
Longfellow, 62, 63
—— Life of, 13
Longman, 44
Longstaff, 83
Lord Chancellors, Lives of the, 23
Lorrain, Claude le, 9
Lotze, 75, 76
Lover, 65
Low and Pulling, 46
Lowe, 50
Lowell, 62, 72
Lowndes, xviii
Lubbock (Antiquities), 3
—— (Biology), 106, 107, 110
—— (Political Science), 90
Lucas, 32, 52
Lucretius, 63
Ludlow and Lloyd Jones, 82
Luigi Cremona, 96
Lunge, 103
Lunge and Winkler, 103
Luther, 73

Luther, Life of, 17
Lyall, E., 69
Lydekker and Nicholson, 111
Lyell, 111
—— Life of, 15
Lyrics (*see* Poetry)
Lytton, 65, 68, 69

MACALISTER, 104
MacArthur, 47
Macaulay, G. C. (Herodotus), 41
—— (Languages), 56
Macaulay, Lord (Essays), 20, 71
—— (History), 45
—— (Lays), 62
—— Life of, 13
Macey, 93
Machiavelli, 73, 92
Machinery (Economics), 79, 80
Mackail, 63
Mackay (The Poor), 87
Mackay, Powell, and Tout, 43
Mackenzie, 47
Mackmurdo, 7
Maclear, 40
Macmullen, 53
MacNeill, 86
Macpherson, 89
Magellan, 22, 33
Magnetism, 97, 101
Magnus, 29
Mahaffy, 2, 41, 58
Mahew, 7
Maine, 82, 90
Major, 33
Malay Archipelago, 34
Malory, 72
Malthus, 79, 83
—— Life of, 10
Mammals, 107
Man, Descent of, 104, 105
Mantegna, 9
Manufactures (Economics), 79, 80
Manzoni, 68, 69
Maps, 36
—— **Colonies,** 52
—— **Ordnance,** 36
Marckwald, 105
Marco Polo, 33
Marcus Aurelius, 72
Mariette, 1
Marine Zoology, 106

Market Fluctuations, The Rationale of, 85
Markham, 33
Marlborough, 18
Marlowe, 62
Marryat, 25, 65
—— Life of, 13
Marshall, Alfred, 79
Marshall, A., and M.P., 78
Marshall, John, 8
Marshall, Milnes, 104
Marshall, W. G., 35
Marshall (Life of Washington), 54
—— (Canada), 52
Marsham, 53
Martin and Huxley, 104
Martin and Wetzler, 101
Martineau, Dr., 75, 77
Martineau, Harriet (History), 46
—— (Stories), 25
—— Life of, 13
Marvel, 62
Marx, 87
Mary Queen of Scots, 20
Masaccio, 9
Masai Land, 34
Mascart and Joubert, 101
Mason, 27
Maspero, 1
Massey, 45
Massinger, 61
Masson, David (Life of Milton), 13, 45
Masson, Gustave, 56
Mathematics, 94-98
—— **History of,** 98
—— **Mixed,** 96, 97
—— **Pure,** 95, 96
Matheson, 42
Mathieson, 85
Maurice, F. D., 17
Maxwell, Clerk, 97, 99, 100, 101
—— Life of, 15
May, 46
Mayer, 99
Mayne Reid, 25
Mazade, De, 50
Mazarin, 20
Mazzini, 22, 71, 92
M'Carthy, J., 46
M'Clintock, 35
M'Crie, 16, 47
M'Culloch, 10, 85, 89
Mechanicians, 15
Mechanics, 96, 97, 99

Medals, Oriental, etc., 2
Mediæval History, 42-54
Meissner, 57
Meissonier, 10
Melbourne, 20
Melsheimer and Lawrence, 85
Men of the Time, xviii
Mendelssohn, 15, 16
Meredith, 66
Merivale, C., 41, 42
Merry, 55
Metallurgy, 103
Metaphysics, 74, 75
Methodists, Memoirs of Oxford, 17
Metropolitan Year-Book, xviii
Metternich, 20, 50
Meyer, 103
Michelangelo, 10
Microscope, 106
Middleton, 3, 4
Mignet, 20, 47, 49
Mill, H. R., 31, 33
Mill, James, 53
—— Life of, 10
Mill, J. S. (Philosophy), 75, 76, 77
—— (Political Economy), 79, 88
—— (Political Science), 91
—— Life of, 10
Miller (Chemistry), 102
Miller, Mrs., 28
Millet, 10
Milman, 40
Milnes, Marshall, 104
Milton (Poems), 62
—— (Prose), 73, 92
—— Life of, 13
Minchin, 96
Mineralogy, 111
Mining, 81, 82
—— **Royalties,** 82
Minto, 12
Mirabeau, 20
Mitchell, 2
Mivart, 104
M'Kendrick, 105
M'Lennan, 91
Moberly, 56
Modern History, 42-54
Mohammed, 17
Molesworth, 44, 46
Molesworth, Mrs., 25
Molière, 13
Mommsen, 42
Money, 84, 85

INDEX

Monk, 18
Monro, 55
Montaigne, 73
Montcalm, 18
Montelius, 3
Montesquieu, 92
Montrose, 18
Moody, 7
Moore (poet), 62
Moore, George, 11
Moore, Sir John, 18
Morals, Principles of, 75, 76
More, Hannah, 22
More, Sir Thomas, 45, 73, 92
—— Life of, 13
Morgan (Canada), 53
Morgan (Sociology), 91
Morice, 55
Morison, 12, 13
Morley, H., 59
Morley, J. (Essays), 71
—— (History), 49
—— (Life of Cobden), 19
—— (Life of Walpole), 21
—— (Political Science), 92
—— (Study of Burke), 11, 12
—— (Study of Rousseau), 14
Morocco, 34
Morris, F. O. (Birds), 107
Morris, Lewis, 62
Morris, W. (Lectures), 71
—— (Poems), 62
—— (Socialism), 87
Morshead, 63
Morte d' Arthur, 72
Moschus, 63
Moseley, 34
Mother's Books, 27
Motley, 51
—— Life of, 13
Mozart, 16
Muir, Thomas, 95
Müller, Max, 53, 71
Mullinger, 30, 50
Mullinger and Gardiner, 44
Mullins, Roscoe, 6
Mungo Park, 33
Municipal Corporations' Companion, xviii
Munro, J. E. C., 53, 81
—— (Lucretius), 63
Murchison, 15
Murillo, 10
Murray (Psychology), 76
—— (Sculpture), 6

Murray's Dictionary, xvii
—— Guide Books, 35
Musicians (see Biography)
Myers, E., 19, 63
Myers, F. (Life of Wordsworth), 14
—— (Essays), 71

NAPIER, Sir W. (Peninsular War), 46, 51
—— (Scinde), 53
Napier, Sir Charles, Life of, 18
Napier, Mark (Scottish History), 4
Napier (History of Florence), 50
Napoleon, 18, 19
Nasmyth, 11
Nash and Ll. Smith, 80
Nassé, 82
National Debt, 86
—— **Insurance,** 83
Natural History, 105-107
Natural History Books, Children's, 26
National Gallery, 4
Natural History Handbooks for Collectors, 107
Natural Philosophy, 98-102
Naturalists' Travels, 33, 34
Navy (see Sailors)
Neale and Hughes, 81
Nelson, 19
Netherlands, History, 50, 51
Neuman and Baretti, xvii
Newcomb, 112
Newman, F. (**Butterflies**), 106
Newman, J. H., Cardinal, 17
Newmarch and Tooke, 85, 89
Newsholme, 28, 83
Newton, Sir C. T., 2, 6
Newton, Isaac, 15, 98
New Zealand, History, 52
Nicaragua, 35
Nichol, 42, 59
Nicholson (Economics), 80, 82, 84
Nicholson, H. A. (Biology), 104, 105, 106; (Geology), 111
Nicholson and Lyddeker, 111

Nights, Arabian, 72
Nile, 35
Nineveh, History, 40
Noble, 86
Nordhoff, 87
Nordenskiöld, 35
Norgate, 44
Northcote, Stafford, 86
—— (Lord Iddesleigh), Life of, 20
Norway, 34
—— **History,** 51
Novels, 64-70
—— **Historical,** 68-70
Novelists (see Biography)
Noyes, 87
Numismatics, 2

O'BRIEN, Barry, 48
O'Connell, 20
O'Curry, 48
Odling, 102
Ogilvie's Imperial Dictionary, xvii
Oil Painting, 5
Oliphant, Mrs., 12, 13, 16, 66
Oliver, 108
Oman, 45
Omar Khayyám, 63
Onslow, Lord, 82
Optics, 97, 100
Ordnance Maps, 36
Oriental Antiquities, 1, 2
—— **History,** 39-41
Ornament, 7
Osborn, 35
Osborne, Dorothy, 22
Ostwald, 103
Otté, Miss, 51
Otto, E., 57
Ouida, 25
Outram, 19
Overbeck, 10
Overton and Abbey, 45
Ovid, 56
Owen (Education), 29
Owen, S. (India), 53
Oxford (see Universities)
Oxford Reformers, 17

PAGE and LAPWORTH, 111
Paget, 25
Painters (see Biography)
Painting, History, 4, 5
—— **Practice,** 7, 8
Palæontology, 111
Palestine, 33
Palfrey, 54

INDEX

Palgrave, F. T., 60
Palgrave, Inglis, 89
Palgrave, W. G., 34
Palmer, 34
Palmerston, 20
Panton and Burnside, 95
Papacy (*see* **History, Europe**)
Paris, Comte de, 80
Park, Mungo, 22
Parker, J., 6
Parker, Theodore, 17
Parkes, 28
Parkinson, 97, 100
Parkman, 53
Parliament (*see* **Constitutional History**)
Parliament, Acts of, 38
Parliamentary Atlas, 93
Parliamentary Publications, 37, 38
Parry, Gambier, 6
Parry (Sculpture), 6
Pascal, 73
—— Life of, 13
Pater, 68, 71
Patmore, 25
Patteson, Bishop, 17
Pattison, Mark, 12, 13
Paul, Kegan, 12
Pauperism, 83
Pausanias, 2
Payer, 35
Payne, 52
Payne and Cotton, 93
Peaks, Passes, and Glaciers, 34
Pedagogy, 30
Peel, Sir R., 21
Pendlebury, 100
Penn, 17
People, Condition of, 82-84
Pepys, 45
Percival, 55
Percy (Poetry), 60
—— (Metallurgy), 103
Perini, 56
Periodical Literature, Index to, xviii
Perkins, 6
Perrot and Chipiez, 1
Persia, Antiquities, 2
—— **History**, 40
Perspective, 8
Peschel, 109
Peter the Great, 21
Peterborough, 19
Pétilleau, 56

Petrarch, 14
Pfleiderer, 77
Phear, 85
Phillips (Chemistry), 103
Phillpotts and Cordery, 44
Phillpotts and Jerram, 55
Philosophers, 77
Philosophical Classics for English Readers, 77
Philosophy, 74-77
Phœnicia, Antiquities, 1
Photography, 103
Physical Geography, 32
Physicists, 15
Physics, 98-102
Physiology, 105
Picture-books, Children's, 26
Picture Galleries, 4
Pidgeon, 80
Piers the Plowman, 62
Pilgrim's Progress, 73
Pindar, 63
Pitt, 21
Plants (*see* **Botany**)
Plato, 72, 76, 77, 91
Playfair, 29
Plener, Von, 80, 88
Plumptre, 63
Plutarch, 23, 41, 72
Pocket Atlases, 36
Poe, E. A., 14, 62, 67
Poems, Collections of, 60
Poetry, 60-63
Poetry, Children's, 25
Poets (*see* **Biography**)
Political Economists (*see* **Biography**)
Political Economy, (for subdivisions *see* Table of Contents), 78-89
Political Leaders (*see* **Biography**)
Political Science, 90-93
Political Science, Quarterly, 89
Politics, 90-93
Pollock, 81
Polo, Marco, 22
Poole (Periodical Literature), xviii
Poole, R. L. (*see* Lane Poole)
Poor, State of, 82-84
Poor Law, 83
Pope, 62, 63
—— Life of, 14
Population, Economics, 83
Porter, 82

Portugal, History, 51
Positivism, 92
Powell, York, 43
Powell, Mackay, and Tout, 43
Poynter, 5, 7
Praed, 62
Prantl and Vines, 108
Prendergast, 48
Prescott, 51, 54
Prestwich, 111
Prevost, 68
Price, 81, 82
Prices, 85
Prinsep, 2
Probyn, 50, 93
Procter, 103
Proctor, 112
Profit-sharing (Economics), 81
Promessi Sposi, 68
Protection, 86
Prothero (History), 44
Prothero (Agriculture), 82
Psychology, 76
Public Bills, 37
Public Libraries, xviii
Publications, Government, 37, 38
Puckett, R. C., 8
Pugin, A. W., 7
Pulling and Low, 46
Purcell, 16
Puritan Revolution, Chief Actors in, 17
Puritanism, English, 17
Pym, 21

Quadrupeds, 107
Quain, 105
Quatrefages, De, 109
Quick, 30
Quincey, De, 12, 71

RABELAIS, 14, 68
Rae, 84, 87
Ragon, 56
Railroads, 88
Raleigh, Sir W., 19
Raleigh (Political Science), 91
Rambaud, 51
Ramsay (poet), 62
Ramsay (Antiquities), 3
Ramsay (Geology), 32, 111
Ramsay (Rome), 42
Ranke, Von, 40, 43, 45, 50, 51, 52
Ranken, 52

INDEX

Rankine, 99
Ransome, C., 43, 52
Ransome and Acland, 44
Raphael, 10
Rawlinson, 40
Rawson, 86
Rayleigh, 97, 99
Reade, Charles, 66, 69
Reclus, 31, 32
Records of the Past, 40
Redford, 6
Redgrave (Economics), 88
Redgrave, R. (Art), 5, 7
Redgrave, R. and S. (Art), 5
Reed, 59
Reeve, 14
Reference, Books of, xvii, xviii
Reference Catalogue of Current Literature, xviii
Reformation (*see* **History, Europe, etc.**)
Reformers, Oxford, 17
Register, Annual, xviii
Reid (Ireland), 48
Reid, Mayne, 25
Reid, W., 11, 22
Rejected Addresses, 62
Religion, Philosophy of, 77
Religious Leaders (*see* **Biography**)
Reports, Parliamentary, 37, 38
Returns, Government, 37
Reumont, Von, 50
Revolution, French (*see* **History**)
Representative Government, 91-93
Religious Writers (*see* **Biography**)
Reynolds, Sir J., 10
Rhoades, 63
Rhys, 3, 47
Rembrandt, 10
Remsen, 102
Renaissance (*see* **History**)
Rent (Economics), 82
Reports of Government Departments, 38
Reptiles, 107
Republican Institutions, 93
Ribton-Turner, 83
Ricardo, 10, 79
Rice, 64
Rice and Johnson, 96
Richardson, Dr., 28, 83
Richardson (novelist), 66

Richelieu, 21
Richey, 48
Richter (Chemistry), 103
Ritchie, 56
Roberts, Sir Frederick, 19
Roberts, Miss, 70
Robertson, F. W., 17, 72
Robertson (Scotland), 47
Robertson, W. (Charles V), 50
Robinson Crusoe, 24, 73
Robinson (Gardening), 28
Robinson (Mathematics), 96
Rodney, 19
Rogers, J. E. T. (Biography), 17
—— (Economics), 79, 84, 85, 89
—— (History), 50
—— (Political Science), 92
Roget xvii
Roland, Mme., 22
Rolleston, 104
Roman Empire, 42
Romanes, 105, 106
Rome, Antiquities, 2, 3
—— **History,** 41, 42
—— **Literature,** 58
Romilly Allen, 3
Romney, 9
Rood, Ogden, 100
Roscher, 79
Roscoe Mullins, 6
Roscoe, Sir H., 102, 103
Roscoe and Schorlemmer, 102
Rose, 43
Rosengarten, 6
Rosenthal, 105
Ross, 22, 35
Rossetti, Christina, 62
Rossetti, D. G., 10, 14, 62
Rossetti, W. M., 13, 60
Rousseau, 14, 92
Routh, 97
Royal Commissions, Reports from, 37, 38
Royal Commission (Elementary Education), 29
—— (Public Schools), 30
—— (Schools Enquiry), 30
—— (Technical Instruction), 29
Royal Kalendar, xviii
Royalties, Mining, 82
Rubens, 10
Ruding, 89
Rühle, 57
Rulers of India, 53

Rusden, 52
Ruskin (Art), 5, 7, 8
—— (Autobiography), 14
—— (Economics), 88
—— Essays, etc., 72
Russell, Lord John, 20
Russia, 34
—— **History,** 51
—— **Travels,** 34
Rutherford's Children, 25
Rutley, 111
Rye, 107

SACHS, 109
Sacred Poetry, 60-63
Sailors (*see* **Biography**)
Saintsbury, 12, 18, 59
Sales, Francis de, 16
Salmon, 95, 96
Sand, G. 68
—— Life of, 14
Sanderson, 96
Sanitation, 28
Sankey, 41
Saracens, Antiquities, 2
Sarto, Andrea del, 9
Saussure, 22
Savonarola, 17
Sayce, 39, 40
Scandinavia, History, 51
Scarth, 3
Schaeffle, 87
Scherer, 59
Schiller, 57, 63, 73
—— Life of, 14
Schmidt, 107
Schömann, 2, 41
School Management, 30
Schools (*see* **Education**)
Schorlemmer and Roscoe, 102
Schreiner, Olive (Ralph Iron), 66
Schubert, 16
Schumann, 16
Schürer, 40
Schuyler, 51
Schwegler, 77
Schweinfurth, 35
Science (for sub-divisions *see* **Table of Contents),** 94-112
Science and Art Department, 29
Science-Books, Children's, 26
Science, Men of (*see* **Biography**)
—— **Political,** 90-93

Science, Women of (*see* Biography)
Scotland, Antiquities, 3
—— Geography, 31-33
—— History, 47, 48
—— Philosophy, 77
—— Poetry, 60-63
Scott Sir W. (History), 47
—— (Novels), 66, 68, 69, 70
—— (Poems), 62
—— Life of, 14
Sculptors (*see* Biography)
Sculpture, 6
Secondary Education, 30
Sedgwick and Claus, 104
Seebohm, F., 16, 42, 44, 45, 82
Seebohm, H. (Travels), 34
—— (Birds), 107
Seeley (Biography), 19, 21
—— (Essays), 72
—— (History), 45, 50, 52
Seeley and Abbott, 59
Select Committees, Reports of, 37, 38
Sellar, 58
Selwyn, Bishop, 17
Sergeant (Government Handbook), xviii, 93
Servia, History, 52
Seth, 77
Sévigné, 14
Seward, 86
Seyd, 85
Shaftesbury, first Earl, 21
Shaftesbury, seventh Earl, 22
Shairp, 12, 72
Shakespeare, 14, 62
Shann, 100
Sharp, 56
Shelburne, 21
Shelley, 62
—— Life of, 14
Sheridan, 62
—— Life of, 14
Shirreff, 30
Short, 8
Shorthouse, 66
Siberia, 34
Siddons, Mrs., 22
Sidgwick, A., 55
Sidgwick, H. (Economics), 78, 79, 88
—— (Philosophy), 75, 76
Sidney, Sir Philip, 14, 73
Sime, 13, 49
Simeon, Charles, 17
Sinai and Palestine, 34

Sismondi, 50
Sister Dora, 22
Skeat, xvii
Skelton, 47
Skene, 47
Smiles, 11, 22
Smith, Adam, 79, 86
—— Life of, 10
Smith, Barnard, 95
Smith, Bosworth, 22, 39
Smith, C. (Mathematics), 96
Smith, G. (Art), 5
Smith, Goldwin, 11, 12, 21
Smith, Hamblin (Mathematics), 95, 96
Smith, Llewellyn (Economics), 87
Smith, I.L., and Nash, 80
Smith, Philip (History), 39
Smith, P. V. (History), 46
Smith, R. Murdoch (Art), 2
Smith, Sydney, 14, 17, 72
Smith, Toulmin, 80
Smith, Dr. W., 41
Smollett, 66
—— Life of, 14
Socialism, 87
Social Economy (for subdivisions *see* Table of Contents), 78-89
Sociology, 90, 91
Socrates, 72
Soldiers (*see* Biography)
Somerville, Mary, 15
Sonnenschein, xviii
Sophocles, 63
Sorley, 82
Sound, 97, 99
Southey (Life of Wesley), 17
—— (Life of Nelson), 19
—— (Poems), 62
—— Life of, 14
Sovereigns (*see* Biography)
Spain, Art, 5
—— History, 51
Spanish Dictionaries, xvii
Sparkes, J. (Art), 8
Sparkes (America), 54
Sparling, 60
Sparta, History, 41
Species, Origin of, 104
Spectator, The, 73
Spedding, 11
Speeches (*see* Biography)
Speke, 35
Spencer, Herbert (Economics), 87
—— (Education), 30
—— (Philosophy), 75, 76

Spencer (Political Science), 90, 91
Spenser (poet), 62
—— Life of, 14
Spinoza, 74
Spottiswoode, 100
Spruner-Menke's Atlas, 36
Stael, Mme. de, 22
Stainton, 106
Stanford's Maps, 36
—— Compendium of Geography, 31
Stanhope, Lord, 21, 45, 53
Stanley, Dean, Life of, 17
—— (Architecture), 7
—— (History), 40
—— (Life of Arnold), 22
—— (Travels), 34
Stanley, H. M., 35
Stars, 112
State Interference, 88
State Socialism, 87
Statesman's Year-book, The, xviii, 93
Statesmen (*see* English History)
—— (*see* Biography)
—— Twelve English, 44
Statics, 96
Statist, The, 85, 89
Statistical Abstracts, xviii, 38, 52, 53
—— Society, Journal of, 82, 89
Statistics, Parliamentary, 37, 38
—— Vital, 83
Staveley, 106
Stead and Hug, 51
Steele, 72
—— Life of, 14
Steele and Tait, 97
Stein, 21
Stephen, Sir J. Fitzjames, 91
Stephen, Sir James, 17, 49
Stephen, Leslie (Biography), xvii, 10, 13, 14
—— (Essays), 72
—— (History), 46
—— (Philosophy), 75, 77
Stephens, Morse, 49
Stephenson, George, 11
Sterling, John, 14
Sterne, 66
—— Life of, 14
Stevenson, R. L., 25, 66, 72
Stewart, Balfour, 98, 100, 101

Stewart (Scotland), 48
Stieler's Hand Atlas, 36
Stirling (Philosophy), 75
—— (Physiology), 105
Stock Exchange, 85
Stokes, Sir G., 100
Stokes, G. T., 48
Stokes, M., 3
Stone, 99
Stopford Brooke, 13, 17
Stories, Children's, 24, 25
Story, 48
Stowe, Mrs. Beecher, 67
Strafford, 21
Strasburger and Hillhouse, 108
Strikes (Economics), 80
Stubbs, W. (History), 44, 46
Stubbs, C. W. (Land), 82
Studies, Lectures, and Essays, 70-72
Sue, 68
Sullivan, A. M., 48
Sully, 30, 76
Sumner (Protection), 87
—— (Individualism), 86
Suvaroff, 19
Sweden, Antiquities, 3
—— **History**, 57
Swift, 72, 73
—— Life of, 14
Swiss Family Robinson, 25
Swinburne, 62, 63, 72
Switzerland, History, 51
Symonds, J. A. (Biography), 12, 13, 14
—— (History), 43, 50
—— (Literature), 58, 72
Symes, 78

TAIT, 97, 98, 100, 102
Tait and Kelland, 96
Tait and Steele, 97
Tait and Sir W. Thomson, 98, 99
Tales, Children's, 24, 25
—— **Historical**, 68-70
Taussig, 86
Taxation, 85, 86
—— **Local**, 85, 86
Taxidermy, 107
Taylor, Cooke, 80
Taylor, E. R. (Art), 8
Taylor, I. (Geography), 32
Taylor, J. E. (Aquarium), 106
Taylor, Sir H., 63
Taylor, R. W. (Latin), 56

Taylor, Sedley (Political Economy), 81
—— (Sound), 99
Teaching, Home, 30
—— **School**, 30
Technical Education, 29
—— National Association for Promotion of, 29
Tegetmeier, 27
Temperance, 83
Tenancy, 82
Ten Brink, 59
Tennent, 34
Tennyson, 63
Testament, Old and New, 40
Testard, 56
Thackeray, W. M. (Fiction), 66, 69, 70
—— (History), 46
—— (Stories), 25
—— (Studies), 72
—— Life of, 14
Thackeray, Miss, 66, 70
Theocritus, 63
Thermo-dynamics, 97
Thiers, 49
Thomas, 2
Thomé and Bennett, 108
Thomson (poet of 'Seasons'), 63
Thomson (poet), 63
Thomson, Joseph (traveller), 35
Thomson, J. J. (Physics), 102
Thomson, Sir W. (Physics), 97, 99, 101
Thomson, Sir W., and Tait, 98, 99
Thompson, Sir H. (Food), 27
Thompson, Kate (Art), 4
Thompson, S. P. (Physics), 101
Thoreau, 72
—— Life of, 14
Thorpe, 102, 103
Thorvaldsen, 10
Thrift, 83
Thring, 30, 72
Thucydides, 41, 55
Thursfield, 48
Tilden, 102, 103
Timbs, 7
Tintoretto, 10
Tip Cat, 25
Titian, 10
Tocqueville, De, 54, 93

Todhunter, 95, 96, 98
Tolstoï, 68, 70, 88
Tooke and Newmarch, 85, 89
Topinard, 109
Tossell and Jeffcott, 56, 57
Toulmin-Smith, 80
Tout, Powell, and Mackay, 43
Town-holdings, 82
Towns (*see* **English History**)
Townson, 57
Toynbee, 79
Tozer, 32, 41
Trade Unions (Economics), 80
Trade, 84, 86, 88
Trade, Fair, 86
Trade, Foreign, 85
Trade, Free, 86
Trade, Board of, Journal, 89
Trade Unions and Strikes, 80
Trade Unions, Reports of, 80
Travellers (*see* **Biography**)
Travels, 33-36
Trench, 60
Trevelyan, 13
Trigonometry, 95
Tristram, 34
Trollope, A., 66
Trotter, 53
Tulloch, 17
Turgenieff, 68
Turkey, History, 52
Turner, J. M. W., 10
Turner, Ribton, 83
Tuttle, 50
Tyler, M., 59
Tylor, 90, 109, 110
Tyndale, 22
Tyndall (Life of Faraday), 15
—— (Physics), 99, 100
—— (Science), 102
—— (Travels), 34

UEBERWEG, 77
United States, History, 54
—— **Literature**, 59
Universities, 30
University Extension, 30
Upcott, 2
Urbanitzky, 101
Utopia, 92

VAMBERY, 34, 40
Vandyck, 10

Vasari, 5, 10
Vaughan, 63
Velasquez, 10
Venn, 76
Verne, 25
Vernet, 10
Victor Emmanuel, 50
Village Communities, 82
Villari, 17, 50
Vinci, Leonardo da, 8, 9
Vines, 109
Vines and Prantl, 108
Viollet le Duc, 7
Virgil, 63
Voltaire (Fiction), 68
—— (Life of Charles XII), 18, 51
—— Life of, 14
Voyages (see **Travels**)

WAGES (Economics), 80, 81
Wagner (musician), 16
Wagner (Chemistry), 103
Wakeman and Hassall, 46
Waldstein, 6
Walford, 56
Walker, F. A., 78, 80, 82, 84
Wallace, A. R. (Geography), 32, 34, 35, 52
—— (Biology), 105
Wallace, D. Mackenzie, 34, 51
Walpole, C. G. (Ireland), 48
Walpole, Horace, 14
Walpole, Sir R., 21
Walpole, Spencer, 46
Walters and Cockshott, 95
Walton, Isaac, 73, 107
—— (Life of), 17
War (see **Biography—Soldiers and Sailors—and History**
Ward (Austria), 49
Ward (Psychology), 76
Ward, A. W. (Chaucer's Life), 12
Ward, T. H., 60
Ward and Baddeley, 36
Warner, Miss, 25
Warwick the Kingmaker, 19
Washington, 21
Watteau, 10
Watts (Chemistry), 102, 103
—— (Gardening), 28
Wauters, 5

Webb, 87
Webster's Dictionary, xvii
Wedmore, 8
Weismann, 105
Wellesley, 53
—— Life of, 21
Wellhausen, 40
Wellington, 19
Wells (Travels), 35
Wells (Political Economy), 79
Wesley, John, 17
Wesley, Samuel, 17
Wesley, Susanna, 17
West, Dr. C., 27
Westgarth, 52
Wetzler and Martin, 101
Wharton and Freshfield, 36
Wheeler, 53
Whitaker's Almanack, xviii
White, Gilbert, 107
White, W. F., 107
Whitfield, 17
Whitelaw, 63
Whitman, Walt., 63, 72
Whitney, xvii
Whittier, 63
Whitworth, 95
Whymper, 34
Whyte-Melville, 68
Wicksteed, 78
Wiclif, 17
Wilberforce, Bishop, 17, 22, 25
Wilberforce, Wm., 22
Wilde, 3
Wilkie, 10
Wilkins, 2
Wilks, 53
William the Conqueror, 21
William III., 19, 21
Williams (Travels), 34
Williams, Mattieu, 27
Williamson, 96
Wilkinson, 83
Wilmot, 5
Wilson, A. J. (Political Economy), 86
Wilson, J. M. (Mathematics), 95
Wilson (Health), 28
Wilson and Fowler, 75
Window-gardening, 28
Winkler and Lunge, 103
Witt (Myths), 25
Witt, Madame de, 56
Wittich, 57
Woermann and Woltmann, 4

Wolfe, 18, 53
Wolsey, Cardinal, 21
Wolstenholme, 98
Woltmann and Woermann, 4
Wood, J. G., 26, 106, 107, 110
Wood (Gardening), 28
Woods, Miss, 25, 60
Woods, Mrs., 66
Woolsey, 91
Wordsworth (poet), 63
—— Life of, 14
Wordsworth (Greece), 41
Working Classes (Economics), 80-84
World's Great Explorers, 33
Wornum, 7
Worsaae, 3
Wright (Optics), 100
Wright, Guthrie, 27
Wright and Hobhouse, 86
Wright and Hornsby, 84
Writers, Literary (see **Biography**)
—— **Religious** (see **Biography**)
—— **Scientific** (see **Biography**)
Würtz, 102, 103
Wylie, 44

XAVIER, FRANCIS, 16
Xenophon, 41, 55

YARRELL, 107
Year-books, Colonial and Foreign, xviii
Year-book, Metropolitan, xviii
Year-book, the Statesman's, xviii, 93
Yeats, 33
Yeo, 105
Yonge, Miss (History), 49, 51
—— (Life of Patteson), 17
—— (Stories), 25, 69
Young, Arthur (Political Economy), 88
Young (Netherlands), 50
Young (Labour), 79
Yule, 33

ZANZIBAR, 35
Zeller, 77
Zoologists, 15
Zoology, 104-107

SELECTED LIST
OF
EDWARD STANFORD'S
GEOGRAPHICAL AND SCIENTIFIC PUBLICATIONS.

Dedicated by permission to Her Majesty the Queen.

STANFORD'S LONDON ATLAS OF UNIVERSAL GEOGRAPHY; exhibiting the Physical and Political Divisions of the various Countries of the World. Ninety Maps, with a Geographical Index. Imperial folio, half bound in morocco extra, with gilt edges, and thumb index to facilitate ready reference, price £12. Full bound in morocco, £15. Size when shut, 16 × 23 inches. Weight, 21 lbs. A box lined with swansdown is given with each copy.

CONTENTS

1. The World in Hemispheres, with a series of sections.
2. The World on Mercator's Projection. The Eastern World.
3. The World on Mercator's Projection. The Western World.
4. The Countries round the North Pole. With Names of principal Arctic Navigators and Dates of Exploration.
5. The World, showing the British Possessions.
6. Europe.
7. The British Isles. A Stereographical Map.
8. ,, A Hydrographical Map.
9. ,, A Geological Map.
10. ,, A Parliamentary Map.
11. ,, A Railway Map.
12. ,, A Series of Rainfall and Temperature Maps.
13. ,, A Series of Statistical Maps.
14. England. General Map.
15. ,, N.E. Counties and Municipal Boroughs.
16. ,, N.W. ,, ,,
17. ,, S.E. ,, ,,
18. ,, S.W. ,, ,,
19. Inner London. Local Government Divisions.
20. Outer London. City and Metropolitan Police Areas.
21. Scotland. General Map.
22. ,, N.E. Counties and Municipal Boroughs.
23. ,, N.W. ,, ,,
24. ,, S.E. ,, ,,
25. ,, S.W. ,, ,,
26. Ireland. General Map.
27. ,, N.E. Counties and Municipal Boroughs.
28. ,, N.W. ,, ,,
29. ,, S.E. ,, ,,
30. ,, S.W. ,, ,,
31. Denmark and Sleswig-Holstein. Iceland.
32. Sweden and Norway.
33. German Empire, Western Part.
34. ,, Eastern Part.
35. Austria-Hungary.
36. Switzerland. The Railways and Principal Passes.
37. The Netherlands and Belgium.
38. The Countries around the Mediterranean Sea.
39. France in Departments. France in Provinces.
40. Spain and Portugal.
41. Italy, North. Sardinia.
42. Italy, South.
43. Greece.
44. The Balkan Peninsula.
45. The Bosphorus and Constantinople, the Dardanelles and the Troad.
46. The Sea of Marmora.
47. Malta and the Ionian Islands.
48. Cyprus.
49. Russia and Poland.
50. Sketch of the Acquisitions of Russia since the Accession of Peter I.
51. Asia. 52. Turkey in Asia.
53. Central Asia. 54. Palestine.
55. India, Northern Part.
56. ,, Southern Part.
57. Burmah. 58. Ceylon. 59. China.
60. Japan. 61. The Eastern Archipelago.
62. Borneo. 63. Africa.
64. Egypt. 65. Central Africa.
66. South Africa. 67. North America.
68. Newfoundland.
69. Quebec, New Brunswick, Nova Scotia, Prince Edward Island.
70. Ontario and Quebec Western.
71. Manitoba.
72. British Columbia and the North-West Territory.
73. The United States of North America.
74. The West Indies.
75. Jamaica.
76. The Bahamas.
77. The Leeward Islands.
78. The Windward Islands.
79. South America.
80. The Falkland Islands.
81. Australia, East.
82. ,, West.
83. Queensland.
84. New South Wales.
85. Victoria.
86. South Australia.
87. Western Australia.
88. Tasmania. The Fiji Archipelago.
89. New Zealand.
90. The Pacific Islands.

Each Plate may be had separately, price 3s. in sheet coloured, or 5s. mounted to fold in case for the pocket, except No. 7 (Stereographical British Isles), which is 5s. in sheet, 7s. in case; and No. 9 (Geological British Isles), 10s. 6d. in sheet, 12s. 6d. in case.

EDWARD STANFORD, 26 & 27 COCKSPUR ST., LONDON, S.W.

GEOGRAPHICAL AND SCIENTIFIC PUBLICATIONS.

STANFORD'S LONDON ATLAS OF UNIVERSAL GEOGRAPHY.
Quarto Edition, containing 46 Coloured Maps, carefully drawn, and beautifully engraved on steel and copper plates, and an Alphabetical Index to the Geography of the World. *Third Edition.* Revised and enlarged. Imperial 4to. Half morocco, cloth sides, gilt edges, 30s. Size when shut, 15 inches by 12¼. Weight, 4 lbs. 8 oz.

CONTENTS.

1. World on Mercator's Projection.
2. Europe.
3. British Isles, Orographical.
4. British Isles, Hydrographical.
5. England and Wales.
6. Scotland.
7. Ireland.
8. Sweden and Norway.
9. Denmark.
10. Germany, West.
11. Germany, East.
12. Austria-Hungary.
13. Switzerland.
14. Netherlands and Belgium.
15. France.
16. Spain and Portugal.
17. Italy, North.
18. Italy, South.
19. Balkan Peninsula.
20. Mediterranean, West.
21. Mediterranean, East.
22. Russia and the Caucasus.
23. Asia.
24. Turkestan, West.
25. Turkestan, East.
26. China.
27. Japan.
28. India, North.
29. India, South.
30. Ceylon.
31. East Indies.
32. Holy Land.
33. Africa.
34. Egypt.
35. South Africa.
36. North America.
37. Dominion of Canada.
38. Canada, East.
39. Canada, West.
40. United States, East.
41. United States, West.
42. West Indies and Central America.
43. South America.
44. Australia.
45. Tasmania.
46. New Zealand.

Alphabetical Index of Towns, Villages, etc. etc.

All the Maps in the above Atlas can be had separately. Price, coloured sheet, 1s. 6d.; mounted in case, 3s.

"New friends and new loves are capital things, provided they are not allowed to displace the old, and for our part we have no intention of ever putting out of its place Mr. Stanford's 'London Atlas,' the third edition of which in quarto form is now before us. We have used it constantly for years, and we have never found it surpassed for the combined merits of handiness, cheapness, accuracy, and clearness. The maps, of course, are fewer and on a smaller scale than those of its larger rivals; but this drawback is perhaps compensated by greater ease of reference. We are not sure ourselves that a compendious atlas, supplemented at different times by the sheet maps, which all the best publishers issue at times when a particular district is of interest, is not a better thing than a more extensive volume, which, after all, never can pretend to extreme detail on the small scale. However this may be, all good things are good in their own way, and in its way the 'London' is one of the best."—*Saturday Review.*

A PHYSICAL, HISTORICAL, POLITICAL, AND DESCRIPTIVE GEOGRAPHY.
By KEITH JOHNSTON, F.R.G.S., Editor of the "Africa" volume in "Stanford's Compendium of Geography and Travel;" late leader of the Royal Geographical Society's East African Expedition. *Fourth Edition.* Revised by E. G. RAVENSTEIN, F.R.G.S., with numerous Maps and Illustrations. Large post 8vo. Cloth. 12s.

"Mr. Keith Johnston's text-book of geography is a work of much thought, wide research, and no inconsiderable literary skill. It contains a vast amount of information on the physical features of the countries of the world, their climate and productions, commerce and industry, political institutions, administrative divisions, and leading towns. A set of maps, coloured so as to distinguish forest regions, agricultural lands, steppes, and deserts, forms a welcome addition to this judiciously-planned and carefully-written text-book."—*Athenæum.*

BY THE SAME AUTHOR.

A SCHOOL PHYSICAL AND DESCRIPTIVE GEOGRAPHY.
With Maps and Illustrations. Crown 8vo. Cloth. 6s.

"This admirable little book is a short edition of the late Mr. Keith Johnston's larger work. It contains all the strictly geographical matter of its predecessor, but the curtailment has been effected by omitting the historical sketch, with many of the costly and beautiful maps. Its philosophical arrangement, broad grasp of physical science, and wide conception of the interaction of terrestrial agencies upon one another, and on the life of man, mark it off at once from old-fashioned routine text-books as something different not merely in degree but in kind. It throws a real interest into geography; and that interest is of the highest and most intelligent sort."—*Pall Mall Gazette.*

EDWARD STANFORD, 26 & 27 COCKSPUR ST., LONDON, S.W.

GEOGRAPHICAL AND SCIENTIFIC PUBLICATIONS.

STANFORD'S COMPENDIUM OF GEOGRAPHY AND TRAVEL,
for General Reading. Based on HELLWALD'S "Die Erde und Ihre Völker." Translated by Professor A. H. KEANE, M.A.I. A series of volumes descriptive of the Great Divisions of the Globe. With Maps, Ethnological Appendices, and several hundred Illustrations. Large post 8vo. Cloth.

Price £6 : 6s. the set, in cardboard box, or 21s. each Volume separately. The Volumes are also kept in stock in calf binding, 28s. each; or morocco, 32s. each.

I.—**EUROPE.** By F. W. RUDLER, F.G.S., and G. G. CHISHOLM, B.Sc. Edited by Sir ANDREW C. RAMSAY, LL.D., F.R.S. With Ethnological Appendix by Professor A. H. KEANE, M.A.I. With 15 Maps and 60 Illustrations.

"Taking it as a whole, this volume on 'Europe' is the best of the series, and in some respects indeed is comparable with the very best works on the same region in no matter what language."—*Academy*.

II.—**ASIA.** With Ethnological Appendix. By A. H. KEANE, M.A.I. Edited by Sir RICHARD TEMPLE, Bart., G.C.S.I., C.I.E. *Second Edition.* Revised. With 12 Maps and 73 Illustrations.

"The design of the work is to supply an exhaustive account of the geography as well as of the material and political condition of the continent, and to present the reader, in as concise a form as the magnitude of the subject will admit of, with a faithful and attractive picture of the countries of Asia. In this Sir Richard Temple and the author, Mr. Keane, have attained a complete success."—*St. James's Gazette*.

III.—**AFRICA.** Edited and Extended by KEITH JOHNSTON, F.R.G.S., late leader of the Royal Geographical Society's East African Expedition. With Ethnological Appendix by A. H. KEANE, M.A.I. *Fourth Edition.* Revised and corrected by E. G. RAVENSTEIN, F.R.G.S. With 16 Maps and 68 Illustrations.

"Nothing so complete on the subject of Africa has yet been published. Every region of it—the Atlas district, the Sahara, the Soudan, the Nile Valley, the Equatorial Lakes, the Southern Colonies—is treated severally. Climate, population, products, are all separately described. Every region has its own careful map, besides a number of physical diagrams illustrating the rainfall, ethnology, and philology of the country. It is, in short, a complete encyclopædia of the continent, which will be very useful to all who wish to follow the track of recent discovery."—*Guardian*.

IV.—**NORTH AMERICA.**—**United States.** Edited and Enlarged by Professor F. V. HAYDEN, of the United States Geological Survey.

Canada. By Professor A. R. C. SELWYN, F.R.S., Director of the Geological Survey of Canada. With 16 Maps and 48 Illustrations.

"The maps are excellent, and altogether this volume is one of the best and most widely interesting of the series."—*Athenæum*.

V.—**CENTRAL AND SOUTH AMERICA.** Edited and Extended by H. W. BATES, F.R.S., Assistant Secretary of the Royal Geographical Society; Author of "The Naturalist on the River Amazons." With Ethnological Appendix by A. H. KEANE, M.A.I. *Third Edition.* With 13 Maps and 73 Illustrations.

"Open it where you will the attention is arrested, and you are irresistibly tempted to read on; while its methodical arrangement, with the copious index, must make it exceedingly valuable as a work of reference. The volume is infinitely more entertaining than many novels that are far above the average, while it contains in itself the materials for any amount of romance."—*Pall Mall Gazette*.

VI.—**AUSTRALASIA.** Edited and Extended by ALFRED R. WALLACE, LL.D., F.R.S., Author of "The Malay Archipelago," "Geographical Distribution of Animals," etc. With Ethnological Appendix by A. H. KEANE, M.A.I. *Fifth Edition.* With 20 Maps and 56 Illustrations.

"We doubt if in any one work so much trustworthy information is obtainable on a part of the world always interesting, and about which knowledge generally is defective, and most inaccurate."—*Times*.

EDWARD STANFORD, 26 & 27 COCKSPUR ST., LONDON, S.W.

GEOGRAPHICAL AND SCIENTIFIC PUBLICATIONS.

STANFORD'S LIBRARY MAPS.

The Publisher begs to announce the issue of New and Revised Editions of these fine Maps, which have hitherto held the first place as Maps for the Libraries of Gentlemen, Public Offices, and Libraries, or for Commercial purposes.

The Maps have undergone a thorough revision to bring them up to date, and the cost of production having been considerably reduced by the use of new machinery, it has been decided to make a substantial reduction in the prices at which they have hitherto been sold to the Public, in the hope of extending their circulation and usefulness.

The Maps of which New Editions are now ready are:—

EUROPE. Scale, 50 miles to 1 inch. Size, 65 by 58 inches.
ASIA. Scale, 110 miles to 1 inch. Size, 65 by 58 inches.
AFRICA. Scale, 94 miles to 1 inch. Size, 58 by 65 inches.
NORTH AMERICA. Scale 83 miles to 1 inch. Size, 58 by 65 inches.
SOUTH AMERICA. Scale, 83 miles to 1 inch. Size, 58 by 65 inches.

The Prices of each of these Maps will in future be as follows:—

Four Sheets, Coloured, 35s.
Mounted on Rollers and Varnished, 45s.
Mounted to fold in Morocco Case, 60s.
Mounted on Spring Rollers, £5.

The other Maps in Stanford's Library Series are:—

THE WORLD ON MERCATOR'S PROJECTION.
ENGLAND.   CANADA.
SCOTLAND.   UNITED STATES.
IRELAND.   AUSTRALASIA.
LONDON.   AUSTRALIA.

For particulars of Price, Size, etc., see STANFORD'S CATALOGUE OF MAPS, etc., 200 pp., sent post free for 3d.

EDWARD STANFORD, 26 & 27 COCKSPUR ST., LONDON, S.W.

GEOGRAPHICAL AND SCIENTIFIC PUBLICATIONS.

OUTLINES OF GEOLOGY: an Introduction to the Science for Junior Students and General Readers. By JAMES GEIKIE, LL.D., F.R.S., Murchison Professor of Geology and Mineralogy at the University of Edinburgh. With 400 Illustrations. *Second Edition*. Revised. Large post 8vo. Cloth. 12s.

"The style is clear, simple, and unpretending; the author has evidently striven to put the subject fairly before students rather than to express his own views, and has thus produced a book which cannot fail to be of great service."—*Saturday Review*.

BY THE SAME AUTHOR.

THE GREAT ICE AGE, AND ITS RELATION TO THE ANTIQUITY OF MAN. *Second Edition*. Revised. With Maps and Illustrations. Demy 8vo. Cloth. 24s.

"The book shows everywhere the marks of acute observation, wide research, and sound reasoning. It presents in a readable form the chief features of the Great Ice Age, and illustrates them very amply from those great tracts of Scotland in which glaciation has left its most distinct and most enduring marks."—*Spectator*.

PREHISTORIC EUROPE. A Geological Sketch. With Maps and Illustrations. Medium 8vo. Cloth. 25s.

"Dr. Geikie's object in the present volume is to give an outline of what appear to have been the most considerable physical changes experienced in Europe since the beginning of the Pleistocene or Quaternary period, the period immediately preceding that which is now being wrought out, and which Dr. Geikie divides into Post-glacial and Recent. He attempts to describe, in a more systematic manner than has hitherto been attempted, that succession of changes, climatic and geographical, which, taken together, constitute the historical geology of Pleistocene, Post-glacial, and Recent times. This he does in a more thorough and complete manner than, we venture to think, has ever been done before."—*Times*.

CONTRIBUTIONS TO THE PHYSICAL HISTORY OF THE BRITISH ISLES; with a Dissertation on the Origin of Western Europe and of the Atlantic Ocean. With 27 Coloured Maps. By EDWARD HULL, M.A., LL.D., F.R.S., Director of the Geological Survey of Ireland. Medium 8vo. Cloth. 12s. 6d.

"Professor Hull has rendered a signal service to students of geology by preparing and publishing a series of maps of the British Islands, in which he indicates, by distinctive colouring, the distribution of land and water at successive periods of geological history. No such series of maps, so far as we know, has ever before been published, or even attempted."—*Academy*.

BY THE SAME AUTHOR.

THE PHYSICAL GEOLOGY AND GEOGRAPHY OF IRELAND. Part I. Geological Formation of Ireland. Part II. Physical Geography of Ireland. Part III. The Glaciation of Ireland. With Maps and Illustrations. Post 8vo. Cloth. 7s.

COAL-FIELDS OF GREAT BRITAIN; their History, Structure, and Resources; with Notices of the Coal-fields of other parts of the World. *Fourth Edition*. Demy 8vo. Cloth. 16s.

"In comparing the present with the previous edition, which was published in 1873, we find that the volume now before us has been for the most part rewritten, and records added of important events which have transpired since the issue of the third edition. . . . Such a volume as the present is indispensable to colliery proprietors or students of carboniferous geology, and ought not to be absent from the library of any literary man."—*Colliery Guardian*.

THE AUTOBIOGRAPHY OF THE EARTH: a Popular Account of Geological History. By Rev. H. N. HUTCHINSON, B.A., F.G.S. Crown 8vo. Cloth. With 27 Illustrations, 7s. 6d.

"Mr. Hutchinson has successfully carried out a difficult design on an admirable plan, and has adhered to that plan throughout. His sketch of historical geology has a genuine continuity. It is so written as to be understood of plain people, and it is illustrated by some very good woodcuts and diagrams."—*Saturday Review*.

EDWARD STANFORD, 26 & 27 COCKSPUR ST., LONDON, S.W.

GEOGRAPHICAL AND SCIENTIFIC PUBLICATIONS.

CHARTS OF THE CONSTELLATIONS, from the North Pole to between 35 and 40 Degrees of South Declination. By ARTHUR COTTAM, F.R.A.S. Popular Edition, on a reduced scale, with three new Key Maps, an Introduction, and extensive Notes.

Thirty-six Charts (each 15 by 22 inches), sold bound as an Atlas, half-roan, or loose in a Portfolio. Price 21s.

"Many excellent maps of the stars have been constructed, but the star atlas of Mr. Cottam is far superior to all its predecessors. The plan of appropriating a map to each constellation renders them exceedingly handy for a systematic study of the heavens."—*The Globe*.

CHARTS OF THE CONSTELLATIONS, from the North Pole to between 35 and 40 Degrees of South Declination. By ARTHUR COTTAM, F.R.A.S. Second Edition. Price £3 : 3s.

Thirty-six Charts (each 30 by 22 inches), printed on Drawing Paper, so that observers can make additions at any time. They can be supplied, folded in half, in a Portfolio, or flat if preferred.

"Surely this is the very luxury of stellar cartography, for from the days of Bayer downwards nothing has appeared comparable with the splendid series of charts now before us for the special purpose for which they are intended. . . . No astronomical library or observatory of any pretensions can afford to be without it."—*English Mechanic*.

(A detailed Prospectus, with Opinions of the Press, sent post free on application.)

POPULAR WORKS ON NATURAL HISTORY.

THROUGH MAGIC GLASSES, and other Lectures. A Sequel to "The Fairyland of Science." By ARABELLA B. BUCKLEY (Mrs. FISHER). Crown 8vo, cloth extra, with nearly 100 Illustrations, 6s. ; bound in calf, 11s.

"A sequel to that very delightful book 'The Fairyland of Science,' and deals with the marvels revealed by the telescope, the microscope, and the photographic camera. For young people or scientific tastes a better book could not be found than this. The author's exposition is perfectly clear and simple. She possesses the art of interesting the young in matters remote from their ordinary experience, and of rendering complex questions perfectly intelligible to children. The chapter on the spectroscope, for instance, and that on volcanoes, are models of luminous, unpedantic, yet strictly scientific interpretation of natural laws and phenomena. The work is illustrated with many beautiful engravings."—*Saturday Review*.

WORKS BY THE SAME AUTHOR.

THE FAIRYLAND OF SCIENCE. Twenty-third Thousand. 6s. ; calf, 11s.

LIFE AND HER CHILDREN. Thirtieth Thousand. 6s. ; calf, 11s.

WINNERS IN LIFE'S RACE. 2 vols. 4s. 6d. each.

SHORT HISTORY OF NATURAL SCIENCE. Fourth Edition. 8s. 6d. ; calf, 14s.

WORKS BY THE LATE JAMES CROLL, LL.D., F.R.S.

"A keen investigator, an able writer, a great thinker."—*Daily News*.
"A deep and original thinker."—*Academy*.

Uniform in Size and Binding.

CLIMATE AND TIME IN THEIR GEOLOGICAL RELATIONS. A Theory of Secular Changes of the Earth's Climate. Large post 8vo, with Illustrations, cloth, 10s. 6d.

DISCUSSIONS ON CLIMATE AND COSMOLOGY. A Supplementary Volume to "Climate and Time." Large post 8vo, with an Illustrative Chart, cloth, 6s.

STELLAR EVOLUTION AND ITS RELATIONS TO GEOLOGICAL Time. Large post 8vo, cloth, 5s.

THE PHILOSOPHICAL BASIS OF EVOLUTION. Large post 8vo, cloth, 7s. 6d.

EDWARD STANFORD, 26 & 27 COCKSPUR ST., LONDON, S.W.

www.ingramcontent.com/pod-product-compliance
Lightning Source LLC
Chambersburg PA
CBHW030338170426
43202CB00010B/1165